Gifted GROWNUPS

The Mixed Blessings of Extraordinary Potential

To Susan Bower

Marylou Kelly Streznewski

Marylou K. Streznewski

12/4/2000

John Wiley & Sons, Inc.

New York • Chichester • Weinheim • Brisbane • Singapore • Toronto

Published by John Wiley & Sons, Inc.
Published simultaneously in Canada.

This publication is designed to provide accurate and authoritative information in regard
to the subject matter covered. It is sold with the understanding that the publisher is not
engaged in rendering professional services. If professional advice or other expert
assistance is required, the services of a competent professional person should be sought.

Library of Congress Cataloging-in-Publication Data:

Streznewski, Marylou Kelly, 1934–
    Gifted grownups : the mixed blessings of extraordinary potential /
by Marylou Kelly Streznewski.
        p.   cm.
    Includes bibliographical references.
    ISBN 0-471-29580-9 (hardcover : alk. paper)
    1. Gifted persons.   2. Gifted persons—Case studies.   3. Creative
ability—Social aspects.   I. Title.
BF412.S77   1999
153.9'8—dc21   98-29536

Printed in the United States of America.

10 9 8 7 6 5 4 3 2 1

For
Grasshopper
and
for my sister, too late.

Preface

If you think that gifted children are a misunderstood minority in American society, try looking up "gifted adult" in a good library; but do so only if you enjoy watching librarians twirl. I have written, as far as I can tell, the only book by and about gifted grownups that is intended for a general audience. It includes the children, but the focus is on you, the adult. How you read it will depend on who you are.

If you already know that being gifted is your special blessing/burden in life, or if you have wondered about the strange reactions other people have to things that seem perfectly ordinary to you, you may laugh a lot in the coming pages—recognition laughter. Hopefully, if you see yourself in the mirror of these interviews, you will find practical help in negotiating the maze of this world.

This book is also designed for people who are reacting to, and interacting with, gifted people in their daily lives, either personally or on the job: the construction worker whose girlfriend scares him when she uses big words; the parent with a high school education who is trying to raise a child with a 160 IQ and jokes that the genes must have come from the milkman; the employer who wonders why that bright young worker just quit; the sincere teacher who doesn't understand that the "pest" in her classroom may be desperately trying to tell her something.

Gifted Grownups began with me, as an outspoken advocate for a gifted program in our senior high school. I was a mature woman, mother of four bright adolescents, a writer, an educator with years of experience behind me, and I was frustrated. I could not get others to see what was obvious to me: that some of the students in my advanced placement English class needed special help. Year after year, a significant number of them arrived in my class at the end of a long road fogged with what they called boredom. They complained of inability to concentrate, lack of motivation, feelings of failure, and were obviously wasting a great deal of talent. The decision to write about this problem was made when I realized that many of these young people were managing to achieve reasonable enough grades to keep their parents and other teachers happily unaware that anything could be wrong. Was the damage and waste I saw a temporary phenomenon of adolescence? Would my talented charges "bloom" in college the way all the adults assumed they would?

Specific research on the gifted has concentrated almost exclusively on educational development and how parents and teachers can help children in schools. What could gifted adults tell me about the world that awaited my gifted students? The complexities of adult life in the twenty-first century would certainly stimulate, but would it nurture them? Would society have the benefit of their many abilities?

I began to look around me, asking about what happens when smart kids grow up to be gifted adults. Within a two-week period I had, literally, the same conversation with three very bright people who described lack of stimulation in their work and feelings of isolation and loneliness because, "There is no one to talk to—no one reads the same weird books I do!" Common enough problems to hear from gifted kids, but the ages of these three were 17, 55, and 79! Any book about gifted people could not stop at high school graduation. A smart kid becomes a gifted grownup.

The Questions

The research problem I set myself was based on the following questions: (1) If I were to speak to a broad cross-section of gifted adults, would they say the same things I had been hearing from my students? (2) If I were to choose those adults according to the informal criteria my own observations had developed for spotting gifted students in the classroom—speed, sensitivity, complexity and sophistication of thought, energy, and humor—would I turn up high IQs, people who were in fact smart kids grown up? (3) If their problems as students remained the same when they became adults, what did that imply about society's understanding of how it is possible to waste one of our most precious resources? (4) What could be done to change things? To answer these questions, I decided to take the academic knowledge of experts in the fields of human learning and gifted studies and interweave it with the experiences of those I interviewed. Thus, the major portion of this book presents the voices of real people talking about their lives.

The Interviews

In all, I interviewed one hundred gifted grownups from 18 to 90. They were diversified by sex, family background, education, occupation, geographic location, ethnic origin, social class, and race. The first forty were selected by my perception of the personal characteristics I had used to spot gifted students over the years. These were such qualities as mental speed, sophistication of thought processes, sensitivity, drive, and sense of humor. My purpose was to educate the public about ways in which they could tentatively identify gifted persons (including themselves). If my thesis were correct, that such informal identification by friends, parents, lovers, teachers, and employers is both possible and necessary, then statistical measures such as IQ would *not* be helpful in choosing the interviewees.

Some of the remaining sixty people were recommended by professionals who knew about the project. The interviews for Chapter 8 were arranged by criminal justice professionals. Many came from the interview subjects themselves, who passed me on to a college roommate, a colleague's husband, or the landlord's niece. Some contacts were made by mentioning the book on a computer network.

The volunteers were given a set of index cards that contained statements from gifted students, quotes from the literature, and my own observations and questions. These cards covered topics such as self-image, family life, education, jobs, dating, marriages, metaphysical experiences, and obligations to society. The gifted grownups were asked to respond only to those cards that interested them; thus, threatening questions were avoided. Some responded to over one hundred cards (the set contained 104); others only to ten. However, almost all of them talked for a two- to three-hour period.

What emerged from the hundreds of hours in which these grown-up smart kids talked about their lives? I found people who had indeed been part of gifted programs, or who had operated like gifted children—in both positive and negative ways. In all cases, they had some sense of themselves as "different" at an early age. Where IQs were known, they fell in the range appropriate for giftedness. What they reported was consistent with what the research on children says about the problems and pleasures of being smarter than 95% of the population. They revealed that the process of managing a high-powered brain/mind can create difficulties in school, work, and society, and can make finding friends and partners a challenge. However seeing the complex relationships between things and always questing for more stimulation, more information can make for a rich and rewarding life.

The interviewees also made statements that validated my original observation that the problems and pleasures of being gifted do not change, only the context in which they are experienced as one grows older. They confirmed my suspicion that a great many talented people are being underutilized, or even wasted by society. The happy and successful gifted people in this study are proof that such waste can be prevented.

An unexpected bonus for those interviewed was a fresh perspective on their own lives. Many expressed amazement that the cards contained statements that they themselves had made. Others were relieved to find that feelings that had caused worry and unhappiness were explainable in terms of giftedness. That a large number of subjects made negative statements about certain aspects of their lives did not lead them to the conclusion that being highly intelligent is somehow undesirable. Most seemed to agree with the designation "mixed blessing."

Although a number of those interviewed could be termed successful, you will not find here any conversations with famous people. For too long society has believed that if you aren't president of General Motors, you aren't gifted. If the estimates of the researchers are correct, and between 3% and 5% of the population is gifted, then we are talking about several million people. What the interviews revealed was that a gifted person of multiple talents may not be as fortunate as a multitalented Bill Bradley (Rhodes scholar, basketball star, senator, author). He or she may be struggling through a series of false starts into careers and college majors, trying desperately to find the one that clicks.

Many of those I interviewed never made it as far as college: They gave up on school because the lower grades were never challenging, they couldn't afford college, or they didn't consider college an option. Lee Iaccoca is proof that all of the brains in this society are not concentrated in the middle class. Some of the smartest kids had learned to hate school so much that they could not tolerate its confinement in any form. The lucky ones found something that suited them better and constructed a life with their own talents. Some of the unlucky ones were interviewed in jail.

Implications for Society

Based on what the gifted grownups told me, some of my students would be very successful in using their gifts. They would go off to major universities and emerge four years later to make outstanding contributions to American corporate, artistic, or academic society. However, the interviews also documented that there are large numbers of frustrated gifted adults, who can be located by a person who knows what to look for, and who do not find outlets for their potential. We don't pay enough attention to trying to teach people who are highly intelligent how to cope with their lives in the adult world. Far too many of them find their drive and creativity thwarted by persons or establishments who regard them as either silly or threatening.

The implications of what these grown-up smart kids tell us about themselves are threefold. First, it is obvious that many gifted people lack even basic knowledge about their own nature. Counterproductive actions, which waste their gifts in personal relations and employment, can limit the personal happiness they may attain and blunt their possible contributions to the progress of society. Knowledge of how and why gifted persons function as they do can lead to greater utilization of their gifts for the benefit of all.

Second, a gifted person must not be studied as an isolated instance, but as a member of a family, a student in school, a worker within some larger setting, a participator in human relationships, and a citizen in a society.

The need for change is the third implication of what these valuable individuals can tell us. We cannot afford to waste our human resources. We need to forget the stereotypes and learn the true nature of gifted persons. While improving our schools' ability to nurture feisty minds, we must understand that multitalented people may require many years to discover what they really want to do, and even then will require stimulation and change. Recognition of the special nature of what these citizens have to offer can improve the lives of all workers, of bright women, and of gifted older adults.

While calling attention to the problem of underutilization of gifted people in American society, this book hopes to be a consciousness-raising statement that encourages discussion and dialogue in those areas of society where solutions need to be worked out over many years. Not only families and schools, but government, industry, universities, and the helping professions must be part of this process. If you are a gifted person, think of yourself as a catalyst, one with valuable special properties for the creation of the future.

MARYLOU KELLY STREZNEWSKI

Contents

PART ONE

THE GIFTED
GROWNUPS

Chapter One

What Makes You Gifted?

They told me I was smart, and I cried. I wanted to be sexy, or glamorous!

Alison, 54

I go through life wanting to say to people, "What's the matter, are you a turtle, can't you do that faster?"

Nina, 17

I learned the whole job in six weeks, and now I'm bored. I guess I'll have to go back to school.

Jean, 38

I'll give anything a try!
Lewis, 68

Who are the gifted? There are millions of them, and they look much like everyone else. Can one spot gifted people just by looking?

Bernice is wearing a deep red knitted dress, and large, dramatic jewelry; her pepper-and-salt hair is carefully styled. She stands with an acquaintance in the lobby of a Philadelphia hotel. A group of football-playing behemoths trundles by and she giggles delightedly, "I can't wait to get home and tell my husband I saw the Eagles!"

Ian has long hair, a beard, and is wearing a paint-stained shirt, fatigues, and work boots. Leaning back in his chair, he raises a bottle of beer and begins a conversation.

Joel walks down the hall of his former high school. A skinny kid, his loose-jointed, bent-kneed stride and his slightly drooping shoulders don't indicate energy. His jaw is slack, lips slightly parted, eyes seem vacant.

Faith has natural flaxen hair, cut in the latest fashion. She's wearing big dangling earrings, a gold choker, a plaid shirt, and jeans. She leans over to the boy next to her and whispers in his ear. They giggle for most of a class.

Jonathan has a beard and glasses; he's a little bit skinny. He has a heavy-looking backpack as he rides his bike across a college campus at 3 A.M. The computer center is less crowded in the middle of the night, so that is when he works.

If you discount appearances and watch what they *do*, it is easier to spot them. Bernice is in that hotel lobby because she is making a presentation at a conference. She has a Ph.D., a husband and family, and she heads a department in a major university. Ian begins that conversation about ballet. He's dressed that way because he is the director of construction projects. He likes his job because he can design the work himself, and he needs new things to design all the time. Joel's eyes look vacant because he hates his glasses and he doesn't have his contacts in at the moment. His skinny body belies his wicked tennis game. He thinks a lot, partly about his summer job representing his father's company on the East Coast. At 19, he is a student at a major university and is in that hallway because he has come back to visit some former teachers. One of Faith's fascinations in life is clothes. She designs outfits for herself each day and can create any style she desires. She is an accomplished musician, an award-winning writer, a merit scholar, and Harvard, Yale, Brown, Princeton, and Swarthmore all wanted her wide blue-eyed smile to grace their campuses last year. The kid she is giggling with is one of the top sixty young scientists in a large eastern state. At least Jonathan looks the part; he is an honors scholar at his university, and his appearance fits the stereotype. He is expected to graduate in four years with both undergraduate and graduate degrees.

What do all these people have in common? They have a large capability for seeing patterns, a restless drive to enlarge their world and to know, know, know. I met Bernice, Ian, Joel, Faith, and Jonathan in the course of conducting my long-term study of the gifted. They are helpful in understanding what happens to the "smart kids" in our society when they grow up.

That segment of the population that can be classified as gifted constitutes between 3% and 5% of the population, depending on who is asked. Some would describe a person who has a finely tuned and biologically advanced perception system and a mind that works considerably faster than 95% of the population. Others would say that the gifted are those whose IQ, if measured correctly, would be over 130. One study, conducted over a fifty-year period, claimed that they are healthier than the average person. That study concluded that, given the proper environment in which to grow, they will be taller and stronger, live longer, get divorced less, and have happier marriages than most people. They are also supposed to be more community-minded, more athletic, more notable, and richer than average.

The trouble with that fifty-year study, done by psychologist Lewis Terman of Stanford University, is that it was based on a selection of people who were already rather successful in the California schools of the 1920s, so it naturally reflected some very accomplished individuals. We will discuss Terman's work in more detail later. Other researchers have reinforced his findings, but Terman was probably the first to dispel, with hard facts, the notion that highly intelligent people are weak, sickly misanthropes of doubtful mental stability. Terman provided a valid explanation for the Hillary Clintons, the Christa McAuliffes. His work makes sense, not only of their amazing multiple accomplishments, but also of their joy in living life on a seemingly different plane.

As Different as Snowflakes

In spite of the volumes of research that exist on characteristics of the gifted, they do not appear in any kind of standard form, any more than any other segment of the human race does. Truly, they are as different as snowflakes. Based on my observations in the classroom and the general population, I concluded some years ago that the gifted can be grouped into three rough categories. It was a surprise to come upon the same categories in a documented study by psychologist Elizabeth Drews. I called them, informally, strivers, superstars, and independents. Remembering these categories can help to explain some of the confusion that surrounds impressions of the gifted. It can also prevent some of the snap judgments that are made at the mere mention of the word "gifted." From the previous section, we might categorize Joel as a striver, Jonathan and Ian as independents; Bernice and Faith are certainly superstars.

Strivers

In the first category are what have been called the "high-testing teacher-pleasers." When I was in college, they were known as "grinds." They work tremendously hard at school or their job. At the behest of corporate, parental, or academic authority, they will meet almost superhuman requirements. Their peers in school or the workplace do not have much influence on them. They have high test scores most of the time; high grades, and high accomplishments. They like structure and direction. One will rarely find creative contributions to science and art here, but certainly the endless taking of pains to do things right. They are often those adults who consider their jobs as their lives.

At 35, Daphne is one of only a handful of female corporate general counsels in the nation. She grew up in a quiet professional household in an unspectacular Washington, D.C., neighborhood. She remembers her then-traditional mother teaching her skills such as cooking, while her brother learned what were considered "masculine" skills, sharing gardening and repair chores with his father. "But the intellectual was never neglected," she recalls. "My mother loved wordplay. We are the only family I know of who kept a dictionary in the kitchen!"

A brilliant college and law school student, Daphne now works long days, evenings, and weekends. I interviewed her on a Saturday afternoon in a deserted conference room. It was midsummer. Her high salary has purchased a beach house, which she has too little time to enjoy. Marriage? Daphne smiles and says, "I'm told I terrify men. But then I'm told I terrify everyone. It never occurs to me to try to hide my intelligence." She is "married" to her job and seems quite content to be so.

Superstars

Another broad group encompasses what could be called superstars. They are the one-third who make the rest of us look bad—people expect all gifted people to be like this. They live up to the image created by the famous Terman studies of people who are taller, healthier, handsomer, wealthier, happier, and nicer than most people—because they are! They work hard, but play hard too. Concern for social relationships makes them popular with classmates, coworkers, employees; they often take their values from the concerns of the peer realm. Their high marks and high accomplishments seem to meld into the whole picture of their overall zest for life. They are often the scholar-athletes who seem to have it all. Whatever field they enter, they can be found in the same place: at or near the top.

In contrast to Daphne is Lauren. She too was a brilliant law student and is now occupying a position with a prestigious Wall Street law firm. She too is 35. She looks 25. "Both my parents were Navy. My mother got her degree in music education on the G.I. Bill. A great role model, she taught me that learning is fun. Even in law school, I took random courses in things like languages and painting."

I interviewed Lauren over drinks in a quiet bar. She seemed equally interested in discussing her prospects for a partnership, backpacking, shopping at Bloomingdale's, and how much she enjoys the theater in New York. "Marriage? Oh, there are plenty of men to marry, I'm just not interested in being tied down right now. I have a lot of men friends, good buddies, and notwithstanding that I come from Virginia, having a date is not the ultimate—there are other influences!"

Independents

So far, we have two groups of people who are a delight to those around them, either because they are fun or because they always have the work finished. What happened to the obnoxious, irritating, know-everything types? They are next, but take a second look before locking them into a negative stereotype. They are often the least understood but the most accomplished.

This third category Elizabeth Drews calls the "creative intellectuals." To coworkers, fellow students, parents, bosses, and teachers—in fact, to anyone who represents authority—they are more likely to be termed a pain in the neck. They work hard, often brilliantly, at what interests them. They may ignore the rest, regardless of the consequences. Their locus of control comes from deep in their inner value system. They are seldom popular, or leaders, and usually they don't want to be. In a classroom they often ask, as Drews says, "below the surface, or, depending on how they feel about the teacher, below the belt questions." They have a zany sense of humor.

They tend not to fit into the neat little slots of our corporate society; consequently, their careers may have a very irregular development indeed. But from their ranks come scientists rather than engineers, inventors rather than manufacturers, artists rather than competent performers. They may drive you absolutely crazy if you fail to understand their way of relating to the world. Having one in the family, as either child or spouse, will guarantee that no one will be bored!

Mark's well-built muscular body says "football," as does his athletic walk. The clothes say "Jock" right down to the Docksiders. The handsome face makes girls sigh, "He's so quiet." Mark uses his well-developed arm muscles for tennis, golf, karate, bowling, sailing (none of it on a school team) and lugging around thick physics books.

"Even when I was little, I knew I was hurting my parents, but I could do my sister's third-grade math homework in my head. I simply refused to do my first-grade homework for 'those people' (teachers) who couldn't understand that I already knew it. From kindergarten on, my teachers couldn't stand me, and they let me know it. I must have driven them crazy with questions! I just assumed that school was supposed to be a miserable place.

"In eighth-grade math I'd daydream and really not know what was going on, so I'd make up my own way to do a problem as I walked up to the board. The teacher would announce sarcastically (because my crazy methods sometimes worked), 'Mark will now show us how to do this problem.' That year I tested off the scale in math achievements. I also failed math. If anybody bothered me, I hit them. I think I expressed myself physically because no one would let me express myself intellectually."

Mark did not go to a big-name school; his grades were barely passing in some courses. The minor college that accepted him provided no challenge. Yet, he could discuss Einstein, Mozart, and T. S. Eliot with the aplomb of a college professor. (After a decade of struggle, he is presently a Ph.D. candidate in astrophysics.)

Here we also find candidates for a fourth category, one we don't like to think about. Those who drop out of organized society do so in a variety of ways. There is the 155 IQ who is washing dishes and going nowhere. And always, because this is the way it is with people who have fast and feisty minds, there is the 155 IQ who is washing dishes because it frees his mind to concentrate on becoming a professional chess player. Some of those who drop out become stock clerks; some become criminals; some commit suicide. In a later chapter, we will discuss how one arrives at the ultimate waste of the best and the brightest.

Gifted Behaviors

Is it possible for an ordinary observer to come to a tentative conclusion about gifted people? Yes. There are specific ways in which they behave, both as adults and as children. The first people interviewed for this book were selected by using a list of indicators that are very useful for spotting gifted people almost anywhere. This list could be compressed into traits like energy, curiosity, speed, concentration, sensitivity, sophistication of thinking, persistence, humor, and something about their eyes. Don't laugh. The last item showed up in interview after interview in response to the question of how to spot another gifted grownup. It was often prefaced by "I know this sounds odd, but . . ."

Might you be one of them? Think back into your own childhood as well as your present life for clues. If the following descriptions do not fit you, perhaps there is a person in your life, either at home or at work, who irritates, delights, puzzles, or otherwise intrigues you. You may be looking at a gifted grownup. It could be your boss or the lowest-ranking shipping clerk; a friend, an in-law, your spouse, or your own child. If it turns out that you find these descriptions fitting your child, look again at yourself. Those genes had to come from somewhere! Is giftedness something you inherit? Partly, but more about that later. Let us look more closely at how one can identify the gifted by their behavior.

Curiosity and Energy

Linda P. Moore, in a wonderfully wise and funny book called *Does This Mean My Kid's a Genius?*, asks if there is anyone around in your life who is "more energetic, more inquisitive, quicker than most and a bit of a mystery." For example, an ordinary child comes upon a colony of ants. She may ask questions and will probably accept the answers of an adult willing to give them, watch the ants with fascination for a while, and go on to something else. The smart kid will probably watch for a longer time; she will certainly ask more questions, especially those beginning with "Why?" or "What if?" A 7-year-old may ask questions that the adult can't answer. If the adult is wise, this will lead to a trip to the library for a book on ants, because the questions may go on for days! And don't look now, but there may be an ant farm in the future.

Or look at the college student who cuts his finger, seriously, and has never had a wound of any consequence before. The cut and the stitches will be examined, speculated about, and checked daily with a magnifying glass. It may be only a cut finger to anyone else, but to a gifted person it's a whole new area to be curious and learn about.

Some people might regard finding a huge dead sea turtle on the beach as horrible; this particular 50-year-old regarded it as interesting. Careful visual observation was done, along with lots of speculation as to why it was so far north. Did it come ashore to lay eggs or to die, and do the barnacles on its body indicate age? She took pictures. She got a book on sea turtles from the library and sent the author a note and a picture because she thought it might interest him.

Discovering new philosophical concepts is always fun for an active mind. A retired executive in her seventies encountered Thoreau's *Walden* in a used book store. "How could I have missed this wonderful man?" she demanded. Then she went about cleverly integrating his ideas into all kinds of conversations and situations, having a delightful time for days. Fortunately, she has an understanding family.

Besides energy and curiosity, it seems, about everything, many researchers agree that gifted grownups seem to be able to retain large amounts of information and to concentrate for long periods of time. Trying to get the attention of a completely absorbed gifted person can be a challenge. Whether it's a 10-year-old studying the stats on her favorite team or a 40-year-old lost in a laboratory experiment, they can be very good at actually shutting out the world around them.

Margo reports, "When my mathematician husband is bored at parties, he sits quietly in a corner and does equations in his head. Only I know that he is no longer in the room. I can tell by his eyes and the contented look on his face."

Speed

Seeing relationships and patterns, putting very complex ideas together, and doing it faster than others are special talents of the gifted. I remember a 6-year-old who would sit, feet swinging, putting together the pieces of an adult-level jigsaw puzzle almost as fast as her little fingers could pick them up, all the while singing "The Kookaburra Song" over and over.

In work situations, it is easy to spot the gifted adult when a new project or a new piece of equipment is introduced or a new problem arises. It may be regarded by fellow workers as marvelous or maddening, but the gifted person is the one who grasps the idea immediately or can already operate the equipment while everyone else is still stumbling around—like the secretary who comments "They sent me to school for three days to learn how to use the word processor. I understood it all on the first day. On the third day, I found a flaw in the program. I wrote the software company a letter; I thought they'd want to know."

Dorothy Sisk of the University of South Florida points out some additional elements of the behavior of gifted grownups. They have a strong tendency to be nonconformist and to think independently. They may have a reputation among peers for having wild and silly ideas or ideas that are off the beaten track. However, a prominent trait is a considerable sensitivity to both emotions and problems.

Sensitivity

Researchers have consistently reported that highly intelligent people exhibit unusually high ideals and values. Gifted people often report being criticized for overreacting to beauty in nature or art, to frightening or horrifying news events, or to moral wrongs in society.

Very young smart kids often worry about evil or world peace before they actually have enough vocabulary to discuss it. One woman who works with underachievers of all ages describes the long series of talks that can be necessary to find out what is troubling such a child. In these long talks, she feeds them, little by little, the vocabulary they need to tell her what is bothering them.

Sometimes, a gifted person finds that the demands of a moral imperative outweigh all practical considerations. A high school student is offended by the principle behind a classroom regulation and, in spite of any efforts by the teacher or other authority figures, chooses to be punished rather than conform. Later on, this sensitivity to moral considerations can lead to dramatic changes in lifestyle or dramatic resignations from jobs.

In the past, this heightened sensitivity was associated with mental illness. We carry the image of the mad genius in our minds as well as in our late-night movies, despite the fact that research has shown the rate of psychopathology to be about the same for the eminent as it is for the general population.

Heightened Perception

A different and more helpful explanation for the supersensitivity observed in many highly intelligent people was developed by the late Polish psychiatrist and psychologist Kazimierz Dabrowski, whose brilliant work is slowly becoming known in America. His work has shown that they have, in fact, more highly developed perception systems in all areas. For this phenomenon, Dabrowski coined the term "overexcitability" (OE), and divided these OE's into five areas of functioning:

1. Psychomotor OE—includes physical movement and the seemingly endless energy that characterizes many of the gifted.
2. Sensual OE—includes an extra measure of delight in the use of all the senses and greater sensitivity to touch, taste, smell, hearing, and sight.
3. Intellectual OE—the quality most noticed, and a good example of confusing the part with the whole. Most people associate high intelligence with the probing questions, the insatiable curiosity, the endless learning seen in gifted people of all ages.
4. Imaginational OE—can be seen in the free play of imagination, in daydreaming, and in the important skill of visualizing.
5. Emotional OE—can manifest itself in anxieties or joys, with extreme highs and extreme lows, both characteristic of those of high intelligence.

American psychologist Michael Peichowski declares that the heightened development of these perception channels can cause conflict and tension in gifted persons, but that it also intensifies, even enriches, that person's mental and emotional development. Thus, this heightened sensitivity and the problems it sometimes engenders are not to be considered neuroses to be cured, but rather stages through which the gifted person must be helped to pass as he or she realizes increasing potential as a human being.

Heightened sensitivity sometimes manifests itself in what appears to be very insensitive behavior. As the reader will observe in subsequent chapters, life as a gifted person can teach you, very forcefully, to protect yourself at all times. Consider how the overexcitability described in the previous paragraphs might be received by classmates, teachers, fellow workers, bosses, or even in-laws, and the need for protection becomes understandable.

Sophistication and Humor

Joseph Renzulli and T. Hartman are two educators who have developed a scale for rating students' behavior to spot gifted children in schools. Again, selected items may call up an image of someone you know or remind you of how it is in your own life. They look for kids who "see more" in a story or film, ones who "read a lot" and are "easily bored with routine tasks."

People who perceive humor in situations that do not appear humorous to others may be more attuned to the incongruities in life. Many of the gifted I interviewed use this perception to find or create humor. Even young gifted children can be found indulging in the making of sophisticated puns; by high school age, they are often adept at triple puns. Some studies report that humor seemed to be the chief element setting creative gifted people apart from others. I once watched two highly gifted teenagers exchange jokes at the beach by writing equations in the sand. One interviewee defined gifted as "people who laugh at the same things I do."

With all these advantages, how could gifted people have any problems? How could they possibly expect any special treatment? How could they dare request any special understanding of or compassion for their unique needs? And, really, shouldn't they expect to be resented?

Being Different

Human nature being what it is, being different can cause some type of problems. Being healthy is no crime, but being taller and stronger than your age-mates in elementary school does not always make you popular; sometimes, it just makes you a good target or an irresistible challenge. The interviews confirmed that gifted people work faster, question more persistently, make more connections, think more deeply, annoy more people, and have greater highs and lows than the average person. The interviews also revealed that they carry around a great deal of hidden anger about the way they are treated. Their happier marriages may be the result of a long and painful struggle to find someone compatible enough to be able to marry. Being rich or notable is often the result of an energy level that drives the individual, whether he or she likes it or not. There is no single gifted type, and the misunderstanding of that fact is one of the biggest burdens a gifted adult has to carry.

A New and Expanding Definition

At this point, the reader may feel that we have not definitively answered the question of who the gifted are and how we can distinguish them from the general population. Do we really know? Paul Torrance of the University of Georgia explains that we are dealing with an expanded definition and developing the research to justify it. For instance, we now know that whatever else it may be, IQ is not the full measure of giftedness.

The IQ test and the concept of identifying as gifted anyone whose IQ is above a certain number—even the concept of intelligence itself—have undergone many changes in the twentieth century. Few of those changes have reached the general public. Many educators continue to view intelligence in a very narrow way. Yet, reducing the whole spectrum of what is now known about human intelligence to a single round number has great potential for damaging lives.

At the end of a pleasant interview, Nina, a frustrated high school senior, says, "It was so refreshing not to be asked about numbers! I liked being able to talk about other things. I could tell you my IQ, but I am not my numbers—my SATs and all that stuff. There is more to me than that!" The IQ, in spite of almost a century of research, is often the sole criterion used to designate gifted children in our schools.

Many children and adults reject, even fear, being labeled gifted. Psychologist Mary Racamora says that the emphasis on IQ (fearing that you are your numbers?) may be part of the cause. Once it is explained that giftedness involves a broad personality profile, she says, many of her clients lose their resistance and are willing to accept this identification.

If you have been a victim of the tyranny of the IQ, these pages are for you. If up to now you have sincerely believed that people *are* their numbers, perhaps we can change your mind about those you interact with, perhaps even about yourself. It is true that the differences between gifted persons and the rest of the population can be, to some degree, measured by certain kinds of tests of certain kinds of performance. The excessive use of qualifiers in the previous statement is deliberate. We now proceed to open the Pandora's box of tests and measurements, chief among them the IQ test.

The Origins of Testing

"Intelligence is a concept created by Western culture that stresses its important values," according to Joseph Khatena in *Readings in Gifted and Talented Education*. He explains that, in our culture, we test intelligence by evaluating how quickly people can solve relatively unimportant problems without making errors. In another culture, according to Khatena, intelligence might be measured by seeing how well people can solve important problems, allowing for errors, and with no time limit. When an IQ test is administered, whether to an individual or a group, what is being tested? The debate over what is being measured continues to the present, with one additional concept gaining wider acceptance: Intelligence, whatever it is, is not the whole scope of giftedness.

One of the earliest ideas about intelligence—and, unfortunately, one of the hardest to discredit—has been the concept of fixed intelligence: You are born with it. Either you have it or you don't. It never changes. You can never lose it. Thus the educational cliché, "Gifted kids can take care of themselves." With this concept still firmly entrenched in the public mind, it is easy to see how many of the resentments experienced by gifted people arise. If each of us is born with a certain unalterable capacity, then it follows logically that (a) people might resent those who did well in the genetic lottery; (b) parents of highly intelligent children could smugly assume future success for their offspring; (c) intelligence would manifest itself, by itself, no matter what the schools did or did not do; and (d) taxpayers would resent paying for programs to help people who are automatically assured of the best of life's goodies anyway. That is not the way the reality works.

Alfred Binet

Although the actual term "intelligence quotient" was coined in 1912 by William Stern (who later decried the pernicious influence of his invention), the story begins with French psychologist Alfred Binet. Around the turn of the century, Binet was asked by the French government to develop a test that would sort out the *slower* children as they entered school so that they could be helped. What Binet actually did was develop a series of real-world tasks involving verbal analogies, abstractions, problem solving, and causal relationships at the levels on which children of various ages were known to be able to operate. Based on the task a particular child could do, he or she was assigned a "mental age."

The intelligence quotient (IQ) expresses the relationship between mental age and chronological age. If your IQ is 100, it means that your mental age and your chronological age are just about the same. "Normal" range is usually conceived to be 1 standard deviation (15 points) on either side of the central figure. From these two points, "average" intelligence begins to shade into above average and below average. At about 130, so the wisdom goes, one begins to enter the category of what is currently called gifted. Shading downward toward 70, mental retardation appears. Roughly, that is the concept underlying the IQ test.

Binet's test gave us the first straightforward method for identifying those with high ability in certain areas. It is worth noting that Binet himself did not put much faith in the tests, because they were subject to error, and he himself did not believe in the concept of fixed intelligence. How ironic that, based on the test that bears his name, so many others have continued to do so!

Terman and the Termites

In 1916, Binet's tests were revised by Lewis Terman, working at Stanford University, for use with American children. Thus, they came to be known as the Stanford-Binet Intelligence Scale, and the testing industry was born!

Terman wanted to study gifted children. He didn't believe in the stereotype of the skinny, sickly, semi-crazy prodigy or the then conventional wisdom of "early ripe, early rot." He designed one of the most ambitious longitudinal studies ever done; it is still being completed. Starting in 1921, when Terman received a large grant from the Commonwealth Fund of New York City, a team of researchers fanned out over California to find suitable subjects. They chose 1,528 subjects, based on the new Stanford-Binet test. Terman and his associates measured every conceivable facet of their lives, from the size of their heads to the number of books in their homes. They collected extensive anecdotal records on each subject from parents and teachers.

In discussing his subjects, whom he called "high-testing children," Terman noted that he found them to be "appreciably superior in physique, health, social adjustment; markedly superior in moral attitudes . . . vastly superior in school subjects . . . 2 grades, sometimes 3 or 4 [above average]." As the "Termites" moved through various stages of life, new studies were done. Ninety-eight percent of Terman's "geniuses" have continued to cooperate with the study. The result is a mountain of data, only now being completely assessed via computerization, and five volumes, *Genetic Studies of Genius*, which are considered classics in psychological research.

Although their names have never been revealed, they are an impressive group of people. They have published numerous books and articles, including fiction and nonfiction. They hold 150 patents. Seventy-eight are Ph.D.s; 48 are physicians; 85 are lawyers; 74 are involved in university teaching; 47 are listed in American Men of Science. However, though 150 are engineers doing applied research, only 51 have done basic research. The study has not produced any Nobel Prize winners, no major poets, artists, or musicians. In spite of many criticisms which have been leveled at both Terman's professional behavior and his work in recent years, Terman dispelled forever the myth of the freaky genius and showed us that the "Terman gifted" were healthier, stronger, handsomer, smarter, more educated, more civic-minded, more physically active in later years, more happily married—just about more everything! Terman's subjects seem to fit the category of superstars, described earlier.

The Age of Tests

By the 1930s and '40s, we believed we could measure almost anything. The masses of men who had to be processed through the Armed Forces in World War II provided a testing ground for a wide variety of human traits. During those decades, the idea of the Terman gifted held sway among most educators, and a whole series of erroneous concepts became firmly entrenched in the public mind. Some of them are still there.

IQ tests were good predictors of school achievement. They gave a nice, definite number with which to work; even if there were doubts about the accuracy of the score, a second test could always be given.

Notice, though, that the continued success of this idea depends on the two concepts mentioned earlier: that IQ never changes and that an IQ test really measures giftedness in all its aspects. As researchers worked within these assumptions, they began to find evidence that neither concept was necessarily true. Initially, the data that piled up were either denigrated or ignored. Then work by major researchers began to change the way intelligence was viewed.

The 1950s and Beyond

Piaget, a Swiss psychologist who initially gathered data by watching his own children, viewed intelligence as the ability to make adaptive and integrative choices. As the growing child's world is enlarged, he interacts with and comes to understand ever more sophisticated data and makes choices about responses. Although this growth is continuous, it takes place in recognizable stages. According to Piaget, a child's mental activity is dominated first by overt actions (0–2 years), then perceptions (2–7), then intellectual operations (7–11), and finally by theoretical or abstract thinking (11–15). Thus, "development" became a legitimate word to use in connection with intelligence.

Later, in the United States, J. P. Guilford's study of the nature of intelligence produced the Structure of Intellect concept (SOI), which postulates a series of intelligences. He defines intelligence as "a collection of abilities for processing information of different kinds in various ways." He was able to show that there are cognitive processes that conventional tests did not measure, such as problem solving and divergent thinking.

Educators Jacob Getzels and Philip Jackson studied 500 adolescents and discovered that those designated creative and those designated high-IQ had the same academic achievement—even though they tested as much as 23 points apart on an IQ test. They concluded that a single number was too restrictive, that it could blind us to other forms of excellence, especially creativity.

Paul Torrance, author of *Education and Creativity*, has moved this idea forward with his work in developing methods of assessing creativity. He agrees that if we establish a single measure of giftedness, we will eliminate many extremely gifted individuals who have different areas of ability.

Educator Benjamin Bloom contributed a taxonomy of levels of the thinking process which is widely used in the development of curriculum today. His studies revealed that only 80% of the IQ is developed by age 6, doing further damage to the idea of a fixed and unchanging IQ. Other research documented the growth in IQ as lifelong, as long as proper stimulation takes place.

Perhaps the most exhaustive work in widening our concept of intelligence has been done by Harvard's Howard Gardner, who has postulated a series of seven "intelligences." Spatial intelligence involves the ability to operate upon what we perceive in the visual world, and is seen in artists, sculptors, and architects, for example. In actors, dancers, and athletes, we see the flowering of bodily-kinesthetic intelligence, which is the ability to use one's body in skilled ways both for goal-directed and expressive purposes. Grouped with these two as object-related, we find logical-mathematical intelligence, which is first shown in the forming of relationships among objects and develops into the forming of abstract relations among patterns of actions. Gardner groups linguistic and musical intelligences in a category called object-free. Linguistic intelligence involves the ability to both make and experience language, as exemplified in poets. Musical intelligence involves sensitivity to musical tones and phrases as well as the ability to know how these fit together in patterns and forms, as seen in composers and performers. Finally, Gardner presents two personal intelligences, internal and external. The former involves the ability to access one's own inner feeling life. We see this in the wise elder who can use this inner knowledge to help the community. Political and religious leaders manifest the external intelligence which allows them to deal skillfully with others by sensing their needs and desires. It is obvious that these abilities could not be assessed by a simple IQ test.

So we can see that, in contrast to the original idea of equating high IQ with giftedness, contemporary psychologists and educators are saying what sensitive parents and teachers have always known. Barbara Clark of the University of California calls reliance on the IQ as a sole criterion for giftedness "unnecessarily damaging." She adds, "unfortunately many people, including too many educators, believe that the IQ score gives an accurate representation of a person's capacity. It does not."

As new concepts of intelligence develop, the challenge to measure them increases. In comparison to the task of measuring a quality as elusive as creativity, the IQ test seems a relatively simple instrument. Educator Paul Torrance concludes, "We do not know the end of the complexity of the human mind and personality . . . it is high time we began developing the strategies, methods and materials that have built into them an acceptance of this complexity." Nina was right: You are not your numbers.

Signs of Giftedness

Since the whole point of this book is to encourage greater recognition of the gifted grownups among us, how might you go about trying to spot the gifted adults in your world? Try the following checklist.

You might be looking at a gifted adult if you encounter a person who:

- Does things faster than anyone else. "I saw the whole concept in ten minutes—it took the company president two weeks!"
- Has more energy. "I hit the floor running every morning—it drives my husband crazy!"
- Has an endless curiosity for new things. "My husband bought me a telescope for my birthday. Now I have a whole new field to explore!"
- Uses up jobs. "I learned the whole job in six weeks and now I'm bored. I guess I'll have to go back to school; I need more training before they will allow me to do the interesting things."
- Is sensitive both to beauty and to pain. "I can't watch the news; the pain is too much for me."
- Has genuine empathy and sensitive perception. "People seem to know that I am a good person to talk to, even when they first meet me; I should have been a psychiatrist."

- Is not afraid to be regarded as an oddball or a weird person. "Existence is filled with opportunities . . . departing from tradition may invite stress but [I am] willing to accept a certain amount of stress in the belief that a new order will be created."
- Is playful. "You are led through your lifetime by the inner learning creature, the playful spiritual being who is your real self." (One suspects that Jonathan Livingston Seagull, as well as Richard Bach, is a gifted being.)
- Has a very highly developed moral sense. "When I believe that something is wrong, I must oppose it, no matter what."
- Has more insight and intuition than others. "Some people might want to call it psychic. To me, it's just what I do, and it is perfectly natural."
- Expresses a feeling of being out of sync with the rest of the world. "Sometimes I think I must have come from another planet!"
- Sees patterns and analogies and can do abstract thinking.
- May not have scored above 130 on an IQ test. May have scored above 130 on an IQ test.
- Just seems more complicated than other people. This complex human being may be at once "more naive and more knowledgeable, being at home equally to primitive symbolism and rigorous logic. He or she is both more primitive and more cultured, more destructive and more constructive, occasionally crazier, and yet adamantly saner than the average person."

That was a rather elaborate portrait. Did you recognize anyone? Perhaps yourself?

In this chapter, we have shown how to identify gifted grownups by observing the differences in their behavior. We have also considered the origins of some of the long-held beliefs that have limited our perceptions of gifted people. Now that there is some general agreement among psychologists and educators about the ways gifted persons are different from the general population, it is disheartening to discover so much lack of understanding in the general public, and in gifted people themselves. I often hear people say, "I know someone who acts that way, but she isn't gifted." Look again. If the person consistently exhibits gifted behavior, no matter how unlikely it may seem, give serious consideration to revising your estimate of that person's capability (especially if you are looking in the mirror). If that person is your student, your employee, or your child, look many times. You may be very surprised at what begins to dawn on you.

One more important concept should be noted. It is essential to remember that gifted persons are found at all levels of society. It is true that larger concentrations of gifted persons can be found where income is above average, but that is mostly because that is where giftedness has had the best chance to be recognized and to flourish. In different geographic areas, in a wide variety of occupations, at all ages and economic levels, I discovered gifted people. In the inner cities, in small towns, on isolated farms, in Native American and other culturally diverse communities, among our newest immigrants, among our disabled adults—the drive, the speed, the sophistication, the sensitivity can be found by anyone who knows how to look. Once we are armed with knowledge about the characteristics of gifted people, it would seem to be a simple task to recognize them, deal with their needs, and allow their gifts to enrich their lives and ours. We will spend the remainder of this book demonstrating that it is not simple at all.

Chapter Two

Inside the Gifted Brain/Mind

. . . we cannot separate gifted children into bits, as if they were really normal children who fit the usual mold but with some extras tacked on like lace adornment. Gifted children are not simply decorated normal children. They are indeed, fundamentally different . . . the brain that drives them is so fundamental to everything about them that it cannot be separated from their personhood.

James Webb, Elizabeth Meckstroth, and
Stephanie Tolan, *Guiding the Gifted Child*

In sixth grade the books stopped making sense. I was very frightened.

Mathematician, 28

 W hat fuels giftedness? Is it possible that there is some actual biological difference between the brains of gifted grownups and those of others? Dr. Barbara Clark, author of *Growing Up Gifted*, writes, "From animal and human brain/mind research we can now postulate that individuals with high levels of intelligence, gifted individuals, show measurable biological differences."

Fascination with the human brain/mind has been with us for a very long time, and not necessarily connected to questions about what constitutes a gifted person. The mysterious mechanism that sits behind the eyes yields its secrets slowly, but in the past twenty to thirty years amazing bits of information, many long suspected, have begun to form into coherent theories about brain function. Research in areas as widely divergent as physics and psychology have revealed these ideas over many years.

It will be helpful to keep certain concepts in mind. The human perception system is based on motion; these perceptions come to us through our five senses. They are processed by the brain/mind, a marvelous biocomputer consisting of an incredibly complicated network containing billions of nerve cells. The brain/mind functions in a series of phases activated by the stimulation received from the environment and controlled by a specific part of the brain. This system continually requires new content. New combinations of cell assemblies need to be formed for the brain/mind to stay organized and continue to function. Deprived of new content, brain activity begins to shut down and becomes progressively more disorganized. The person experiences a disruption in the ability to learn, even to think. Prolonged deprivation can result in irreversible damage. The level of activity required is different for each person. It also depends on how highly developed the brain is in the first place. Thus, a healthy level of stimulation for an average person may be well beyond the damage point for the high-powered brain of a gifted person.

Perceiving the World

Brain/mind researchers have shown that perception of anything outside of oneself is based on differences. Our world is made up of the perceived discontinuities in everything around us, which come to us through our five senses. The edge of the paper feels different from the surface of the desk. The ink is a different color from the page. The pen creates a weight in the hand. The scratch of the point is different from the lack of sound that surrounds it. Experiments have demonstrated that the human eyeball undergoes constant minute vibration. By arranging a series of reflecting mirrors so that the motion is stilled, experimenters were able to induce a temporary loss of vision in their subjects.

The processing of information works in somewhat the same way. Piaget describes learning as the accommodation that must be made between what already exists in the system and the new input. Differences are the source of stimulation: No difference, no novelty—no stimulation. This is probably what the junior high student meant when he pleaded with his parents, "But I'm not learning anything!" He wasn't. The material being presented in his math class was material he had mastered several years before. He could not "learn" it again. None of us can, gifted or not.

In the biocomputer we all carry inside our heads, the basic unit of the human perception system is the nerve cell, or neuron. We have billions of them. These cells are connected by means of tiny fibers called dendrites which reach out in all directions to receive transmissions from other neurons in an unimaginably complex array of interconnections. Impulses are received, processed by the neuron, and passed on, by a larger, tougher fiber called the axon. The dendrites of the next cell receive what the axon sends without ever touching. The tiny electrical impulses that constitute mental activity leap across microscopic space at a point called the synapse.

Neuroglial cells constitute the chemical connectors between neurons. An increased level of neuroglial cells allows for faster movement of impulses from cell to cell. As this endless cyclical process produces more spines in each dendrite, the neurons become "biochemically richer," resulting in more complex networks and patterns of thought. A variety of researchers have concluded that a gifted person actually has more neuroglial cells, more dendritic spines, more complex connections of neurons at the synapses, and more accelerated synaptic activity. This means that in the brain of a gifted person, ever more complex patterns can be followed, and followed faster.

Here is a possible physiological explanation of why gifted people think faster than others in many situations. Their minds do, literally, race. We might think of this as a kind of mental "warp drive" that allows for the making of connections so rapidly. A high school teacher who is a gifted grownup explains, "A suggestion is made at a meeting and six ideas go off in my head—fast! I start popping out solutions— the mind goes galloping ahead of everyone else, seeing the point, making the application, remembering it for next time—and wanting to go on to something else. How can you express in words feeling your mind go into overdrive? You become the big mouth, the chatterbox, the kid who is always raising her hand."

Bernard is unusually articulate in describing his own mental processes, using images from his work with computers. "My attention span is measured in seconds. There is a term in computer science called 'multiplexing'—which is basically the interleaving of time-dependent subjects. A crack about me is that I seem to be able to think of three or four things at once. I'm really multiplexing at a very rapid rate." But there is a price to be paid: a constant interplay of speedy perception, understanding, analysis, and then more questioning, more speedy perception, and so on, endlessly, it would seem. "It only stops when I sleep," Bernard admits.

Gifted minds also "get" things, including jokes and puns more quickly, and see more in stories than the average person. Intuitive experiences, or hunches, also seem to come to them more easily. This peculiar human quality has been explained as processing done so quickly that one is not aware of the processing, only the end result. A young woman reports, "Whenever he is in a situation where calculations must be done, my brother just gets this odd look on his face and almost instantly blurts out the correct answer. He claims not to know how he does it."

It can be an eerie feeling, sensing the machinery going into "warp drive"; ideas, possibilities, connections pouring forth faster than pen can get them down, often faster than tongue can articulate them. "Your mind works so much faster than your tongue!" I say to a gifted teenager who stumbles when he talks. The light in his eyes says, "Yes!"

Thinking

The measurement of brain waves, the sweep of the electrical impulses through the brain, has also yielded information about the functioning of highly developed brain/minds. When a so-called alpha pattern is evident, the person is said to be in an alpha state. This state allows for more concentrated and relaxed learning. It also allows for better integration of the two hemispheres of the brain.

(They are the intuitive, creative right brain and the linear, verbal, measurement-oriented left brain.)

In general, the brain waves of gifted persons tend to be more synchronized and coherent, which allows for "high levels of mental functioning." However, interrupted in the middle of a long session of thinking, a gifted person may accuse the disturber of crumbling a whole edifice of thought before it reached completion. This is one of the reasons gifted grownups truly need time alone, and regularly.

Margo, a writer, relates how she avoided yelling at her children when she was trying to work. "I trained them, from an early age, that unless there was an emergency, they should stand next to my typing table and wait until I stopped typing before speaking. It saved a great deal of grief, both for me and for them!"

Serious contemplation of the possibilities of the human mind can leave one awed, and certain that limitless human development is possible. But there is a catch. This amazingly rapid array of natural wonders is dependent upon the principle that the human perception system is based on motion. Moreover, once set in motion, the brain develops increasing levels of speed, power, and complexity, which then require increasing levels of speed, power, and complexity. It also needs something to direct all that traffic. That is where the reticular formation comes in.

The reticular formation is "a tiny nerve network approximately the size of the little finger," located in the midbrain. It acts as a kind of routing system for our perceptions. The reticular activating system (RAS) is responsible for alerting us and focusing our attention, and it needs to maintain a certain level of excitability in order to function. This level is based on the requirements of a particular brain for input, through the motions on which the perception system is based. When this does not take place, when there is not enough "traffic" in that particular brain, a kind of gap or void is created, and the mental system actually strains to keep going. It's a bit like trying to ride a bicycle *very* slowly.

Thus, when stimulation falls below the level necessary for that particular person's neural development, she may become what we on the outside describe as bored, restless, distracted, annoying. That "little devil" in the third grade is not consciously trying to give his teacher a headache; he is simply trying to keep his own RAS going! And if he is a smart kid, the level he requires could be fifth grade and beyond. Left to his own devices, he may choose withdrawal, disruptive behavior, or having a stomachache every morning. And if, as Clark says in *Optimizing Learning*, anxiety affects brain function, that child won't even learn much on the third-grade level.

The Brain/Mind Needs Stimulation

An underachieving high school student laments, "I can feel my brain rotting." Such a young person may not be lazy or merely bored. He may sense the physiological processes in his own perception system grinding to a halt, but be powerless to do anything about it because he doesn't know what is happening to him.

A precocious young woman moans, "The calculus class is so slow! I mean, one explanation is enough. Sometimes I have to wait while the teacher explains it twice, or even three times!" Her frustration may be perceived by her classmates, or even her teacher, as arrogance.

In *The Universe Within*, Michael Hunt, a psychologist, explains, "Stress input takes up most of the mind's conscious equipment and so impedes the retrieval of information from the short-term memory." The classic parental demand, "If the course is so easy why aren't you getting an A?" may be explainable in light of the stress caused by boredom, which may lead to poor performance in class.

Over and over, my interview subjects said, "I am happiest when I am learning something new." As an adult, it is difficult to describe the nameless fog that spreads throughout the perception system when, whatever the job situation, one tries to cope with repetitive tasks that provide nothing new. Many find themselves saying with that seventh-grader, "But I'm not learning anything!" Psychologists may point to "inhibition of the RAS when novelty is absent," but an employer will use terms like "lazy" and "uncooperative" to label an underemployed gifted adult.

Lack of Stimulation Can Cause Damage

Much has been learned about the brain/mind in experiments in which the subjects are deprived of *all* stimulation—lying in bed in a white room, floating in the sealed dark of a sensory deprivation tank. In his essay "Physics and Perception," David Bohm reported his amazement at what happens when the sensory deprivation is extreme: "The general structural attunements built into the brain since early childhood tend to disintegrate when there is no appropriately structured environment for them to work on. If we compare these attunements to some kinds of skills . . . perhaps it is not entirely unexpected that they should decay when they are not used. But what is still surprising, is the extremely great speed with which skills built up over a lifetime can deteriorate." Depth perception, color perception, and reading ability can all be temporarily affected. In terms of the amount of stimulation a high-level brain requires, some jobs, and many classrooms are experienced by gifted people as a form of sensory deprivation.

Research carried out by D. O. Hebb at McGill University in Canada led him to conclude that "psychological development is fully dependent on stimulation from the environment. Without it, intelligence does not develop normally." Have you ever heard an adult say, "You know, I was really smart in elementary school. I don't know what happened. I just lost interest I guess"?

Hebb's studies also indicated that the absence of stimulation could destroy motivation as well as induce strong emotional states. As this girl relates: "They put me in the lowest math group by mistake in sixth grade. I just turned myself off, put all wrong answers on some tests just to amuse myself. It took me three years to turn myself back on. I only did it then because I decided I wanted to go to college." Other researchers go even farther in describing deterioration in learning ability, problem solving, and reasoning. They even report "restlessness, irritability and occasionally fear of panic proportions."

Kimberly, stuck in a job that required that she spend whole days doing nothing but standing at a duplicating machine, reveals, "I began to have nightmares, irrational fears. I awoke one morning and could not decide what dress to put on. Then I knew my job was making me crazy." The high suicide rate for gifted teenage boys comes to mind; the bright dropouts, the drug-addicted might be explainable in light of some of this information. "I got a bad job review and was told I'd be fired if I didn't improve," says a women with a 155 IQ trying to cope with a job which consisted of typing and stuffing envelopes all day. When she asked her supervisor if she could possibly have more to do, he gave her more envelopes!

How many of the difficulties on assembly lines can be traced to this information about how the brain's functioning, or lack of functioning, depends on a stimulating environment? This much is true for all kinds of brains, all kinds of people. Mentally challenged persons are quite happy doing repetitive work in sheltered workshops precisely because it is not monotonous to them; with their limited ability, even a simple job becomes an endless and delightful challenge.

The gifted adult who fights the system and annoys everybody, but doesn't seem to care, pays a high price. Perhaps she knows, or at least senses, that not fighting would extract an even higher price; some researchers say the damage may be irreversible. A troubled high school graduate who fought everyone who tried to help her explains, "Fighting is the only way I have to feel alive."

Integration of Brain and Mind

It may seem from the discussion so far that the emphasis on stimulation of the perception system does not square with our earlier discussion of the different types of gifted persons. It may seem to reinforce the idea that all one needs to do is give the little "egghead" tons of intellectual work to do and everything will be fine. In school, just give the average child two worksheets and the gifted one four. On the job, just give the adult more envelopes. If we humans had only one dimension to our brains, the intellectual one, that might be fine; but we have what might be termed three separate brains. Each has different needs and functions but depends on integration with the other two, in order to operate successfully.

The concept of the triune brain, developed by Dr. Paul McLean, director of the Laboratory of Brain Evolution and Behavior of the National Institutes of Mental Health, goes something like this: At the top of the spinal chord sits the oldest and the most primitive brain, which is known as the reptilian brain. It is in charge of the automatic (autonomic) system: heartbeat, breathing, blood pressure, circulation. It is this portion of the brain that can be accessed in biofeedback. It is, if you will, the internal part of the brain. It has no language faculty, but is in charge of regulating a great deal of our physical well-being.

Sitting atop this brain, close to the center of the inside of the skull, is what has been called the old mammalian brain, the emotional mind, or the limbic system. Here, biochemical reactions trigger what we call feelings of rage, anxiety, affection. Our pleasure centers are here, *not* in the highest brain. Most important, it is the gateway to the next system, where the thought processes which distinguish us as humans occur. Those processes can be enhanced or inhibited by the opening or closing of the chemical gates activated by our emotions.

Surrounding these two older brains, fitting over them like a large crumpled gray cap, is the neocortex, the cerebrum—the new mammalian brain. Physically, it takes up most of the space in the skull. It is here that we process data from inside and outside our bodies, where we experience what we call our senses; where we think, plan, analyze, remember, and have insight and intuition. It is the only part of the system that can communicate in language, the language area being located in the more analytical left brain. It is this thinking part of the brain that we usually designate as mind, *but*, the chemical triggers that can inhibit its function are located in the limbic system, where the emotions reside.

Thus, if maximum speed, complexity, and power are to be developed and then used after development, all three systems must be working in active integration. The physical and the emotional support the higher brain functions. According to educator Barbara Clark, the triggering systems that shut the biochemical gates to optimal functioning are "boredom, threat, anxiety and sameness." The turn-ons? "Pleasure and challenge."

Limitless Potential for All?

We all have potentially much larger capabilities than we now use. Some believe that these can be increased by stimulation. "Intelligence is the birthright of all humans. It is much more normal for the human brain to grow and expand than not," says Clark. "Because parenting has not been given priority, most parents do not know these things. From conception to infinity, we have the possibility for developing potential." If intelligence is both environmental and genetic, and capacities can actually be increased by stimulation, this bodes well for all.

But if we accept, as almost a century of research indicates, that those persons who are closest to the top end of the spectrum of human abilities actually do develop more complex brains, then certain other elements in both our thinking and acting must be changed, as we realize that "brain processes present at birth will degenerate if the environmental stimulation necessary to activate them is withheld . . . the genetic contribution provides a framework which, if not used, will disappear"? This other side of the coin is crucial in thinking about gifted persons. Without stimulation, nurture, recognition, and care, the initial genetic advantage is not only not developed, but may result in an actually impaired human being. Gifted persons do have a more highly developed perception/processing system—a different brain, if you will. Stimulation sufficient for an average person may not be great enough to prevent damaging sensory deprivation for a gifted person in school, on the job, in the conduct of personal life, and in the contribution that person could make to society. The brain we have been describing continues to grow. The more it grows, the more it requires. An often repeated statement by Abraham Maslow, could be the motto of this book: "Capacities are needs."

But sometimes needs conflict. Specifically, smart kids and gifted grownups are often forced to choose between their need for stimulation of the brain/mind and their emotional need to fit in. Many of them avoid such conflict by hiding their gifts.

Chapter Three

In Hiding

For the majority of sensitive people, the true self remains deeply and thoroughly hidden.

Alice Miller, *The Drama of the Gifted Child*

Many gifted people have discovered that life is easier if you mask all or part of what you are. Fear, rejection, and bitter experience can drive some people to conceal the very qualities which make them unique and valuable. Disguising their talents in a wide variety of ways, many of the gifted begin this process in early childhood. The covering up, in order to fit in, can last a lifetime.

Amy has big blue eyes and a whispery voice; her flaxen hair is tied with a ribbon. Pink shorts compliment her lacy white blouse. A successful journalism major, her delicate hand forms a fist which slowly pounds the cushion of the sofa between us. "I'm sick of being a sweet little girl!" she exclaims. Amy is afraid to allow her family to see the person she really is, because she has defended herself all these years by being the sweet little girl her Southern family expects. "I learned early that aunts liked hugging; so I hugged. And Daddy didn't like little girls who lost their tempers, so I didn't."

Amy remembers trying to give up the cover. She and her brother, veterans of multiple corporate transfers, decided that the move to a new eighth and ninth grade was going to be the one where they changed their images. "I was going to stop worrying about what people thought of my brains and try to be more social. My brother was performing what he called 'character surgery' on himself and was

35

going to stop being a brainy wimp, lose twenty pounds, and take karate lessons. The emotional strain was so great that on the first day in the new school we both got sick and had to be sent home.

"Actually, no one ever was jealous of my good grades because I was so *nice*. . . . You can't just acknowledge that you are smart and go on from there because people don't like that . . . you get tired of playing the game. You want to be totally honest and say, 'Look, this is the way I am and if you don't like it—tough!' . . . but at the same time you want someone to say, 'I like you' . . . you get caught in the game and lose the person underneath. Even though I know it's only a game, I'm tired of it . . . Could I stop? Do I know anything besides the game?"

Losing Yourself

In *Passages,* Gail Sheehy describes the game rather well: "With the debut of the first separate sense of self about the age of two, we are endowed with an extraordinary gift: the makings of our own individuality. The price of cultivating this seed is the separation, the gradual and painstaking process of separating the inner reality of ME from the glorified images of THEM. Therein lies the rub."

Gifted persons are, from childhood, more sensitive to the vibrations of those around them. They can sense tension, acceptance, and rejection at an early age. And being highly capable, they learn fast; they learn how to survive. If being sweet gets the best results, you are sweet. If playing dumb means getting more friends, then you play dumb.

As part of the quest for self, the child learns whether his little world accepts the asking of questions or punishes those who ask with laughter and abuse. If the former, he can pass GO and take his chances with the world of school and playground. If the latter, he will have to begin to make some of the most important decisions of his life (never mind that he may be only 6 years old): He has to begin to decide what he is willing to trade for what; how much emotional pain he can stand; and how much of the self he is willing, quite literally, to bury. This is not done consciously, of course; by the time the conscious stage is reached, it is often too late. The process is described in an anonymous letter in Maslow's *Toward a Psychology of Being:* "How is it possible to lose a self? The treachery, unknown and unthinkable, begins with our secret psychic death in childhood—if and when we are not loved . . . it is the perfect double crime in which he himself also gradually and unwittingly takes part . . . Oh they love him, but they want him or they force him or expect him to be different! Therefore he must be unacceptable. He himself learns to believe it and at last even takes it for granted. He has truly given himself up. No matter now whether he obeys them, whether he clings or rebels or withdraws—his behavior, his performance is all that matters." Maslow comments, "the child, faced with the difficult choice between delight experiences and the experience of approval from others, must generally choose approval from others, and then handle his delight by repression, or letting it die, or not noticing it, or controlling it by willpower."

Conforming

She wants to know, to work to learn more. "They" won't let her. They make fun of her if she insists, or punish her for creating problems—must be something wrong with her. "They" are parents, teachers, siblings, peers, supermarket clerks who resent being asked how the cash register works. If the emotional pain is too much, she can always become like the other kids, at least outwardly. It has been reported so many times that it has become a classic story: the parent visits the first grade classroom to find the precocious child stumbling through a first grade reader in perfect imitation of her classmates.

The child conforms, but the urge is still there. She can feel, as gifted advocate Barbara Clark says, "the power you are never allowed to use." Some gifted people expend a great deal of energy devising very clever covers in order to get through their lives. Perfecting that cover can use up so much energy that it is not until some later identity-questioning time (at 17 or 47) that the person realizes that the covering has been going on for years.

Being Cute

The sweet cute cover is especially useful for girls, but is often a trap, as Amy discovered. "That's me!" exclaims Joyce, "I was a nice kid. I should have been a rebel. What I should have done was tell everybody I was bored so they would give me something else to do, so I'd shut up. I was loud when I was little. It was just that I finished everything ahead of everybody else and I wanted someone to talk to. I became too quiet in junior high in an effort to change my image . . . now I think I'm at a happy medium."

As a teacher, I can recall being appalled when a senior, whom I had known since kindergarten as "such a sweet person," revealed that she had been teeth-gritting, fist-clenching angry since second grade at "people who wouldn't let me *do* things!" Her Oriental family expected respectful acquiescence, not challenging of teachers. She took out her frustrations on hockey fields and basketball courts; she didn't know that it was all right to be the way she was until she was 17 years old.

Sometimes one just doesn't talk. A high school senior confides, "My ideas are always so different from everyone else's that it's not worth the hassle I'll get if I open my mouth." And a 20-year-old says wistfully, "In high school, my mind said so many things that my mouth never did." A middle-aged gifted woman says succinctly, "I didn't get teased. I kept my mouth shut. For thirty years."

Manipulating

Very clever gifted children, especially boys who are not physically impressive, describe a cover consisting of careful suggestion and manipulation. In school, he gets others to discuss a topic by asking very naïve questions in such a way that the questions he wants to ask are raised by others, at least to the point where he can ask the one thing he wanted to know without seeming out of place, or out of line. The group to be manipulated almost always includes the teacher. Interviews yielded reports of this system being used successfully as early as third grade. One can become a well-liked adult this way. One can also get an ulcer.

Being Helpful

Another defense against the pain of rejection is to allow oneself to be used, to become the person everyone asks for help, as early as first grade. One boy reports that, not knowing any better, he simply gave the answers to workbook problems to anyone who asked. The distribution of his largesse was halted by an understanding mother who tactfully explained that this wasn't what was meant by being helpful. Now a computer science major, he still has trouble saying no to people who want help with programs.

No matter how helpful you are, the resentment lurks just below the surface. It appears in school when the tests are handed back. Here is revealed the double bind that gifted adults live with all the way up through the corporate board room. It is expressed by a high school student receiving a perfect score on a test, but it describes what he has lived with for many years and what he knows he can expect in the future: "The number 100 has eyes, glaring like the rest, at you . . . When asked, turn the paper over, revealing the eyes, and without bending mouth, utter IT in a mumbly way . . . Just be sure to ask for theirs first, or your grade rises up into their eyes beyond the reach of inquiry, pity, or helpfulness . . . Yet you wait for the swell of murmurings when you tell the person two aisles away that you got a C. Anything less than an A is half-teasingly considered a failure."

One is not allowed to enjoy accomplishments, but one is not allowed to be average either. Somebody always seems to be waiting for you to fail so they can gloat. A retired executive still remembers how a gifted grownup was treated in the retail clothing business, especially because she happened to be a woman in a man's field: "It's the same at school or in the workplace; if you do it better than anyone else, they glare. Indicate that it was easy, and they glare more. But if you do an average job or you fail, they laugh. People almost seem to wait for you to stumble. It's supposed to be conceited to enjoy your accomplishments, but you aren't allowed to be ordinary."

A smart kid learns to walk very carefully if he or she wants to get anywhere.

Being Nasty

Inevitably, there comes a time when being helpful isn't cool for the male of the species, and being kind is something only girls can get away with. The mouth can become a cover if the fists can't measure up. The class clown, no matter how high his grades, is allowed to be one of the boys. The class nasty can frequently defend himself by grinding people into the playground asphalt almost as well as an adult—verbally. He or she pays a terrible price in loneliness, possibly for a lifetime. The glib tongue becomes a formidable weapon against both peers and teachers, and later against subordinates and even spouses. The smart(-aleck) kid threatens, often successfully, any teacher he considers beneath him, and that is most of them. Often, it seems to be a way of lashing out at the adults for not providing what these children know they need: a more stimulating environment.

Inside the class nasty is often a lonely and, even more sadly, a delightful person aching to find someone with whom he can feel at home. At 18, one such young man said softly after an uncharacteristic burst of real emotion, "There's so much inside, sometimes a little of it leaks out." Now at 20, after two years at a major university where his intellect is appreciated and his teachers are sometimes world authorities, he is quieter. He can tease a friend gently and even admit to being nervous about spending a year abroad. Hopefully, he has lost the need for the armor he wore all through school.

Substances to Ease the Pain

If the pressure of being different becomes too much, there are, by junior high school at least, people and activities and substances that can use up all your energy, provide you with new and fascinating experiences, and ease the pain, all at the same time.

After Martin showed up drunk in a tenth-grade Spanish class, his teacher read his folder, looking for clues, and found: "Martin seems to have lost interest in school [in third grade]"; "brilliant original science report on shells he collected at the beach but he is constantly behind in his workbook and does not hand in his math homework." It was a familiar story from there on: bored, listless, he was cutting class, failing everything, and considered that it was all his fault. "I can't do anything," he replied when asked about his interests, ignoring his capable guitar playing and his knowledge of art and literature. He could engage his teacher in a sophisticated discussion of the ideas revealed in *Animal Farm* ("I read all my sister's books in eighth grade"), but he was failing a slow English class. He was solving the problem of perfectionist parents who didn't understand that he needed more, not less, by retreating into alcohol and pretending to have no abilities at all.

Chris was the classic "druggie," or so it seemed to his teachers. Product of an abusive father and a chaotic home life, he exhibited the ragged clothes, uncombed dirty hair, and tell-tale idiot grin at the wrong times. But in spite of knowing giggles from other students, he would persist in trying to participate in class discussions even when he couldn't finish a coherent sentence. His first essay, passed up from the seat farthest away from the teacher, was a well-done drawing, no words. The second was an extremely well-written analysis of *One Day in the Life of Ivan Denisovich* as a criticism of Marxism, in a class where students were learning to write in complete sentences. The third paper revealed his desire, which he had no hope of realizing, to be an architect. The fourth detailed what he would like to do to the people who run "the system." It was excellently written, violent and frightening. He fell madly in love with a smart girl in the last months of his senior year and transformed his appearance. His intellectual interests were accepted; he was even "allowed" to study. But his old friends mocked his girlfriend and taunted him. After graduation, he moved into an apartment with them and retreated behind his psychedelic cover again.

College Covers

After surviving the rigors of secondary school, a gifted young person may find that even college is a life space best negotiated by masking at least part of who you really are. At 20, Farah has already worked on a cancer research project as a summer job. She describes her life as an affluent student in an Ivy League school: "I can't let myself be a dumb little fluff. But I have to be careful so my boyfriend won't think I'm competing—brains are supposed to be emasculating, you know. And I'm careful so my girlfriends won't think I'm showing off. I guess I just don't want to make other people feel bad. And yet, one day my roommate just lashed out at me, 'It's not fair that you should have looks, money and brains too!'"

Being a smart kid at a mediocre college can be a painful way to get an education—in isolation as well as academics. Once designated a DCR (damn curve-raiser) in freshman year, the person may be labeled for four years. Nora has done graduate work at a European university, but the school she originally attended featured large doses of boredom with weak courses and resentment from both students and faculty of her academic standards for herself. "I liked asking questions in class. I think people got hostile because the prof and I seemed to be having a good time. After a while, it got to me and I just shut up. My sociology prof didn't call on me deliberately because he said I did too much work for the level of the course. When I came to him with my term project all planned in advance, he was actually nasty. Social life? I have to be careful about dates. The last person was angry with me for using big words—and he had a master's degree in business!"

An intense student at a highly respected Catholic university, Bob enjoys discussing serious issues, but he finds it very lonely at parties because, he theorizes, bright girls have fallen for the myth that to be popular you have to cover your brains. "To go to parties you have to do without discussing things you really care about and be more trivial. I have begun interesting conversations with girls I know are very smart, only to have them turn it off if they think someone else may be listening."

Job Disguises

Tricia explains some of the reasons for protective coloring on the job. "In the office, they began to call me the walking dictionary, so now my speech adapts to the people around me. It makes me feel fake, but I have to do it. I know I am not like the people with whom I work. My mind gets stagnant and wants to do something challenging. My whole body gets restless." Tricia is grateful that her secretarial job will last only until she has enough money to return to art school. "I should understand that others are only protecting their egos, but I have worked hard for what I have, so don't insult me for using it." In spite of her efforts at a cover, she admits, "I probably do give too much information when I am asked a question."

Government service can require the use of at least a temporary cover for your smarts. A young National Park Service employee reports that she has to be "more sweet, less sharp" on occasion to get older superiors to listen to her ideas. "Then I can go back to my immediate boss, who is really smart, and we have a great time carrying out our ideas."

Even your outside activities are sometimes better covered. A grandmotherly type, Gloria decided to go to college in her fifties. This seems to have disturbed her coworkers' image of a diffident personnel secretary. Absenting herself from the lunch table gossip to do her homework has prompted sarcasm-laden remarks, such as "Well! Where was our little student today, off with her books?" She has decided, "Next course I take, I'll work at home."

Uncovered

There are some who, in spite of the consequences, refuse to hide, from their earliest years. Whatever the world dishes out, they can take, both absorbing and causing pain. They hang on to that self at all costs. They are maddening to teachers, parents, coworkers, and peers. They simply will not be bullied into behaving according to someone else's standards. A brilliant medical student says, "I was never tolerant of people. If I wanted to learn something, my parents simply had to get me the books I needed to read. You can't go through life worrying about not offending people."

When interviewed at 18, Nora was in the middle of a difficult transition; her widowed mother had married into a warm but uneducated family. "My stepbrothers get hostile because they think I'm showing off. But I have gotten a lot noisier in the last year. I state my opinions. I'm sick of going along. It isn't worth it."

A 47-year-old mother of five describes it this way: "After thirty years of being a good little kid, the change (outspoken opinions, college degree, rejection of family religion) was a real trauma for my family. But you have to go through the rebellion sometime. One advantage of doing it later in life is that you don't care what anyone thinks. I don't cry much any more!"

Robert, a college poetry professor who has driven trucks and installed boilers, grew up in a tough city neighborhood. From seventh through tenth grade, he says, "I almost had it beaten out of me that what I had was valuable. But in eleventh and twelfth grades a change took place. The toughies-but-dummies who had beaten us up all those years had trouble passing the fire department examination. Three or four of us who were smart didn't laugh, and suddenly they treated us differently. They knew that we would be the ones who got the good jobs." Robert has never had to use a cover because he has found a way to run his life. "Even in tough situations where macho is important, you can't be effete, but you can be respected if you know what you are talking about. You would be surprised at how many well-read truck drivers there are in this world."

"I have never been allowed to hide," says Laura, an actress, writer, and radio personality. When her first-grade teacher discovered that she could read, she was trotted around her parochial school like a circus freak until her mother put a stop to it. "At various points in my life, if I had had a cover, I would have presented a very pleasing facade which would mask the mind that frightens people. Lacking that, I try to establish some sort of frame or context in which people can understand me. Part of my exercise in my current radio job is to see how unusual I can be and get away with it."

Memories can remain a long time. In the middle of an interview, a retired educational administrator flashes back to the pain of a day in sixth grade when he realized that his best friend resented his good grades. "We were lifetime friends, and he's been dead for ten years," he muses. "Why should I think of that now?"

Alison raised five children while experimenting with painting, sculpture, and interior decorating. Then she acquired a Ph.D. while teaching full time, which certainly advertises her status as a gifted grownup. But even she says, "You have to have a good cover. Mine was (and is) a good little kid. But," she adds with a grin as the interview ends, "it's important to let one or two people read the book."

True. All you have to do is find one or two people who understand the language in which you are written. One of the most poignant discussions of covers takes place in a short story by Wilmar Shiras called "In Hiding." A child who is an incredibly brilliant mutant hides his abilities in fear until a psychologist helps him to see that there must be other mutants scattered around the earth, the results of the same radiation accident that altered his genes. All the loneliness of living with a cover is depicted in just a few sentences: "'You mean—there may be more? I'm not the only one?' he added in great excitement. 'Oh Peter, even if I grow up past you I won't have to be lonely?'"

If a puzzling person is part of your life, consider the possibility that he or she is a gifted grownup with a good cover. If you are a gifted person, remember that one of the places to be yourself and to find others is at home. There is comfort, as well as an interesting dynamic, in a household composed of varied and powerful people.

PART TWO

WHEN THE SMART
KIDS GROW UP

Chapter Four

The Gifted Family

Home is the place where when you go there, they have to take you in.

Robert Frost, "The Death of the Hired Man"

A good crucible for brightness . . . all those years of a loving, warm, open family!

28-year-old

When I tried to find someone who would understand me, and was ridiculed, my parents were there to understand.

40-year-old

A gifted person of any age needs what we all need: a circle of loving persons who will accept you for what you are, and who will help to ease the pain when most people don't understand, and a few others who are like you, to make life fun and keep you from being lonely. That sounds like a good description of a warm, loving family.

We often forget that a family is the context in which adults as well as children work out their lives. A single individual cannot be isolated like a butterfly specimen and studied dead still. Gifted people of all ages are acting within the framework of some sort of structure. Each individual is moving, or not, toward growth in self-worth, personal maturity, education, lifestyle, and relationships. Dealing with the family as a unit has many advantages.

Gifted children are very likely to have gifted parents. If these parents can see themselves as part of a dynamically interacting group, they may be able to reach back into their own childhoods to gain crucial empathy with other family members. A very bright child who is feeling rejected at school or in the playground may derive consolation from knowing that a parent went through the same difficulties. For the adolescent impatient with the imperfections of others, looking at parents and other family members as gifted people can provide important insights, not to mention better family relations. Living through the trying twenties, whose storms are multiplied for the gifted young person, may be easier on mothers and fathers who can admit to undergoing similar storms themselves. Viewing grandparents in this light can lead to greater family harmony. A retired gifted adult needs fuel for the machinery within. What is dismissed as aging crankiness may be as profound a cry for help as that of a misbehaving third-grader.

Unfortunately, some smart kids are born into families where intellectual needs are neither understood nor accepted. For some boys, brains are considered nonmasculine. ("What do you mean, you tried out for the chess team?") For some they are nonpractical. ("You want to be a physicist? How can you believe that someone would pay you to think for a living?") In other families, brains are nonfeminine. ("Let the boys win once in a while, or you'll never have any dates.") For some parents, a woman athlete is safer than a daughter who is suspected of being smart. And some just never understand the need for mental stimulation. There is the man whose mother berated him for spending his depression-era allowance on "foolishness!" (books). A college student reports a mother who commented, "For what you spend on books, you could go to a lot of parties."

Mark, a young man whose life has been a struggle to cope with a world which did not believe how sophisticated a child's ideas could be, recalls that he made his father feel threatened. "When I was about ten, I remember overhearing my father say, 'That kid thinks I'm stupid. I can't stand having him think I'm dumb!' I guess I had said something pretty precocious."

During the course of my interview with Mark, it was readily apparent that what we had here was two gifted people, in the same family, neither one of whom understood how the gifted function. The same curiosity, independence of method, and need for stimulating work characterized both father and son. How much better it could have been if that father had been able to see that the defiance of authority which his son exhibited in going his own way academically (failing boring courses because they insulted him) was the same defiance he engaged in when he quit a successful sales job and started his own company because his employers refused to make use of his talents. The son was clearly aware that what was bothering his father was "He's bored; he's used up all the challenges." Somehow, he never connected it to his own difficulties.

But families, supportive families, are crucial for the development of a gifted child's potential. If parents are wise enough to help each member maintain a good self-image by making room for the way each one operates, then those people outside the family who do not understand can be dealt with. However, to create this kind of healthy atmosphere, it is necessary for the gifted adults to have knowledge of their own needs and be able to work toward satisfying them.

Life Stages or a Special Rhythm?

In families with highly intelligent people, it is especially important to remember that the need for constant growth continues throughout life. As far back as Shakespeare's "Ages of Man," the concept of growth stages in the lives of both adults and children has been explored. Gail Sheehy modernized the concept in her book *Passages*.

However, both men and women report another factor that seems to override these stages, at least in gifted adults. These people focused on accomplishing one goal and moving on to another, regardless of any stages. I concluded that gifted grownups experience a constantly repeating cycle of renewal and growth which does not seem to be keyed to any life stage. Indeed, there seems to be a special rhythm to which a gifted life moves, must move, if the adult is to feel fulfilled and contribute to society.

That endless drive, that feeling of always having so many things one wants to get done, is evident in George, as he describes himself as a father in his early forties. "I still feel very 'adolescent' in many ways—as if there are still all these things I want to get done. I don't feel as though I'm on the downside of anything. It feels somehow, in the last few years, as if 'it' has finally arrived, and now we can start."

However, the feeling of being *adolescent* can leave a parent, especially a father, feeling guilty if he does not understand that it comes with the territory. He may worry because he cannot seem to settle down the way most fathers do. Working one's way through the ordinary life stages can be trying for anyone, gifted or not. Various contemporary writers have defined these growth stages, which describe us as we break away from home, establish families and careers, reevaluate ourselves in middle age, and adjust to aging and retirement. Trying to balance living to the rhythm of a cycle one does not quite understand with the emotional responsibilities of growing children and the need to support a family can leave a very bright parent angry and torn.

Dr. James Webb, the psychologist who co-founded SENG (Supporting the Emotional Needs of the Gifted), explains, "Just because we pass age 21 does not mean that we have finished going through life stages. Gifted adults seem to hit the stages earlier and more intensely." These are the periods in a gifted parent's life when he or she may find it extremely difficult to deal with the demands of spouse and children.

Father's Needs

Viewing the family as a collection of interacting high-powered minds requires attention to parents as both givers and receivers of what a family can provide. Is the father impatient, fast-thinking far beyond anyone in the household? As a result, does he tend to lose patience with others, demanding far too much of his children? Or does he simply provide, in a dynamic way, the "fast track" atmosphere a gifted family needs? Is he the quiet self-absorbed type, who withdraws, and does that result in emotional awkwardness for his children? Or does he provide the intense understanding that a like-minded offspring may crave? Is he simply doing his best without knowing what his best really is?

Frank was a Harvard graduate student at 19 and is a successful young executive at 30. He managed to make it through regular elementary school. "I always got As. I goofed off once in fifth grade, and got a C. I don't remember if it was the belt or the fist, but my father allowed me to know that I wasn't to do that again." He talks very little about his childhood, but he does say, "I had two very smart friends in school who never amounted to much, because they had no one to look out for them. My father was always beating on the school—he made them change my courses. He got a nearby university to let me take math courses when I was only fifteen." Frank's recounting of being hit for receiving a C indicates a father of the first type.

Eric is the self-absorbed type; his family has become accustomed to his "tuning out" in social situations. There is simply something more interesting, to him, going on inside his own head. However, his idealism and perfectionism have led him to demand all-or-nothing achievements of his children. His daughter reports, "I always remember the time I came home with all As but one. I had worked hard for those grades and all I got was, 'Why did you get a B?'" None of Eric's children has become an underachiever, the frequent result of overly demanding parents, but each has grown up with the feeling that, "No matter how much I do, it's never enough."

A father who is extremely frustrated with his own life can also be hard on his family, as Myra explains. "My husband is a very bright man. He is stuck in a dead-end job, which he hates, and he is taking it out on the boys. They are bright, but he is incredibly demanding of them." In this family, marshaling resources to allow for further education for the father may be best for everyone's development.

More Complex for Mothers

In today's society, a gifted mother has an even more complex set of circumstances with which to cope. This seems to be true regardless of her age. At 52, Margo explains, "I have little patience with growth stage theories, mostly because they all seem to stop somewhere in the fifties! I feel that I am just now entering a new stage, and I intend to keep entering new stages until I die. I do not intend to fade away into some mythical 'sunset' stage any time soon!

"Of course, I can look back and see those stages in my own life. I didn't 'break away' soon enough in the trying twenties. I did solidify my life with home and family in my thirties. I felt the accomplishments of the renewal stage with my master's degree. Along the way, 'empty nest' pangs appeared, very mildly in my case, as my children launched their own lives. But all of these stages occurred like background functions. The overriding drive, all my life, has been 'What's next?' What is there that I can do that will be a learning experience? I am currently planning a major career change, and possibly a geographical move; I am also thinking about going back to school."

Theresa is an example of a woman who moves to the special rhythm of the gifted cycle of growth. She left her practice as a pediatrician to be with her two daughters for six years. "I stayed home with my children because that nurturing is more important than twenty years of medical practice. I am raising the future mothers of America, and that will outlast me for many generations. I need to be home with my gifted daughters to give them the special opportunities they require. My kitchen is a mess because they need to glue and cut and create things—a housekeeper would never put up with that! I enjoy being there for the new idea, when they are excited and want to share—a caretaker could not provide that feeling which adds to their self-worth. I would like to make them each a rock inside, very secure. When you have that inner security, you can deal with the world's unkindness."

In typical gifted fashion, Theresa is asking "What's next?" for herself. "I have exhausted all I want to know about flowers and trees—we designed our own swimming pool and that took time. I've explored the intricacies of cooking, grooming, and decorating to the depth which satisfies me." At the time of the interview, she was deep in plans for her new office; during her time at home she kept up with her field by reading, and gained some new ideas about pediatric medicine. She laughs, "People think I'm nutty. They ask, 'Don't you ever stop?' I admire Thomas Jefferson; he dabbled in everything!"

Moving to this rhythm is different for Alison, who has grown children, who are parents in their own right, as well as a demanding job as an elementary school principal. She is always looking for a new project, a new something to learn. "You work yourself to a frazzle and once it's done and you reach a point where you could tread water (after finishing a doctorate), and you're out looking for something new to kill yourself with! The things that kept me sane when my (five) kids were growing: tiling the kitchen wall, sculpture, painting, sewing, collecting antiques, decorating. I just wanted to see how they worked. The fun is in the challenge. Life is a juggling act—with three eggs!"

Alison recalls an instance when she drove her family to distraction with her fascination with antiques. "I bought a chair, and when I got it home I launched into this big explanation to the children of all its important features. Finally, one of the boys said, as politely as he could, 'Mom, this is really boring.' I tried to behave myself after that!"

Today's Young Parents

Alison's daughter Kate is now an attorney and the mother of two boys. Her husband is also a lawyer. They are an example of gifted adults being conscious of the necessity of being good parents while they satisfy their own needs. "I realized that I couldn't stay home and be satisfied, so I have a job where I can bring the baby if I need to. My husband and I juggle a lot of things. On weekends, he works with my sister in a furniture refinishing business, and he takes our son with him, so he can see his father work with his hands and understand that."

Another busy young mother, Meg, has found a kind of liberation in the juggling act which is a professional mother's life. "I used to discipline my entire being. Now I can let it all out. The kids and I love being noisy at home. We have a good time. The children, my work at graduate school, restoring my house—I have a built-in boredom factor. When I use up a job, I add complexity, or find new jobs."

As Meg's two boys mature, they will be good companions for one another, if the world does not appreciate the results of all the freedom to grow which their mother and father try to give them. Meg's husband, Ian, works long hours as a construction supervisor and coaches his sons' soccer team, but he still finds time for what nourishes his own intellect—ballet and classical music.

Parents as Role Models

It is essential for parents to know that regardless of their educational background, they probably share their gifted children's abilities and can help them to make their way in the world. What seems to make the real difference in what parents can give their gifted children is not so much shared activities, but the role model provided by a parent who does his or her best, but who *does*.

In Rita's case, respect was built early; revelation of talent came later. "My father always impressed on us, 'I can't tell you what to do, but I will show you by what I have done.' He was never intimidated by my smarts, but he knew early on that he couldn't really help me. However, we still influence each other. At 65, he began to paint—with such sophistication of line and color! I went back to painting, after ten years."

Delores credits her gifted father with rescuing her education. "Dad was a policeman who did a lot of public relations work with schools. I had a chance to apply to the special academic high school in our city and turned it down. A couple of months into the year, I realized how bored I was and just casually mentioned that maybe I should have taken the opportunity to go to a fast-paced school. He used his contacts with the school system to pull some strings and within a week I had changed schools. I had a wonderful four years."

Interviews also yielded many single young women who not only understand, but respect the things their mothers have done. "My mother is more than just a housewife," Cindy maintains. "She enjoys contributing to society. I enjoy thinking, philosophical people and I'm really very comfortable around adults; my peer group often has trivial conversations. When I get home, I'm glad my mom is there to talk to."

An educational administrator with two master's degrees, Julio describes his steelworker father as "very bright, very well read; the kids used to call him 'professor.' Even when we couldn't afford it, we had books. He was so proud of my small collection, he built a shelf for my room. He would take people up there and show them my books. When he died I found notebooks for self-improvement with entries like, Read all of Wilkie Collins . . . Read all of Shakespeare." Julio recounts the waste of a gifted person simply: "The steel mills killed him."

"My father has little education, but he taught me much. He built our house," says Cindy, a photographer. Heather adds, "My father never went to college, but he goes on book binges—we feed them to him!" A musician and hardware store owner, Morgan's father was, she recalls, "always a big reader, even though he left school at fourteen when he came here from Canada."

Ned concludes, "My father taught me higher values; my mother taught me how to survive in the world with them." Kimberly enjoyed "matching wits with Dad; the result is, we're both good at it." Respect was built in Brad's case: "We always played games, but the first time I could beat him was as an adult." Sometimes, it is the child who has to cope with a parent's accomplishments. Jahmal is a street-smart weight lifting coach who says, "I have trouble relating to my mother sometimes—she's the one in college!"

Parent–Child Conflict

However, even very bright parents can encounter conflicts with their children in terms of styles of behavior. Colin is a brilliant, if quixotic, computer scientist. He describes a high school career filled with bizarre science projects and the collecting of electronic gadgets. "My friend in twelfth grade was allowed to build a science fair project in his bedroom. His parents let him take up two-thirds of the room with tubes and he even cut a hole in the wall for wiring. I was very envious; my parents always made me put everything away each time I worked on a project."

Though intelligent professionals in chemistry and medicine, Colin's parents never quite understood his passion for electronic gadgetry. "I remember one birthday, I had received twenty dollars as a gift and I went right down to the electronics surplus store because a piece of equipment that I wanted cost exactly that. Not bothering to remember carfare, I had to walk home (three miles) lugging this big thing, and I was late for my own birthday party. My mother screamed at me—she just couldn't understand that buying this hunk of junk meant more to me than being at my party."

The younger child who is math/science-oriented but who is also nonverbal needs particularly careful handling, if he or she is not to become what Barry, a Ph.D. candidate, has termed a "science brat." He explains that, "Sometimes, science-oriented smart kids, like me, feel empty because they lack development in the arts." Being verbal aids in social development, and a nonverbal child, with all the same needs and responses as anyone else, may have difficulty expressing them. If care is not taken to provide an open, caring home life, both school and home can conspire to convince such children that it is safer not to let feelings show. As the adolescent begins to consider behavior options, he or she often believes that a separation must be maintained between feelings and intellect, and that intellect is somehow worth more. If that happens, we should not be surprised when a "cold" adult or "science brat" is the result.

Tim and Adrian, Gifted Parents

Adrian and her husband, Tim, are an active young couple who understand the dynamic of a gifted family. Both had difficult childhoods. Tim recalls, "My parents didn't approve of me. My father called me a 'No good goddamn kid' all through elementary school. I had to go on my own to sign up for the special high school I attended in Detroit; my parents refused to fill out the forms. It was the teachers I trusted in that special school who explained to me what it meant to have an IQ of 165. I was poignantly honest about who I was in college. I still say things out of place sometimes."

Adrian recounts a bleak childhood of another kind. No one ever allowed her to know that she was bright. "I went to kindergarten expecting to play in the sand and sing, but one day they took me to another room, with older children I didn't know, and I was expected to read. No one ever explained. I was scared because I thought I had done something bad." When a sensitive aunt suggested that she might have superior abilities, "My mother's only reaction was to say, 'Oh really.'" She drew her own conclusions as she tried to manage her racing mind all alone.

"While the other kids were reading, my mind raced! I'd go to the pencil sharpener, tap my toes, anything. In third grade I went through what I can only describe as a 'mourning period.' I felt as though something inside me was dying, as though I had lost my best friend. In fourth through eighth grades I tried to rally my friend, but I had altered my thinking patterns so far, in my effort to adjust, that I remember thinking that I was at the end of my substance. I felt like I was on the moon and someone took my moon shoes away—I just drifted. Along the way I had become a very bad behavior problem. My parents were pillars of the church, and here I was with this awful reputation. I did things because they made me laugh. It was either that or become a babbling idiot—the laughter released the tension inside me."

Adrian discovered the real nature of her advanced ability only with the help of her super-bright son's fifth-grade teacher. Determined to give her three children a different kind of childhood, she devotes full time to their care. Recalling her own experiences has helped Adrian to view, realistically and sympathetically, the position of her 9-year-old son, who, even in a special program, is unlike anyone in his school. He is a gentle boy, an avid soccer player, respected by his classmates, but he is still "different."

Unlike the blank of her childhood, Adrian talks openly to him about how he will have to make his way through life. "I want my kids to know what the game is up front. I want Jon to know that he'll pay a price, but in the long run he will get wonderful things." The museum trips and the special lessons and the home computer and his butterfly collection are all fine, but sometimes, she says, all she can do is hug him and say, "It isn't easy being so different, is it?"

At those times, "He hugs me back, so tightly, and says quietly, 'No, Mom.'"

If she opts for full-time child raising, as Adrian has done ("I could get ten Ph.D.s with what I've learned raising these kids"), then a gifted mother still has to cope with her own needs for intellectual stimulation. And suburbia, even affluent suburbia, can be a difficult place to find it. "You can't integrate everything inside," Adrian explains. "At some point you have to have a verbal exchange, or your mind gets glutted, like a house in which the windows haven't been opened. You get so tired of trying, looking, hoping, every party you go to, every new house you move into, that you will find someone who is compatible. There are things I need to talk about, and all my neighbors want to talk about is their Williamsburg reproductions."

Never mind that Tim was company vice president at 35; he sits here now in shorts and a T-shirt, teasing his wife about why he fell in love with her. "It was those long legs," he grins, after he points out how bright she is and what good friends they are.

Financial priorities are set carefully, Adrian explains. "It was new drapes or Jon's hockey camp. We felt it was more important that Jon be able to find ways to relate to other kids, because his intelligence can make it hard to fit in at school." They worry about getting old. Since Tim's executive position disappeared in a merger, he has learned to worry about his job.

"We lead such ordinary lives," Adrian comments. They do things together as a family: trips, gardening, reading stories, baking cakes. Their interests and worries are like those of any growing family. Jon may have produced a beautiful mounted butterfly display at 6, and the walls may be graced with Adrian's photographs and Tim's paintings, but they care about love, companionship, a feeling of belonging.

Tim concludes, "As a family, we experience a variety of drives, needs, and opportunities. We also catch butterflies and plant gardens. I paint. We have an awareness and understanding of one another. We want our children to have a chance to develop everything of which they are capable."

The World of the Gifted Child

Even with caring parents, the world must be a very strange place to a smart little kid. Here she is, looking out at the world learning and absorbing the Way It Works, at what seems to be a normal pace. If the whole family is bright, a child may not notice much for the first few years; contacts with the wider world are limited for most 2-year-olds. Inevitably, as playmates, sales clerks, neighbors, and other strangers enter the picture, the child begins to realize that the answer to "Doesn't everybody do that?" is "No."

As interaction with the world beyond Mommy's arms increases, this little being whose brain/mind has been genetically programmed to work faster than most, to absorb more than most, and thus to need more than most, encounters conflict and resistance. The child pushes on the environment, does things faster, makes precocious observations, asks questions adults can't answer, is not tactful about knowing more than others, and does things other kids can't do. From the child's point of view, the other 95% of the world is not doing things "correctly." So begins, to a greater or lesser degree, the realization of being different. The child may be treated as a delight ("You made your bed!"), an annoyance ("Must you ask so many questions?"), a freak ("Look everybody, she can read!"), or a threat ("You think you're so smart, well I have news for you").

At a very early age, *they* can sow the seeds of joy, confidence, and love or doubt, fear, and anger. The questions begin. Am I the only one? Is there anyone else like me? Am I bad? If I'm not bad, why do I make everyone unhappy?

Whether it's parents who slap or strangers who stare, curiosity, questions, and accomplishments one is proud of create a less than enthusiastic response from the world, which is so large. The child, who is so small, begins to conclude deep inside, even if he or she doesn't have the words to say it, "There is something wrong here." The next conclusion may well be "There is something wrong with me. I cause pain to the people around me. Mother frowns when I open all the cabinets, Father looks annoyed when I ask questions, people stare when I read signs in the store, the other kids get annoyed when I can climb higher."

The decision-making process begins early: whether to change, adapt, or deny. Yet, it is not possible to deny completely. The push of the mechanism itself continues. He tries to explain, "I already know how to do that." He may even demonstrate that he does know. "Why can't I be in fourth grade? I like their work better than first-grade work!" Something inside pushes to know, to grow, but "they" punish or ignore or laugh or expect favors. Is the pain worth it? The only way to change this mechanism is to allow it to rot from disuse.

Several of those who described themselves as shy could remember a time when this was not so. As young children, they had been outgoing and in several cases recalled being very talkative and full of questions. Although most could not pinpoint a specific time when they withdrew, several theorized that they must have learned, over time, how to be shy. One recounts, "Along about eleven or twelve, I just wanted to be quiet and fade away and never say anything again because my mouth seemed to get me into trouble."

All children need nourishment, grudging or otherwise. Some survive with a pattern of benign neglect. What they do not need is to be stifled by lack of recognition or deliberately thwarted in their efforts to take the world at their own accelerated pace. Lack of recognition can be accounted for by sincere ignorance, but are there gifted children who are deliberately held back? Of course. Many of them. Referring to information gleaned from the family diaries of Hermann Hesse, the German novelist, psychologist Alice Miller relates: "Like so many gifted children, [Hesse] was so difficult for his parents to bear, not despite, but because of his inner riches. Often a child's very gift, his intensity of feeling, depth of experience, curiosity, intelligence, quickness—and his ability to be critical—will confront his parents with conflicts that they have long sought to keep at bay with rules and regulations. These regulations must then be rescued at the cost of the child's development. All this can lead to the apparently paradoxical situation when parents who are proud of their gifted child, and who even admire him are forced by their own distress to reject, suppress, or even destroy what is best, because truest, in that child."

A teacher of gifted elementary students, Tanya recounts the reaction of one mother to the news that her son was highly gifted, IQ around 185. " 'Oh my God, what do I do now?' she moaned. It was vary hard for her. She had this notion that she might damage this bright being. For a while he became very difficult to handle. His mother was so threatened by that label that she was hesitant to give any guidance or direction. She reasoned that if this person was so bright, who was she to tell him what to do? Eventually she could see that he was still only a first grade little boy and she had to be natural with him. She was able to accept that it was her good nurturing as a mother which had prepared him to take full advantage of our gifted program."

When parents realize that they have a child with "it," they may begin to view the child in a kind of separate way, unconsciously treating the child as if he or she is somehow a different type of human being now that a label has been pinned on the child. It seems possible that this, as much as teasing from peers, is the reason some kids hate the term "gifted." They may sense that stepping back, the disruption of the emotional current that flows between parent and child.

Audrey is a brilliant academician, college professor, authority in her field at 35; she describes her earliest memories as a sense of playing a game. "I must have been just under two. My parents had this set of cards with all the fish in our state on them, and all the birds, and I guess I memorized them. It was my trick at Christmas that year— they'd hold up the card and I'd say the name. I got a reaction from the relatives for that . . . but from around two, my parents treated me like something from outer space. I was three or four when they had me tested, and my IQ was projected at around 200. My parents pulled back—they kept a distance from me in a very horrible way. Because they stood back so much, so early, I had to repress a rage that they didn't treat me better. That rage has never left me."

The emotional space between Audrey and her parents has never been crossed, in spite of family therapy and her own deep analysis in college. She has vowed to treat her own two children differently, but even she reports that it is difficult to do so. "My son is bright and difficult, as is my daughter—she can read at four. She's very inventive, original, and a very strange child. But as soon as I think that I wonder, Am I doing the same thing to my children that was done to me? And I give her a big hug to let her know she is accepted. Recently, my son criticized something I said to my daughter—he criticized me, and I felt a moment of withdrawal from my own child! I worry about that. Children are such victims."

Stimulation: A Necessity

Because the child does not understand his or her own difference, it is usually not possible for younger children to articulate their need for stimulation as easily as, say, the need for more food with a simple "I'm hungry." If they could spell it out, it might sound like Farah's description of the demands she made in junior high: "I hollered a lot. I want to learn things! I want books! I want tutors! I have to absorb all the knowledge of the past! I did scare my parents. My mother tries not to let me know when I intimidate her—my father lets me know."

A childhood rich in stimulation of many kinds does not seem to require anything fancy—although it is nice. It is important that parents take the initiative in providing activities. George is a college professor who grew up in a tiny town in Wyoming. His father is a school custodian. Gaile is a psychologist from San Francisco whose parents worked in factories and raised her in a modest duplex in northern New Jersey. Liesl is a successful illustrator but her father's business interests made her an international traveler by the time she was 12. Yet, all of these gifted grownups emphasized an aspect of their childhoods that they remember as rich and pleasant and that they feel has contributed to their well-being: doing things. They had parents who talked to them, allowed the child to follow them about and share in simple household tasks, encouraged them in learning to fix things, and took them to interesting places at an early age.

George recalls that there were always books and reading in his home. "Dad would take us out into the country about ten miles from town to see the old homestead where my grandparents had begun their life in the West. The house was deserted and falling down, but there was a bookshelf with books still on it, including a copy of *Hamlet*. I remember thinking—I was only about nine—of all the strange things ... homesteading in Wyoming ... scratching a bare living ... and a copy of *Hamlet* on the shelf." Musical ability was encouraged by the small country band his parents had, and George still plays several instruments for pleasure. The richness of his early stimulation allowed him to work his way through majors in music and physics before deciding on teaching literature as a career.

Besides her psychology practice, Gaile is a civic activist and amateur historian. She credits her ability to juggle many activities and to make contributions to early training in problem solving. "My parents simply thought that you should know how to take care of yourself in the world, and not be afraid to take on the challenge of making something on your own. I learned to sew, to cook, to make household repairs. We had little money, so when something broke, I was always challenged to see if it could be repaired or a way could be found around using it. To this day, when I begin a new project, I make many mistakes, but I have learned to deal with them using problem-solving techniques I acquired as a child. Learning to live is as important as learning how to think."

Probably because of their frequent travel, Liesl's family has always been close, and her parents saw to their children's special needs in many ways. "We were never treated as though we were a pain in the neck because we were kids. Our questions were taken seriously, and answered, if answers could be found. My father always took the time to explain monuments and things like that as we traveled. We had a large Lego® set, and each weekend, my father would assign us a structure to build; once it was a spiral staircase! My parents always encouraged discussion at the dinner table. Now that we're older, we have great arguments."

Word-play, argument, verbal wit, jokes, games, puzzles—they are among the least expensive toys a child can have. They also represent the kinds of skills which are crucial for the nurturing of lively minds. One woman remembers, " We had insane jigsaw puzzles to do. One was a Jackson Pollack painting. We played Crypto and Mind

Maze. I hated going to bed because I was always afraid I'd miss something." An older woman recalls, "We always did our homework around the kitchen table, but we always ended with games. I remember Lotto, Chinese Checkers, little Chinese hand puzzles. My father never let you win because you were a kid. He respected us."

Siblings

Siblings can go a long way toward increasing or decreasing feelings of security and belonging in a family. Theresa is one who was conscious of her ability as a threat to her younger sister: "I always had to show her the ropes. I could always beat her, and I was frustrated because I wanted someone to play *with*." Rudy believes, "I may have influenced my sister negatively because she had to live in my shadow; she was always my 'sister.'" Gloria, an aspiring singer, resented being the shining example in the family. "I'm sure my brothers hated hearing, 'Your sister got all As.'"

A sibling can be the ideal friend for a gifted person of any age. Marcelle, a lawyer, says, "I have always been very close to my brother. Neither of us fit into a large set of conventional cousins, uncles, and aunts. My parents were not focused on the larger world 'out there.' We two were the only ones."

Living away from one's family, a sister nearby can be a special blessing, as Kate has found: "For my sister, I don't have to hide my weaknesses. When we were growing up, people used to ask her if she wanted to be like me, because I was outwardly so successful. She'd surprise them with a loud No. She knows me too well. She's one of the few people I could ask for help. We dread one of our husbands being transferred."

Illustrating another facet of gifted sibling relationships, Amy explains, "It's hard to live with a brother who is a constant reminder of your own limitations. I don't like to argue. I know I am no match for my brother. As we were growing up, I was the good little kid, partly because my brother was the rebel. I would eat my vegetables just because he didn't." The notion that gifted kids don't behave like perfectly ordinary kids can be dispelled by comments like these.

Others

One of the most fruitful, nourishing things you can do when you realize, no matter the age, that one member of the family (including yourself) may be a gifted person is to take whatever information you can gather and apply it to the rest of the family. Troublesome aunts and uncles, weird cousins, cantankerous grandparents, and irritating spouses may be more readily understood—and more lovingly treated. How liberating to know that these people also have to cope with being different!

As a gifted person of any age, the people one prefers may sometimes be found among relatives. Mark wonders, "My aunt is much older, but she always seems to enjoy talking to me for some reason. She's working on a Ph.D. in music; I head straight for her at large family gatherings. My grandfather is great to be close to. I spent a whole summer with him when I was 15. He's a factory worker, and that helped me to understand that you can't judge people by their position. He's still a very smart man."

Cecile, a college professor, reports a key influence in a grandmother. "She was a central European matriarch, soul of the earth. She wore exotic clothes, and she read to me. She made occasions to read—Tennyson, of all things, and Longfellow—I can't imagine how she found them." Lillian recalls, "My grandfather was hard of hearing, but he could always hear me. He knew about a lot of things. We discussed Shakespeare."

Career choices can often be influenced by a relative who understands a particular interest. Colin's mother may not have understood his missing his own birthday party, but "I have an uncle with a Ph.D. in political science, who also had a cabin in the Berkeley hills. He was the one person who encouraged my interest in electronics. Some of the happiest memories of my childhood are of time I spent in that cabin playing with electronics equipment."

And Morgan—a gifted grownup who has changed so many of her ideas that "I can't talk to my parents any more; they just get upset"—has found that one person she loves to spend time with is her mother-in-law. "She does things. She is well on in years but that doesn't stop her. She reads, does volunteer work, has accepted aging gracefully. I really enjoy going to museums with her."

Nina's Family

Nina is model slim. Curled up in a chair in her parents' comfortable living room, she looks the part of an affluent young suburbanite. At 18, she is stepping out into the business world as fast as that world will accept her. Her brightness has been nourished with both stimulation and acceptance from the start. Love and affection abound in her family, especially as she is the youngest of five. Stimulation in the way of games, puzzles, music, crafts, trips, and arguments have always been part of her life. Brothers and sisters who taught her anything she wanted to learn provided an outlet for her incredible energy level.

"Everybody was pretty well along mentally by the time I was ready to learn things. By the time I got to kindergarten I could have been in second grade! My brother Todd taught me to read as he learned it, four years ahead of time. My little friends would come over and I'd suggest reading a book and be puzzled because they couldn't read yet. And games, always games! I remember that Mom would play Concentration with me every day before I left for afternoon kindergarten—I could beat her. My siblings did so many things with me. They would take me on dates—to go bowling, to the mall. They taught me to fix a bike, play hockey; I learned lacrosse when I was eight."

School was the only dark spot. Her feisty mind and high energy level made school, especially the last year of high school, a nightmare. "For a while, Mom was the only one who understood. I'd unload on her. She fought with the principal to get me out of one really awful class. If she hadn't been here, I don't know what I would have done. For the past several years she has been my best friend."

At 18, Nina enjoys the responsibility of a full-time job in the retail clothing business. She has detailed plans for her own shop—construction, stock, location—on paper already. "I know I have to slow down a little and learn things like accounting (she's taking courses at the local community college) or I'll fall on my face, but I think I could be ready to move in three years." She concludes with, "It all depends on what is brought out when you are young."

Understanding for Parents—From Children

As part of the interview process, I asked several young adults near the end of college if they could offer any advice to parents raising gifted children like themselves. In letters to me, Heather crafted some practical advice; Mark created a metaphor and shared a poignant understanding of the job any parent has to do.

From Heather: "I'd say that parents should encourage their kids to do well, treat them the same as any other kid, and make sure they are well rounded, with culture, sports, and hobbies. Take an interest not only in their gifts, but in their social life. In high school it's very hard to be intelligent and not feel pressured by your peers who always say, 'You make me sick, you got an A again.' It is really hard to deal with people being jealous. Parents should talk about it; it helps to relieve a problem to complain about it to a sympathetic ear.

"For me, college is much better, because that is where I want to be. My brother is not going to college and he is already making money and loving his work as a carpenter. If a gifted kid has a skill or wants to wait a year or so before college, why not? I don't think my parents ever gave all this much thought. They just encouraged us to do what we really liked as long as it didn't hurt anyone, and it wasn't illegal!"

From Mark: "I would say, direct without forcing. You are the wind, and your child is the sailboat. He or she mans the tiller, and ultimately chooses the course, but while the boat is starting out, you as the wind can influence its possible direction. The tiller belongs to the child. You cannot take it from him or her. But if you see a direction more favorable than others, you can blow in that direction and the child will have no choice but to see it as the path of least resistance. Offer advice from experience without asserting, and free the boat if it becomes beached or runs aground. But above all, no matter how hard the wind blows, the child must feel as though he or she is steering the craft and making decisions. A conscious decision is the only thing in life we can truly call our own. If others make these decisions for us, what do we have? Be careful. If the wind blows too hard, and the storms gets too rough, the sailor may abandon ship . . . the water can look lovely, so dark and deep.

"I myself have made it thus far, a student at a highly accredited institution, and look at all the rough seas I've come through. At some points I was hanging on to the gunwales with a finger, but I have arrived in one piece. I would say that my parents were quite successful, but it is not an easy task blowing on someone else's sail, while trying to steer your own craft, by yourself. This is what I would say to concerned questioning parents of kids in fast racing boats."

The Dynamic of a Gifted Family

Within the dynamic of the family can be found all of the persons who appear in the chapters that follow. Understanding the interaction of their special and sometimes conflicting needs is essential if we are to nourish their abilities successfully. To look at a list of characteristics of the gifted, like the one below, in terms of how a whole family interacts is to understand and perhaps turn to forces for good the high energy that crackles among any collection of high-powered minds:

- Heightened sensitivity, both emotional and physiological.
- Need for challenging work: resistance to routines, authority, low frustration tolerance.

- Increased levels of inner conflict: relentless self-criticism, difficulty in choosing among multiple talents.
- Difficulty in dealing with others: impatience, reluctance to accept criticism, unrealistic expectations, coping with hostility from others.
- Feelings of isolation: hiding talents.
- Deep concern with morality and justice, whether personal or world problems.

These interactions can run the gamut from delightful to painful. A family whose members can see themselves as interacting in a dynamic group can make provisions for these qualities. Heightened sensitivity levels can be understood and provided for by special quiet times or quiet spaces within the household. An open discussion of problems in getting along with a world which doesn't understand can be a safety valve, an expression of love and support, and a means of learning coping skills—for adults as well as children.

Gifted people of all ages tend to make incredible demands on themselves, especially if they are multitalented. Family members can provide support for one who needs to set off in a new direction. Being openly involved in each other's lives can allow parents to assist a college student changing majors. Children can pitch in to help a mother who needs to return to school or grow in other ways. A family group can agree to a more modest lifestyle so that a father can return to school or take the risk of launching a new career. Blunt but loving criticism can help a "scattered" person of any age regain essential balance.

If shared by the family, the high idealism of many adults may be directed outward to help the world, instead of inward to demand perfection of other family members. An extreme attitude toward giftedness is a danger which a family group can help each other avoid. "Pity the poor gifted" will solve no problems; nor will "I'm gifted, so the rules don't apply to me" create a better life for one's children. Striving for the balance of a full person will create an atmosphere in which talents will not be hidden, and feelings of isolation can be relieved.

If you are a member of a gifted family, ask yourself whether all members of that family can find the recognition and shelter they need within that space. Can father come home and complain that no one understands him at work? Are mother's frustrations with lack of stimulation from the carpool acknowledged, and is she encouraged to find ways to feed her mind while she feeds her family? As she pursues her own career, does she receive the support, both practical and emotional, that working mothers need? Can a grandparent freely express frustration with not being taken seriously or treated intelligently?

As more individual situations are explored in the coming chapters, keep in mind that even though the gifted come in all ages, shapes, sizes, and personalities, they do have much in common with everyone else. All of us operate in some kind of context, some kind of structure, which, however unconventional it may be, serves us as "family." It is the place we begin and the place to which we should be able to turn for the shelter and recognition we all need.

Human beings who have these essentials can survive the misunderstandings and adjustments that are inevitable if you are gifted. When and if they meet those educators who can give them what they need in school, they will be equipped to respond. It is so pitifully easy to tell, at any age, if a gifted child has been loved. Those who receive love and validation at home can often bloom in spite of horrors or neglect at school. Those whose families do not provide such validation sometimes are rescued by a sympathetic person along the way who helps to make school or job a validation. But often, too often, such people do not bloom; they survive.

But no matter how loving and supportive a family may be, the day comes when we must leave the protection of the family circle. If one is a gifted child, along with a little lunch box, one takes that powerful drive to know, endless questions, speed, insights—in short, a different brain—and sets off for that most wonderful and most dangerous of all society's institutions: school.

Chapter Five

School: Hard Times, Easy As

*Why are the only things that are important, things that teachers
tell me, and why do teachers only tell me things I already know?*
Smart kid

Picture a Classroom . . .

We have assembled a special class that comes together
only in the imagination, but what they will say is very real. They are
going to talk about schools, where it is well known that some smart
kids can learn more material faster than other students. What is not
so well known is that other gifted children may learn in ways that are
not understood by their teachers, their parents, their classmates, or
even the students themselves.

Drawn from the interviews, the comments of these people paint a
picture that reaches across the geography of the United States and
the span of this century. They are people who have attended schools
from Northern California to South Florida, in circumstances from
battered inner city, to posh and private. The ages of our students
range from 18 to 90; occupations from college student to retiree.
There are Ph.D.s, heads of departments, government officials, secretaries, entertainers, and criminals in this imaginary room.

It is their variety which makes it so uncomfortable to listen to
what they say about life as a gifted child in America's schools. Most
of them see the quality of that experience as poor. Their judgments

upon the educational community are harsh. It would seem that American writer William Saroyan's poignant memory of elementary school could apply to any grade: "I was so bored that I made remarks all day long. (Well, sometimes I didn't. I sometimes fell to dreaming, and kept my mouth shut all day. Or I became both bored and depressed and didn't want any part of the action, at all.) During the ten-minute recess morning and afternoon, I would race out to the playground and ask myself, 'Lord, Lord, what are we to do, what are we to do? It is all so stupid, so boring, so everlastingly slow.'"

Like Saroyan, the gifted grownups I interviewed serve as proof for educator Joanne Whitmore's claim that "Gifted children are the most misunderstood and educationally neglected group in America today." They bear out the statement of Victor and Mildred Goertzel, who wrote about 400 famous people in *Cradles of Eminence*, that many of them had serious school problems. They offer some insight into why, according to psychologist Joyce Van Tassel-Baska of the College of William and Mary, in the Chicago suburb where she once worked, 45% of the gifted students had grade-point averages lower than C, and 14% of the dropouts had IQs over 130.

The sad fact is, a significant number of gifted children fail in school. Why is this so? In his essay in *Psychology and Education of the Gifted*, researcher Paul Witty explains that as far back as the 1920s, we knew that certain children learned so quickly that by fifth or sixth grade they could be two full years ahead of their classmates. But, as they grew older, Witty says, "the attainment of many pupils grew LESS commensurate with their early promise. It became clear that the typical curriculum was unsuitable to offer these pupils sufficient challenge or motive for effective and continuous learning." Less commensurate? Yes, unfortunately, much of the good work done by parents can be undone by the schools.

Are your chances for a good school experience any better if you are one of those described earlier as a striver or superstar? Are you less likely to do well if you are an independent? Not necessarily. Having a particular type of stance toward learning is only one factor. What seems to have made a crucial difference for many students is understanding, supportive teachers. They allowed the superstars to

grow in many directions, validated the hard work of the strivers, and helped to make life bearable for the independents. Watch for those teachers as you read.

The Stages of School

Our imaginary class describes what seem to be three stages in the journey from kindergarten to grade 12. There is initial confusion, coming to terms with being different, and surviving with an adult mind in an adolescent body. If you are one of the grownups for whom school was a nightmare, these stories from your peers can help to put your experience in perspective. Parents and educators should read this chapter as a cautionary tale.

Stage 1: Confusion

The first stage is the confusion and mystification of the early grades as children move out of the home into a larger world and find that their (to them) normal way of operating in relation to the world results in rejection. At the very least, the little person will be confused and far too often will conclude that the self is the problem and begin to distort it.

Helen, a Ph.D. Candidate in Her Sixties. "In upper New York State, I flunked kindergarten! I never knew why. I always thought it was the bunnies—when we drew bunnies I drew lavender ones. After that the teachers talked among themselves very seriously. I was put in another group and for twelve years my best friend could gently remind me, 'But you are a year behind.' Translation: you must be stupid."

Michelle, Career Woman, in Her Thirties. "I spent half the time in first grade in parochial school in Pennsylvania in the back of the room—insurrectionist acts like dropping pencils on the floor or reading ahead in the reading book. I always wanted to do the art

projects in colors different than those dictated by the teacher. If I did it their way I knew I would get the 'glory' of having it hung up. If I wanted it my way, I would have to choose not to be recognized."

Cecile, College Professor, Fifties. "My first-grade teacher in New Jersey was a bitch, and I had no one to save me. It was made so clear to me even at six that teachers loved pretty little girls, not ones with glasses and unkempt blonde hair like me."

Meg, Teacher and Doctoral Candidate, Forties. "In second grade I was asked to cut out the rising and setting times of the sun from the paper. After the first few times I refused to do it—once I understood the concept, I saw no point to it. That year the teacher announced to the class that I was passing by the skin of my teeth. I remember sitting there thinking that teeth don't have skin."

Barry, Chemist, Ph.D., Twenties. "In elementary grades in Georgia they thought I had a learning disability because I had trouble paying attention—I was just bored, and my mind would wander to more interesting (to me) things."

Audrey, College Professor, Thirties. "I was treated so strangely. I remember once in third grade when the class was not behaving well, the teacher took me out in the hall and asked me what I thought she should do about it. Here I was just a kid, and she talked to me like an adult. I was put in the back of the room with the slow learners so I could help them. I hated having to teach the other kids; I wanted to learn things."

Many of those interviewed reported third grade as the most traumatic of their elementary years. The average third-grader is a question-asking machine. It is likely that the sophistication, not to mention the persistency of a gifted child's questions could strain relations with all but the most understanding teacher.

Bernard, Computer Salesman, Twenties. "Of course they were annoyed at my questions! A teacher who has thirty-two kids to worry

about is going to shut you up. You develop the ability to choose not to be hurt."

Heather, College Student, Twenties.   "On parents day, my third-grade teacher told my mother that she should tell me to slow down because she was running out of things for me to do. I was so angry, but I couldn't talk back to the adults."

Heather learned that the true pressure on many gifted children, as well as adults, is to stay with the others—in effect, to under-achieve. An educational administrator observes, "The thing people lose is a sense of wonder . . . by third or fourth grade, we have often wiped it out." We at least make sure that no one draws lavender bunnies.

Goldy.   Goldy is an example of a gifted child who defied all efforts to distort or stifle her quick mind and high energy level. "When I was growing up I perceived things very quickly. I would say what I thought, regardless of who was listening. I argued with teachers, questioning why I had to do certain things. There were conflicts as early as preschool. I have always been involved in art. When we drew, the teacher required that we stop at the moment she said time was up. I would continue to finish what I was working on and she would tear up my paper—a very uptight woman to be teaching! Soon my mother began to ask where all my cute little drawings were and I said, 'Miss————tears them up.' My mother was furious!

"In kindergarten it was necessary to convince the teachers that I could actually learn faster than the other kids if I was allowed to wander around the room or play with a small object while we learned the words to a little song, for instance. I was eventually permitted to draw during class in first grade for the same reason.

"With teachers who didn't understand, I'd be more and more bel-ligerent—I think that is how I preserved my 'self' at that time. If a teacher shut me up, she only shut me up physically. My mind would be racing, little secret conversations with myself . . . all the things I wanted to say and couldn't . . . like a secret wink. As a child, I was constantly reading, never satisfied. If I came across a word I didn't

know, I would have to look it up. I read encyclopedias for fun. I had (and have) an insatiable drive for knowledge."

As the conflicts escalated, along with parental trips to deal with teachers' complaints, it became clear that Goldy could not develop in a regular school. Three years in a special school with a very open learning environment allowed her to gather her resources for a try at a conventional but private school.

The rest of Goldy's education, through senior high, was a struggle. High grades eluded her until college. "I was always put with the 'difficult' kids—and that often meant the slower classes. I had little motivation to work my way up. Whether consciously or not, I seemed to decide, 'OK, I'll behave like someone stuck in a low class and adopt the habits of those around me.' Some classes were open to all levels, and I did well in those. Of course, there are many bright kids, like my sister, who conform easily. But then there are ones out in left field, like me. So many teachers never understood my need for a sympathetic teacher and a slightly different way of learning."

Now a poised and somewhat mellowed graduate student and teaching assistant in organic chemistry, Goldy admits, "For much of my life, it was me against the world, and I wasn't sure I was winning . . . So many people never reach their potential because nobody knows how to deal with them." One can only speculate about what might have happened to her without caring professional parents, special schools, and a sense of humor.

Stage 2: Knowing You Are Different

The next stage in the school experience seems to involve the decisions of the somewhat older smart kid who is learning the painful rules of the game and is beginning to make conscious choices about dealing with the world. When does a gifted person begin to be separated from fellow students, like it or not? I asked ninety average kids when they first became aware that there were people in the world who were smarter than most kids. The answer was surprisingly consistent: third or fourth grade. Gifted grownups recount the realization of the difference this way:

Bob, College Student, Teens. "In third grade my friend and I made our own Western movie. My father filmed it for us at a local park. In fourth grade we organized an intramural soccer league for the whole school, and the principal loved it. But when we went to him with a plan to study more history after school he said that it was not a good idea. We were crushed. We never planned a big project again."

Bill, Convicted Felon, College Student, Thirties. "I never understood why we had to be in school; there didn't seem to be anything much going on, at least in my school in south Florida, and because I was little I was picked on a lot. Once in fourth grade I got all As, but no one reacted. Since there didn't seem to be any difference in getting As or Cs, I went back to getting Cs."

Audrey, College Professor. "By fourth grade they had run out of things for me to do. They took four of us and after we had spent the morning with regular classes, being bored, we got to spend the afternoon in a special room with a lady who came to Michigan all the way from Columbia University. We learned on our own. I read all through the Civil War, ancient history, physics—I loved it, but it ended when elementary school did."

Joan, Poet, and Teacher, Forties. "I had no library until I moved from rural Maryland to Ohio in fourth grade. I seemed brilliant in a blue-collar steel town, but all I remember of fifth grade is the following scene: A hot radiator on the left . . . Alan Mercer reading, haltingly, on the right . . . and the teacher screaming at the top of her lungs, 'Don't read ahead! Don't read ahead!'"

Michelle, Career Woman, Thirties. "I remember once in fifth grade I managed to read a whole book under my desk between 10 A.M. and 2 P.M. When I told the library ladies that I had read the book the same day, they looked at me like I was from Mars. They didn't know how to mark such a thing in their little book!"

Paul, High School Senior, Seventeen.   "In sixth grade I was arguing with the teacher about a math problem and she made the statement, 'A tree branch has a certain length.' It seemed logical to me to point out that since it is growing, the length is constantly changing. I was treated like I was an idiot."

Dora, Computer Scientist, Forties.   "In sixth grade in New York City we had IQ tests. The first time, I came out retarded. I came from a poor neighborhood and was lost among all the sophisticated kids. The second time I was put in a special group. I have trouble to this day dealing with stories, so I was lost in English. I did well in math, but the math teacher would humiliate me in front of the class for not doing my homework."

Frustration Increases.   As the middle school or junior high school grades appear, one can hear the smart kids' disappointment in the system. Already, they are beginning to turn away from school as a source of real learning. Yet, so important is this period in a child's development that one noted educator has said, "If you have a teacher in your school system who can walk on water, put that person in your middle school!"

Bob, College Student, Teens.   "In elementary school you get looks. In fifth grade they call you brain. By junior high you start cutting off— trying not to use the sophisticated words you learn."

Colin, Computer Scientist, Forties.   "Seventh grade was like being in a prison. My mind was elsewhere all the time . . . I thought about sex a lot . . . One teacher gave a little more to do, and that was my first inkling that school could be enjoyable. In actual fact, I could spend 10 to 12 minutes a day on schoolwork, and still get Bs. (My friend and I figured this out, and used to sit and laugh—'Think what we could do if we studied!') My intellectual stimulation in junior high came from reading my mother's college biology books and my father's medical books. I was a typical bright kid: bored with school and doing what I had to do to get by."

Jonathan, College Student, Nineteen.   "In llinois, I would sit there in math, understanding better than the teacher. But you must 'Ponder'—'Think' (it helps if you scribble). You must never blurt out the answer without thinking, because that ruins all the teacher's leading up to things and makes the other kids turn and stare. By sixth grade I had perfected this method: wait long enough, raise hand slowly, and answer in a hesitant voice. When I was finally scheduled into accelerated math in eighth grade, I realized that I had done half of the material in seventh on my own!"

Several studies have shown that it takes a mathematically gifted eighth grader between three and fifteen hours to learn first-year algebra well enough to achieve a good grade on a standardized exam. Most of them are required to sit through 150 hours of classroom instruction to accomplish the same thing.

Rebellion or Withdrawal?   By eighth grade, the gifted student often begins to fight back, asserting the right to be herself, to challenge authority, and to pay the price for doing so. Others choose simply to withdraw from the contest. Either way, it runs a close second to third grade, in being described as "the worst year of my life."

Will, Retired Administrator, Seventies.   "I had the highest grades in the county on the eighth grade exam for high school—but a big red F in conduct; I forget what it was for!"

Bernard, Computer Sales, Twenties.   "Junior high was a conclusive waste of my time. It seemed to me that every teacher I encountered was an idiot. I never found a single one who was interested in learning. By this time you have an adult mind in a kid's body. I wanted answers to the causes of things and when no one helped me, I withdrew. That is when I began to learn how to intimidate people, especially teachers. I did it well and I hated it. More than any time in my life I was isolated."

Cindy, Photojournalist, Twenties.   "In junior high I wore my hippie outfit to the awards assembly even after my mother brought a dress to

school and begged me to put it on. I insisted, 'I earned my grades dressed like this, I'll accept my award like this.' The vice principal said I was incorrigible. I went home and looked it up in the dictionary."

Kerry.   According to one authority, "clinic files bulge with cases of bright children who are regarded as 'maladjusted,' a major percentage of these maladaptive behaviors ensuing from the failure of society, largely through the schools, to enable these bright children to function more nearly in harmony with their potential." He could be describing Kerry.

Kerry speaks very quietly. She is on her way back from a period of almost total withdrawal, fueled mostly by a school experience that was a nightmare of misunderstanding for six years. Currently seeing two therapists, she plans to enter college only part time, until the learning skills that were a casualty of her withdrawal begin to return.

"Until fifth grade I was accepted as one of the brightest in my school in western New York. I still felt different from others, but I was treated so nicely that it was OK. When I moved, the new school did not test me, they simply put me in the lowest group and told me I could work my way up. At the time I was reading on eleventh-grade level, in a group which was reading below sixth-grade level. I began to believe that I belonged there. I couldn't make friends with the slower kids. I asked and asked to be tested.

"The teachers didn't know what to do with me, so they did nothing. When my parents finally convinced the school to test me, my IQ came out at 128—two points below the required number for the gifted program. I was crushed. By the time I got to eighth grade, I was failing things deliberately. You know, many people have said that I did all those things to hurt my parents, but that isn't how it works. You have all this anger inside at the people who haven't treated you right and you want them to know it. But your mind, your intelligence, won't let you hurt people like your parents. You need to hurt someone, so you hurt yourself.

"My Spanish teacher was particularly annoyed at my behavior. If I wasn't working, she would make me stand in a special part of the room. I began to doodle on my book covers—parts of songs, poetry I was

writing, weird perceptions I had—all of it harmless as far as I was concerned. The teacher happened to see it, and I was marched off to the office. Result: the school required that I see a psychologist. I fought the psychologist's efforts to help me for two years—anger again.

"In ninth grade there was only one teacher who helped me get through that year. I was acting so strangely by then. I would just stare at people and refuse to talk. I did make them test me again. The IQ came out high enough, but there was no gifted program in senior high. For a while I thought high school would be my new start, but they put me in average classes because of my grades, and I just couldn't do it."

An ironic contrast is provided by the fact that there was another equally bright little girl in Kerry's Upstate New York hometown who, in the complexities of corporate transfers, moved into the same school district as her little friend Kerry, but did not attend the same school. Unlike Kerry, she was placed in a gifted program and sailed through junior high. By the time the two friends were reunited in senior high, Kerry was barely getting through the days, withdrawn and angry; her friend was a school star. Like some strange experiment, the two little girls who started out with the same potential reached graduation. Her friend went to an Ivy League university. Kerry went to a psychiatrist.

An extreme example to be sure, Kerry's experience points up the very real destructive potential of school for a gifted child. One says, "Average kids are, for the most part, 'school-proof.'" Kerry comments, "If you are smart, you need a bit more from people, and they can't always give it to you."

Stage 3: Adult Mind, Adolescent Body

By the time a gifted teen reaches senior high, modes of conduct have been chosen, survival skills have been carefully honed, and some substantial dues have been paid. Self-images may be beyond repair. More than ever, an adult mind is operating in an adolescent body, buffeted by adolescent emotions. In some cases, that mind is more competent than some of its teachers, and high grades from such a

teacher may mean very little. With each year of high school, the pressure builds for time and space to work like an adult. Examples of nonconformity increase.

Nonconformity.   Smart kids of the stubborn variety often create problems for themselves. Many of them seem to be quite willing to put up with whatever the world dishes out to maintain their own integrity. Their adventures with being themselves can range from comical to poignant to near tragic.

Will, Retired Administrator, Seventies.   "I will never forget my eleventh-grade English teacher—poor skinny old maid in 1929. She put the following sentence on the board as correct: 'Woman, without her, man would be a savage.' I argued that no commas were necessary and made an enemy!"

Audrey, College Professor, Thirties.   "After an elementary school in Michigan where the four of us learned on our own, there was nothing in high school but regular classes. I just couldn't go. I'd stay for a few periods, and then I'd just have to leave. I was truant so often they threatened to send me to juvenile court!" Audrey's interdisciplinary Ph.D. spans three fields.

Nigel, Talk Show Host, Fifties.   "I had been a professional actor since age 7 so I had little patience with incompetence in adults, especially in a high school in southern Kentucky, where I landed because of my father's job. I didn't follow the rules; they were for slow people. I'd read all the books in the first few weeks of school, and that would get me in trouble. I always wanted to correct my teachers. I'd hold out as long as I could, and then bring up something from a later chapter, or bring in another source. I seldom got a positive response. I finally dropped out, joined the navy, and took a GED diploma. Eventually I acquired degrees in English and biology."

Wes, Physician, Thirties.   "In high school I was constantly told that I would fail, that I should forget college. I was never disruptive, I just

hated the regimentation so badly. At 15 I was hospitalized for a suicide attempt. I did much better when, in senior year, I was put in a special program which allowed me to just finish the required work and take college courses the rest of the day. And yes, I hated regimentation in medical school also."

Easy As Mean Nothing.   Being successful without feeling the joy of pushing your limits can create very negative feelings in a bright and idealistic high school student. One termed it "being rewarded for producing garbage!"

Alix, College Student, Nineteen.   "As in an easy course mean nothing. You hand in something you didn't work on and get an A and you feel cheated . . . you are not challenged enough. Calculus? Well, math is like eating Fritos . . . you just get into a rhythm with the crunch, and the next thing you know, the whole bag is gone! Learning faster isn't enough; you have to learn more, or learn more in-depth. Sometimes I wish they'd just give me the book and let me learn it myself while they explain it to the others."

Bill, Criminal, College Student.   "Awards I received, I knew I'd given maybe 50% . . . It made me feel that the rest of the world was completely stupid not to see that. I lost respect for people."

Amy, Ministerial Student, Twenty.   "In high school, I just worked enough to get the grades . . . forget about the class. You get the good grades, Mom and Dad are happy and everyone thinks you're wonderful, and you don't care. You forget most of it anyway."

Playing Over Your Head.   As the reader will note, many of those who speak here have gone on to successful lives and fulfilling careers. This raises the question of whether our brightest minds are developed because of their education or in spite of it. One factor that seems to have made a crucial difference in how people's lives turned out is a concept explained first by Nigel. He called it "playing over your head."

Nigel, Talk Show Host, Fifties.   "My mother was a concert pianist, so I knew a lot of musicians. When I began playing bass as a teenager, I hung around the jazz clubs in Chicago, and one night some of the older men were kind enough to let me sit in with them. I learned more in that one night than at any other time! I was playing way over my head, but playing with people who were better than I was allowed me to grow to a new plateau. Playing out of your class, you are able to move to a new class. It is the excellence of the people you are working with, the demands that places on you, which makes it possible for you to grow . . . You can break limits, set new ones, and break those, but you can't generate that leap by yourself. What smart kids need, especially in high school, are chances to 'play over your head.'"

Scott, Teacher, Thirties.   "I couldn't read properly until fourth grade; I was only clever with numbers. In high school I joined the debate team so I could be near the smart kids—they laughed at me, but I began to learn. My SATs were so bad I went out and got vocabulary books—made my own dictionary. I'd ask the other kids how many pages they could read a night and then try to increase my rate to theirs. I went through those years catching up. I eventually got a master's degree from Oxford."

George, College Professor, Forties.   "School was intermittently painful from beginning to end. I was always in trouble, but I was a star in the county contests in our old-fashioned western town. The world doesn't seep into a place like that much. We had one teacher who would allow two or three of us to meet at his house and read plays, talk about 'literature.' It was as if we had our own academy—my entire intellectual development took place outside of school. That teacher was the difference between my getting a job in town and never going anywhere, and going on to college as a professor of literature."

Colin, Computer Scientist.   "In tenth grade I read Kant and Spinoza and neglected my grades. My parents were upset. After that I had to toe the line in school. The physics teacher was old, coasting toward retirement, but he understood and let me work on my own. The

chemistry teacher let me have the keys to the lab—until I caused an explosion. In twelfth grade our science teacher took several of us to a scientific symposium in San Francisco—it was the high point of our young lives! Real scientists! My science fair project illustrates my scatterbrained approach to things. I had no description, no design; I put my circuit diagram on ten feet of butcher paper. The judges didn't think much of it, but Techtronics gave me free books and parts, because they loved it. I'm still a nonconformist, designing computers."

Many of the students expressed gratitude to those special teachers who allowed them to see larger worlds, to try more sophisticated work, to play over their heads. Those who had to struggle alone seem to have had much more difficulty being successful in college, in a career, and in their personal lives. Even with an understanding family, lack of support from school can take its toll.

Eleventh Grade Is Crucial.   Assuming that a gifted student operates at least two grades beyond his or her peers, it is inevitable that high school will be used up before the traditional twelfth grade is reached. Eleventh grade is often the crucial year, when decisions about the future must be made. It is a fortunate young person whose school recognizes the problem and whose parents are prepared to cope. School authorities have the resources and the power to do great good, or to create great problems for a smart kid.

Laura, Writer and Broadcaster, Forties.   "I wanted to go to college early and was told no by the bishop, who was in charge of the parochial schools. It was explained to me very carefully that they couldn't do it for me because then 'others would want it.' It was as if they were saying, 'My God, we might find that we have others who are bright, lots of them, and that would upset our routine.' I took chemistry in twelfth grade and did not open the book the entire year; I just listened in class. I passed with a 98, and I was so angry . . . this is academic achievement? That experience changed my life. I became cynical, bitter, and angry. I was the archetype of being punished for being different. I finally received an independent college degree at 40."

Fran, Juvenile Detention Director, Thirties.   "Because my family was always on the move, and also because my parents were having marital problems, I was shunted through a series of boarding schools, one of which made me repeat tenth grade. At the end of eleventh grade I was as old as a senior, and I had spent four years in school. I wanted out. I feared that even college would regiment me in the same ways that private schools did.

"My school understood. They got out the list of colleges still looking for students and helped me find a suitable school, open and understanding of nontraditional students. I had never taken SATs or anything like that, so they helped to make arrangements for an interview, at which the college accepted me. If they hadn't helped me, I would simply have dropped out of school."

Gary, Computer Scientist, Forties.   "I used up my school's curriculum by the end of eleventh grade also. But nobody ever gave me any guidance or advice. I wanted to go to Reed College in Oregon, but it was too late to apply. My math teacher tried to set up some independent calculus work for me but it didn't help much. I was on my way to becoming an eminent scholar—that was my ambition. After a year of marking time, I had no educational ambition at all. I made a firm decision that I would go to college to have fun." (Gary's story will be continued in the chapter on criminals.)

Bernard, Computer Sales, Twenties.   "I had an acceptance letter from a major university at the end of tenth grade. My wise parents carefully pointed out the pros and cons of college at that age, and I agreed to wait another year. I was allowed to make my own decision. In high school I had arrangements with some of my teachers that I would come to class when I could; if not, I'd just stop by and pick up the work. It worked fine. They were some wonderful people. Do I regret going to college at 16? I'd be a stone not to have some feelings about the socially important things you miss. But at the time I could make no other decision. I was at the end of the curriculum.

"In the educational sense, high school was a waste for me. The structure and the smart kid are an awkward fit. I didn't understand it all, so I withdrew. But teachers should remember to *look*. Find the

gifted kids. Don't leave them on the outside looking in. See if the system can bear them. There is, of course, a danger here—once you start to nurture that ability, the progression is geometric and it will take off!"

Is early attendance at college the only answer? Definitely not: Gifted young persons can remain in high school and at home quite nicely *if* they are challenged on a level appropriate for their intellectual, social, and emotional maturity. This might include courses at a local college, work with a community mentor, internships or Saturday programs, or intense involvement in art or sports. A student should be strongly encouraged to concentrate on what he or she loves and not be allowed to simply fill time with superficial involvement in too many activities.

Alix, for example, wanted to go away to college. Her parents felt that, socially, she was not mature enough to do so. She spent senior year attending high school classes in the morning and music classes at the local community college in the afternoon. She maintained a full practice schedule with her school band and her own instrument and full social contact with high-school-age friends.

Hitting the Brick Wall.   I have coined a phrase for a problem which may occur in senior high school, which can puzzle parents and frighten a student. I call it "brick wall time." It happens like this: A high-achieving twelfth-grader will appear with a dazed look and announce, "I got three tests back today—a C in calculus, a D in physics, and a C in English. What is happening to me??!"

What has happened is that up until now, the gifted student has not had to struggle to do well in school, the way average students do. He or she could control the schooling process with ease and have top grades simply by deciding to have them. However, as the material becomes more sophisticated, the student reaches a point where concerted mental effort is needed to do well, and this is a new and strange experience. For the person accustomed to breezing through school, it may feel a little like walking into a brick wall.

The student will have to learn how to study harder, but it may take some time to be able to feel, internally, what constitutes "harder." He or she may need extra help with formal study skills. Rather than

scolding and demanding, wise parents will help their son or daughter to understand that this is an inevitable adjustment which everyone must make when they reach their level of challenge. It happens for most people when they enter first grade. There are others for whom it does not happen until graduate school. With cooperative parents, it is far safer for an adolescent to work through this frightening period of self-doubt while still within the shelter of family life. Working it out all alone as a college freshman can be much more difficult.

Nina.   In spite of a nurturing family that helped her through a senior year when she felt "abandoned" by the school, Nina is not looking forward to taking college courses. "I wish I could just *do* the course in a month or two. Some kids can do more, but no one listens. My parents listened, but school didn't want to hear. If you're not average, get out. I was ready to leave that school after tenth grade. I felt that the teachers were holding me back.

"I've always liked being with older people. By eleventh grade there was no one older except the teachers, and I think I scared them. They didn't want to be around kids who had ideas they never thought of, or who could organize things faster and better than they could. The other kids didn't like it either. I often didn't do any homework, but it didn't matter. I could read a book during a class and still get As and Bs on the tests. Now I'm worried that somewhere along the line I'll have to really work and I won't know how because I've been 'cruising' all this time. I spent fifteen minutes on calculus and did all papers the night before—papers I felt were an insult for a senior in high school. They wasted my time and I said so. Here was this kid telling them the assignment was dumb . . . I don't know, maybe they knew it was, or maybe they really thought it was important and I hurt their feelings. I wanted to go to college a year early, but my guidance counselor discouraged me. I listened to him because I thought he knew what he was talking about. He didn't."

Nina can provide helpful insights into that most puzzling of all gifted students, the so-called underachiever. "My boyfriend is a smarter person. He failed math and I had to tutor him. I discovered that he can understand things just as fast as I can, but he doesn't pro-

duce. His parents pay no attention to him; they don't seem to care about anything he does. He's the oldest and he can't yell, or get mad, but he can fail. They never cared about his As, but they sure cared about his Fs! The only time he does well is when I yell, 'Look at what you are doing to yourself!' Then he gets As."

She has also spotted another type of underachiever. "Many kids do well because they've been told that they are smart. But some kids who were never told really are smart. Some of them should have been in faster classes, but they were bored, or did poorly, and were turned off and just gave up. You can tell from talking with them that they have the same feelings I do, but they have given up on school. If you really notice, average kids don't complain; everything is always OK—not the emotional ups and downs that I have always lived with.

"I guess nobody understands that kids like us need as much attention as kids who are mentally retarded. You are treated as average but expected to do more—and they don't believe you when you say you can't understand something! Retarded kids are treated on their level, and they often produce more than is expected. If we were treated on our level, I think we might surprise people. Sometimes I wish I was dumber than average—at least I'd be challenged on my own level. I just wish someone would pay enough attention to me to realize that I really need and want to learn. I feel older, I can do more; I want to get started on my life earlier than most people. I haven't found anyone who understands that.

"I once considered teaching as a career, but I don't like the way teachers are treated. I would like to teach gifted kids and give them the outlet I never had, but that fizzled, because I don't believe I'd ever find a school system that would let me do it my way."

What Could Make It Better?

Were none of the grownups I interviewed able to recall positive school experiences? Some few were able to remember an atmosphere of both challenge and warmth in elementary school. They attended

odd little schools in private homes, with "science class on the sun-porch. We learned high school biology in sixth grade. My friend Peter and I *were* the sixth grade!" These places functioned like one-room schools in that students worked at their own pace, passing through grade levels whenever it suited them. Ironically, this is what the good programs in public schools seek to do.

Our schools are not hopeless, but they do suffer from a lack of understanding of and compassion for gifted students, and a decided lack of actions which would allow someone besides the super kids and the good little kids to function productively. It would be foolish to state that a concerned parent seeking a humane education for a gifted child is facing a hopeless task. It would be equally foolish not to acknowledge that serious national problems do exist, and that making things better requires major exertion from everyone concerned.

Are there actually that many students whose development is not being attended to? According to Professor Robert J. Havighurst, "It seems probable that our society discovers and develops no more than perhaps half of its potential intellectual talent." Information in this field changes rapidly, but at this writing only twenty-three states have legislation requiring special programs for gifted children. Another twenty states have legal provisions for funding, but no requirement. According to estimates by the National Association for Gifted Children, approximately 35% of those identified are actually in some sort of program, but *A Nation at Risk* claimed that less than half of our smart kids are even identified. The portion of the identified gifted who are in effective programs is not known. How many students encounter teachers who know anything about gifted students? Once again, unknown.

Training for Teachers

Lack of understanding behavior on the part of otherwise sincere teachers comes from lack of information. The teacher who solved the problem of a "bouncy" third-grader by putting his desk inside a large appliance box and not allowing him to interact with the class may not be the monster that third-grader remembers. She simply may not

have known that quirky behaviors, combined with certain observable characteristics, indicate a burning desire to learn.

The French teacher who was confronted with an actual temper tantrum by a ladylike top senior didn't realize that when you have done an original translation of a Maupassant short story and written an essay on the art of translation for your Advanced Placement English class, your patience may snap when your French teacher assigns a bulletin board as a senior project.

Confronted with an "impossible" child, or a superkid, any teacher will feel threatened if he or she does not recognize that what is happening here is giftedness. There is bound to be resentment at being put in such a position—and by a child, no less. And even if giftedness is recognized, most teachers are only too well aware of their lack of training in how to deal with these students who demand so much.

As far back as 1983, *A Nation at Risk* pointed out a serious shortage of teachers of the gifted and the appalling statistic that half of our gifted young people do not match their tested ability with comparable achievement in school. In its report, "A Nation Prepared: Teachers for the Twenty-First Century," the task force assembled by the Carnegie Foundation described teachers who can help students to "see patterns of meaning where others only see confusion . . . foster genuine creativity . . . work in groups which decide for themselves how to get the job done." It warns teachers of continuing challenge, "as the knowledge required to do their job twists and turns with new challenges and the progress of science and technology."

A concerned teacher who tries to obtain specialized course work will soon find that there are only a few places scattered around the nation that offer work in gifted studies. The small minority of teachers who have made the education of the gifted their special field often work in new or marginally funded programs. When these are cut, their jobs often disappear. So much for special training. But in states where gifted programs are required by law, some sort of program must continue. It is often assigned arbitrarily, regardless of whether or not the teacher wants or knows how to deal with gifted youngsters. And the situation is right back where it started, with lack of training and resentment again.

Students and teachers alike suffer from the stereotype of the gifted child as a perfect person, easy to deal with, a total joy in the classroom. Teachers assigned to gifted or advanced groups are often told, "Gee, it must be nice to have such an easy job."

One such teacher describes how easy it really is. "I'm paying a lot of dues for the joy and satisfaction I gain in teaching gifted kids: misunderstanding of *my* kids, resentment of them by parents, teachers, and other students, refusal to provide for their needs by ignorant school boards. It comes with the territory."

Judging by the words of gifted students themselves, only a handful of teachers have any training to help them identify gifted students, let alone any training to know what to do with them after that. The combination of the unidentified and the underachiever can be the most frustrating and puzzling of all. Teachers who care about such students are as frustrated as their pupils. One says, "I spend a lot of my time as an educator spotting that little guy in the back row. There's an eye factor here somewhere; bright kids have bright eyes . . . unless they're zonked out on substances; and they are so frustrated. I am currently dealing with three of them, in two classes."

A Teacher Who Found Three.   "The first student moved here from another state and was put into a regular class. I spotted him the first time he asked a question—it was so sophisticated. Testing shows he reads on high twelfth-grade level. The school says they can't move him out of a slow-average tenth-grade class because of schedule problems.

"The second began his high school career in a modified class for slow learners, with a sensitive teacher who booted him up to an average class, where he just turns out 100s and As with no effort. Test scores indicate only marginal intelligence, which simply does not make sense. I am trying to make a case for individual testing for giftedness.

"The third student was a 'flunkee' from last year. He is an alcoholic, very proud that he has been sober for forty-two days. He failed the previous year because he was in a class for slow learners and hated it. None of this squares with the writing I am seeing—you can't write very sophisticated, complex sentences if you are not very

bright. Our current theory (his and mine) is that all the tests which determined his placement over the last two years were taken while he was drunk. I have asked to have him tested by the school district psychiatrist—there is a six-month waiting list.

"What horrifies me is that these are just three kids in one tenth grade, in one school, that one teacher could spot just by knowing what to look for. How many more of them are there in our school, in our state, in the whole country?"

Veteran of many struggles to provide for the best and the brightest, another teacher makes an impassioned statement. "I want more from the richest country in the world. Statistics can never measure the ideas not discovered, the diseases not cured, the problems not solved, the inventions not invented, the music not written. There are no charts of the things which die behind those bright eyes because it seems nobody cares."

High on any gifted student's list of dirty tricks is the experience of getting more in the wrong way. If you finish early, you are not given new work, just more of the same. Gary describes, "one of the worst things that can be done to kids is let them have a taste of something and get all excited about it, and then take it away. You get a fire raging and then quench it; get it going again and quench it . . . it's devastating."

One parent recalls visiting her son's high school to complain about a lack of challenge and careful planning of his program. She watched in horror as the (uninformed) principal calmly took her son's schedule and filled it with Advanced Placement courses. She recalls that he smiled in a friendly way and remarked, "Now I think he will be sufficiently challenged." Left to the chance ministrations of an untrained teacher or an uninformed administrator, this is what gifted students may experience in our schools.

Educating Parents

However discouraging the above may be, we must face the fact that it is parents, informed and involved parents, who can make the difference for an individual child and for education as a whole. Parents

need to understand that they should not be afraid to take an active role in their child's education. If our imaginary class could turn the tables, they might give parents a list of things to do that goes like this: "Pay attention; do your homework; learn your Four Ps; get organized, and be cool about school!"

Pay Attention!   First, talk to your child; or rather, listen when he or she talks to you. Pay special attention if, at any age, your child says, "I'm not learning anything." Kids don't read Piaget, but they know instinctively that there should be a difference between what is already in their heads and what is being presented in class. Their evaluations are important. They may not have the maturity to carry out the suggestions they make, but that is what parents and teachers are for: to provide structure, discipline, and loving guidance.

Anxious parents often wonder if they should insist that their children be skipped ahead; would they rather have fun learning than be with their age-mates? One mother whose four children are now adult professionals in art and science had this observation: "Skipping is not the answer. Teachers need to understand that smart kids learn much faster. The kids in the next grade are not any brighter. My kids usually caught up in two months and were bored again, and just younger. So much is repeated from grade to grade that I almost think bright kids could go every other year!"

Those interviewed for this book were almost unanimous in their objection to skipping grades in elementary school. They point out that programs to challenge gifted students should keep them with their age-mates.

From the perspective of a college student comes the following advice for parents: "Encourage, but don't demand, especially as far as grades go. Positive reinforcement is a hell of a lot more valuable (and valid) than negative . . . I can still remember other kids saying that they were anxious about their parents seeing the *report card,* as if that is all school is about, and as if a C required that the parent soundly chew out the child. I know that if I had come home with a C, my parents would have asked me about the class, but they asked me about my classes all year, not just at term end. They were interested in how

I was doing in a very supportive way. So, be interested. If something doesn't seem right about the class the child is in—too fast, too slow, the kid is bored and not doing any work—go in to the school and find out what is going on. And don't be afraid to stir up a little dust."

Do Your Homework.   Second, educate yourself. It is much easier to ask for help for your child if you know what you are talking about. The references at the end of this book can provide quite a full background in gifted studies. They may also help to give you a better perspective on your own school experience and yourself as a gifted person—because there is a fair chance that you are. Do not be afraid to use what you learn about yourself to help your child.

School reform is a widely discussed issue, and many formulas have been offered to solve our problems. Many of them emphasize rote learning and lockstep test passing, which can be even more detrimental than present systems to a gifted child. Parents should inform themselves completely about current educational restructuring proposals, particularly the elimination of grouping by ability and the extensive use of group learning. In themselves, these practices can benefit all learners, but they can be misused when they are misinterpreted.

Be watchful and concerned that grouping practices are flexible and sensible. Extremes that do not provide any special opportunities above and below the average and that consistently "use" the brighter students to teach the slower ones can be damaging to both groups. Many educators point out that the current focus on education provides an opportunity to press for improved conditions for all learners—so stay informed.

Throughout your child's school career, talk to the teachers. It will be a lot easier if you do your reading homework first. And be polite. Roger Taylor, a funny and compassionate gifted advocate from Illinois, says, "If parents come storming in to me about their kid, they often turn out not to have a clear idea of the child's ability. If they come in politely, they almost always turn out to have a good idea of how we need to help their child."

Educator John Feldhusen advises that parents can be helpful to the school by providing objective information about home activities and

by volunteering to help with special projects and trips from which their child benefits. He stresses that it is also essential to make yourself a part of any group that provides an avenue for parent feedback.

The Four Ps.   If you really want to help your child, you will have to be Prepared, Polite, and Persistently Pushy. And because this is the real world, prepare to become accustomed to *The Look* and *The Sigh.* The first will come from friends, relatives, and neighbors, precisely because you are being pushy. The second will come, unfortunately, from some school officials, who will find you tiresome. Keep smiling, but keep asking. Understand that you are not going to change the world, and go about the business of seeing to your child's needs.

Having done all that, the day comes when corporate America announces a family transfer. I have seen much good work for gifted kids undone by a change of schools, and of course sometimes, but not often enough, the opposite is true. Your work begins in the school you are leaving. Visit the principal and request that you be given all the pertinent information about your child's ability and explanations of all scores and tests. Take notes. If the school will permit it, hand-carry your child's records to the new school, where you should present yourself to the new principal and review the situation with him. Do not be shy about announcing that your child has special needs. Do not forget the Four Ps.

Be Cool about School.   Regardless of whether your child requires radical acceleration or simply advanced classes within the school, secondary school can provide a major challenge to the emotional strength and the personal integrity of the gifted parent. Much of the unnecessary pushing and the hysteria about grades comes from parents who have not taken a good honest look at their own ego needs. It is crucial to your child's well-being that you keep cool about school. Encourage experimenting and the taking of a wide variety of courses, but do not try to turn every enthusiasm into a lifework—especially if it happens to be the field you pictured for your little genius.

Belief in self can be severely damaged by the parent who expects the child to be a superkid just because he or she happens to be gifted.

The fast pace of American society has taken a fearful toll in stress-related diseases in adults. In the past several years, I have noted an alarming number of young people who are attempting to match their parents' workaholic skills. As one comments bitterly, "My father drills it into me all the time, 'It's a tough world out there—you are the best or you are nothing!'" It is distressing to witness the poor self-esteem of a student who is balancing honors courses, sports, church activities, and a part-time job, but who feels that, somehow, it isn't enough.

Understand that for a multitalented person, one who thinks of many sides to every question, not knowing what the lifework will be is the norm. Such a person cannot narrow choices by the same process of elimination as others, that is, by eliminating the things which are too difficult. In some individuals, few things are beyond reach. The gifted student needs room to explore, to some degree at least, each of many possible areas of talent, and needs support while doing so.

Gifted high school students should be allowed to practice making decisions about their own learning. In many cases, they do know what they need and the form in which they need it. They must also be allowed to experience the carrying-through of responsibilities to which they have freely committed themselves, even if, in so doing, they must deal with failure.

Certainly, as a concerned parent, you should work hard at helping your child to select an appropriate college. Check carefully into the school's academic reputation and faculty-student ratio. Find out whether there are special scholars programs available. Take a long honest look (privately) at your own need for status. If an Ivy League university is right for the student, and you can afford it, by all means have him or her apply. But be very sure you are not catering to your own need to tell people at parties that "Johnny is at Yale."

Encourage a gifted student who is struggling for direction to attend a strong college that will allow him or her to begin without declaring a major and will permit several semesters of coursework in which to make decisions. And if the student wants to take a year, or even two, to work or explore other options, allow him or her to do it. Applying to colleges is a way of keeping options open; many college

acceptances are good for three or even five years. Above all, encourage your gifted child to choose a lifework based on what he or she loves to do, and never forget that children have a longer way to travel as they go higher, wider, and deeper into life.

If you have a child whose ability and precocity are so far beyond age-mates' that you foresee very special needs developing, you may want to consider some form of radical acceleration, including early enrollment in college. Authorities are nearly unanimous in their findings that, if properly managed, early enrollment in college can be a good thing.

Julian Stanley, who has worked with accelerated students for many years at Johns Hopkins University in Baltimore, says, "Students who enter college at an early age well prepared academically and well oriented by experience and planning can get an excellent undergraduate education." Others who have done follow-up studies agree. However, they all recommend careful preparation and an appropriate maturity level for success. If you are considering such a move for your child, you might want to contact the National Association for Gifted Children or Supporting the Emotional Needs of the Gifted (SENG), whose addresses appear at the end of this book. Contacting nearby universities is also a good way to start. Johns Hopkins, the University of Washington, and the University of Virginia are among those that have done good work with early admission students.

Get Organized!   As the parent of a special child, you need and deserve the support of others in a similar situation. If there is no parents organization in your locality, start one. Whether banding together for emotional support or to push for better programs in the schools, the organizing of such parent groups is a job for parents, not teachers. Teachers do not have the power to force their own employers to make changes; indeed, in some areas, teachers who are perceived to be associated with "pressure groups" can jeopardize their jobs. If you are unsure about how to organize a parent group, contact the National Association for Gifted Children for assistance. You will find the address at the end of the book.

What you can obtain for your child probably depends on the state in which you live. Some states have well-defined legal requirements for the education of the gifted; many do not. If your school district can't help you with information, write to your state department of education. If you live in a state that does not have requirements for gifted education, consider beginning the work of organizing your whole state. Educated parents who are willing to form serious action groups can make a difference.

In addition, parents and educators need to begin to forge an alliance based on their shared desire to do what is best for all children. It is important that we stop here to pay tribute to the workers in the field of gifted education: the counselors, the teachers, the administrators scattered throughout the country who have been trying to change things for gifted students for years. Whether they are the well-known researchers at universities whose names fill the notes of this book, or the unknown individuals who work in classrooms every day, they are frustrated not only by lack of funds but by the myth that "gifted kids can take care of themselves."

Regular classroom teachers need to have the opportunity to acquire basic knowledge about how to work with these special students. In the face of the glaring lack of coursework available at most universities, the references included here might be a good place to start. Teachers can also be a powerful force for change by working through professional organizations to press for better teacher training in gifted education. School boards need to recognize the need to fund teacher training workshops as well as workable gifted programs.

School boards and administrators, if they are doing a complete job, need to be aware of the nature of giftedness and of state and local policies regarding gifted students. More important, they have a serious obligation to identify the gifted students in their schools and to listen to those teachers who are trying to provide the kind of environment such students need. Laying aside the stereotype which classifies all parents who try to obtain a humane education for their children as troublemakers will not be easy, but it is essential. Educators who are willing to educate themselves and parents who are

willing to become involved will quickly find that they are not adversaries, but partners.

We have listened to a discussion of school experiences by a wide variety of bright people. They have recounted the confusion and hurt of their early years and their gradual coming to terms with being different. Whether they acquiesced to the system and learned to devalue their gifts, fought that system and took the consequences, turned their backs on school as a source of real learning, or even bloomed under the guidance of special teachers, they point up the need for more knowledge of giftedness by classroom teachers, counselors, and administrators. The kids have left a "chore list" for the adults—parents and teachers—and a plea for them to join forces.

Reminders for All Educators

What is the most important thing students would like educators to remember? From one hundred gifted grownups of all ages, reflecting on their experiences as school kids, comes a composite answer:

> Gifted kids always want to *know.* They need more to do, more attention, more stimulation. Talk to them! . . . Even if the kid is smarter than the teacher, the teacher should be able to suggest a place to go for help . . . they aren't meaning to intimidate you or make you look foolish.
>
> Help them to keep a perspective and a sense of humor about their brains . . . a high percentage of gifted kids are shy and don't want to be treated differently; be ready to be supportive but not obvious. Help them to know that they have the power to make decisions about their lives . . . they often know the best way to go about learning something. Let your students know that you are human—that you have an imagination and can laugh . . . Gifted kids *can* take care of themselves, but is that what you want? Don't you want them to grow? . . . Sometimes let them do what they want, even if it isn't exactly what you had in mind—it could be better. Make it so that it can fit the requirements.

Smart kids have a right to be praised in front of everyone, as well as have their faults dealt with matter-of-factly. The class does not have to be protected from them . . . Remember that they *are* children, and immature in many ways . . . All of them are not smart in everything; they could be average in some areas, or even below . . . be able to deal with their insecurities. [said very quietly] Smart kids are people.

To close the discussion of what school has been like for gifted kids of all ages, we will call on the final member of our imaginary class. Calvin is a 40-year-old gifted grownup who works as a machinist while he studies linguistics, psychology, and computer programming and writes poetry. He relates, "As a little child I played with kids at least two years older than I was. When school started, they went off to school, but I wasn't allowed to go with them. The separation cut me off from them for the rest of my school career. I think what I've been doing ever since is trying to catch up to the playmates they took away from me when I was 4."

Composed by Calvin as an adult, the verbal collage that follows seems to speak for many smart kids about the school experience in its answers to the question all parents ask:

What Did You Learn in School Today?

What did I learn in school today?

I was very bored, and the desk smelled like sweaty hands . . . just like it used to, and I had ink on my fingers . . . the teacher broke a ruler on the edge of someone's desk, trying to hit his knuckles . . . That's what I remember, but I didn't learn anything. She was a good geography teacher, but I knew it all from magazines.

I didn't learn anything, but I tore my knuckle on some barbed wire playing football behind the bleachers. Official sports are so boring. My father wants me to play football, but it seems so pointless. The older boys know lots of terms for what is going on

in the football game, but they seem like strangers. The older girls go rah-rah, but it seems so empty and contrived that there must be something wrong with me ... I should be growing up ... but I didn't learn anything today.

I had an idea today that I thought was important, but I didn't write it down, so I forgot it ... I invented three-dimensional pictures today, projecting slides at angles through rippled plastic, but my high school physics teacher said it wouldn't work and my college physics teacher said it had already been done, so I didn't learn anything today.

Do you remember the throwing stick I invented, like the book I saw later said the cavemen used? Why wasn't it important?

Why are the things I wrote in the Navy unimportant? Why are the only things that are important things that teachers tell me? And why do teachers only tell me what I already know?

I didn't learn anything today. I wish I had a bouquet of new knowledge to give you so you would love me. You will not take the flowers I invented. And you ask me again and again, "What did you learn in school today?"*

* Used with permission by Herb Perkins-Frederick.

Chapter Six

Young Adults: The Extra Mile

*The despair of bright young men and women in their lonely
struggle for a satisfying maturity is both deep and dark . . . how
bewilderingly varied is the world of knowledge whose horizons
keep retreating.*
   Joseph Cohen, *The Superior Student in American Higher Education*

*I was only following my nose, and if it looked from the outside
as if I were shifting fields, then it was plain that the outside was
not a good vantage point.*
                              Jerome Bruner, *In Search of Mind*

If getting one's gifted children through the nation's required
schools is problematic at best, watching as they launch themselves
into the young adult years can be traumatic, for both the children
and their families. As the gifted young people leave the relative control of family and school to establish their own lives, the picture can
look very promising or very bleak. Faculties beyond the average take
the person higher, wider, deeper, for longer. Multiple talents require
time to be explored, and it can take at least twelve years to sort it out.
Perhaps that advanced neural system needs time to mature. Perhaps
it never matures, if we mean to imply an end.

   The late John Gowan, educator and psychologist, explained that
gifted persons may learn at an accelerated pace, but their social and
emotional growth may not keep up with academic accomplishments.
He added, "the gifted have farther to go to fulfill their self-actualized
needs . . . Their own longer deeper search for meaningfulness is the
extra mile the gifted have to travel."

In *Passages*, Gail Sheehy describes this as the getaway period and the "trying twenties." How much more trying they are for someone who sees more in situations, feels more intensely, questions continually, and who may have multiple talents. Unless a very fortunate superstar, the gifted young person may be a little behind in relationship-building skills so necessary to making wise choices for marriage and family living. What Sheehy calls the "Merger Self," long denied companionship, may now reach the stage where other bright people are readily available, and the desire for a permanent lover is strong.

However, the "Seeker Self" may still have several exotic options pushing to be explored. The plethora of possibilities opened by multiple talents and multiple interests may make it difficult to select one field to pursue. Add to this a heightened sensitivity, a tendency to feel things deeply as well as to agonize over moral decisions, and it is easy to see why young adulthood can become a whirlpool of conflicting choices, both personal and professional. And all the while, there is the voice, from family, friends, colleagues, lovers, self: "Aren't you ever going to settle on something? Aren't you ever satisfied?"

Where They Were at 18

The people whose lives are explored in this chapter began the journey in dramatically different ways. For example, at 18, Marcelle was an awed Princeton freshman, doing what the stereotype is believed to do: being brilliant at a top school. But Fran was working as a waitress, doubting she would report for classes when they started at Earlham in the fall, and Adrian was quitting Catholic University because she was sick of restraints. Maureen was a high school dropout, working in a factory in California.

Among the young men, Bernard entered Swarthmore after eleventh grade; Frank was a junior at the University of Pennsylvania, on his way to a degree at 19; Mark's low grades barely earned him acceptance at a

third-rate school. Don was enlisting in the Air Force; Julio was packing groceries in a San Francisco supermarket. Colin was sleeping in New York subways, sinking slowly into the drug culture.

The gifted people were interviewed for this chapter at various points on the journey. Some were just out of college; some arriving at 30; others were looking back from several years beyond that supposedly magic number. The many ways their lives illustrate success can provide helpful suggestions if you are one of those who is struggling though this period wondering if it will ever come together. It may also provide both insight and consolation for families, lovers, friends, and even employers who are standing on the sidelines thinking, *"This is gifted?"*

That Special Rhythm

More than anything else, perhaps, getting from 18 to 30 means learning the special rhythm that the parents referred to in Chapter 4. It means understanding your own fast pace, to be sure, but it is more than that. The special rhythm of a gifted adult's life is the constant need to learn something new. When goals are achieved, new goals appear. A field of learning explored through long and arduous study will simply yield new questions, new fields to master. This seems to be true regardless of age or what has already been achieved.

Philadelphia psychologist Dr. Al Levitt divides bright people into two types, based on how they process input from the environment. The first group needs only small amounts of outside stimulation and can work on that for a long time. A scientist, for example, may work on a single theoretical problem for many years and derive great satisfaction from her work. Such a person may not have a very high level of physical energy. The other type requires great amounts of stimulation from the environment and internalizes much less of it than do those in the first group. They need repeated doses of high-interest activity through school, work, an avocation, or even emotional involvement in a cause. They may also have a very high degree of physical energy.

Thus, although bright people may move through their lives to the rhythm of a cycle of required stimulation, they do so at different rates. That scientist may be intensely involved in her work for five years, whereas a high-powered business executive without a new project may be bored in five weeks. What they have in common is that when their particular source of stimulation has been used up, something new is needed in some area of their lives. What may be viewed by others as restlessness or discontent is a norm for a gifted adult. Such understanding needs to be internalized by that person and accepted by those who share the same life space, be they lovers or employers. Bernard says it with a grin, but he means it: "When I'm comfortable, I'm uncomfortable."

Three Tasks

Arriving at 30 in one emotionally and financially healthy piece is an accomplishment for anyone. Gifted grownups seem to have three special tasks: (1) to recognize their difference and learn to value themselves because of it, not in spite of it; (2) to allow themselves to meet their needs by more intense work, more school, a better job, or trying new things; and (3) to avoid the scattering effects of too much of task 2.

Of course, there are the superstars who have had all the requisite acceptance and stimulation along the way and who go off to challenging colleges armed with awards and good study habits. They are the ones we read about in the alumni news. But for far too many gifted young people, continuing education means continuing frustration. Sorting out options and coping with mistakes can use up precious years.

Don, the One Who Hated School

Don was a frustrated smart kid who fought by hating high school out loud while he earned good grades, but rejected further education because he believed it would be more of the same. Misunderstood through twelve years of education, Don survived his senior year in a

special program that allowed him to take honors courses in the morning and work at a mechanic's job in the afternoon. Knowing his own needs, he searched carefully for quality colleges with open curricula. He was accepted and given small scholarships to three such institutions, only to find that he could not agree to enter any of them.

"I have hated school so badly for all these years, that I can't face a classroom in any form," he told his parents. After four years in the Air Force, he had the skills for a high-paying, boring job in electronics, which he declined to use. Working as a successful motorcycle mechanic, then as a waiter, he finally decided to risk college as a music major. At 25, halfway to an undergraduate degree, he said, "For the first time in my life, I am enjoying school." At 27, he graduated from college with highest honors and was accepted at a major graduate school.

Jonathan, the Good Little Kid

Even a bright person who enters college eagerly, at the conventional age, may encounter unexpected problems. Often unnoticed is the Good Little Kid who submits, all unwillingly, to routine, repetitive work and earns top high school grades with gritted teeth, clinging to the belief that college will be better. One danger for such a person is the "awful disillusion of not finding a challenge, and losing idealism."

Jonathan was a Good Little Kid. The university he attended recognized both the speed and sophistication with which certain freshmen could work by organizing a special scholars program. Promising students were permitted to alter their studies to suit their needs, but this was not always enough to really help them. The habits of a Good Little Kid can inhibit the release of the person's full capabilities and put the student in danger of becoming a disillusioned dropout.

From the vantage point of his fourth year, Jon lamented, "All the time I wasted not taking advantage of what I could do. I took introductory courses, and they were just like high school. I could have taken a third-year statistics course, but I was cautious. I went through a very rebellious period when I realized that after two years, I had, in effect, left undergraduate work behind. I wasted those two years!"

Taking time off to explore the real world, Jonathan worked for a large computer company. Returning to school as part of another special program, he was a teaching assistant and graduate student in computer science, when, to everyone's amazement, he stopped going to class, failed courses, and spent much of his time writing programs just because he liked them. He let his hair grow long and took to listening to the music of the Sixties. Not even his closest friends, gifted students who were doing well at top universities, understood. Jonathan himself smiled helplessly and said, "I don't know; I just seem to have lost all motivation . . ."

Michelle, who is older, understood perfectly. "He's angry. I know. I did exactly the same thing in my freshman year of college. You can allow yourself to be pushed around by systems just so long, and then you have to rebel. Being a Good Little Kid just takes its toll."

Should rebelliousness of this type be encouraged in high school to avoid it later? Jonathan thinks not. "Two factors must be considered concerning rebellion in high school. A 16-year-old can damage the future if left alone. It isn't wise to trash your grades, because the world looks at them, and next thing you know, you're a sanitation engineer!"

Besides insisting on careful counseling and access to challenging courses, Jonathan advises parents of bright high school students to be tolerant of the small rebellions. "Kicking a door, loudmouthing a teacher can provide a real 'charge' for a high school student. Unfortunately, when you are older, you have to do something like trash a master's degree in order to get the same feeling."

Now able to assess his behavior after "escaping" with an undergraduate degree, Jon says, "I was angry at missed opportunities, the things I was too shy to take advantage of. There should have been better counseling at my university to help me make those decisions. Things came easily no matter what I did, and I think that was part of what happened to me. When I returned from working outside of school, I suddenly saw everything as bogus—money, jobs, the school itself. I needed a period to free-fall. All family and friends can do at a time like that is try to cushion the landing by being concerned, while they let the 'kid' thrash out the problems on his own.

"Now that I've sneaked out with a degree, I can start over and do things right. My eyes are open and I'm facing many decisions. I'm looking for more than a job. I want to find a place I will like to live, someone to be with, and a job which will challenge me more than part of the time. I want to design new programs."

College Isn't Always Better

J. M. Tolliver and David Willings are two Canadian researchers who have studied gifted and creative people in the university and the workplace. Willings studied thirty-five university students from England and Canada, and was able to follow fifteen of them for ten years. He found their lives to be marked by uncertainty and struggle. One highly intelligent student's penchant for analysis caused her to see deficiencies in research systems and led her to try to work out her own methods for accomplishing required tasks, and this often annoyed professors. These bright undergraduates had a penchant for criticizing others, and this usually included their professors.

But the gifted young adults tended to be even more critical of themselves, setting impossibly high standards for workload and grades and feeling like failures when they didn't meet them: "Everyone in the original sample [35] felt cheated at the university and that . . . [it] was an alienating experience . . . a process of ingesting facts and reproducing them on examinations. They had all expected something better. They had not expected to be equally bored at university as they were at school . . . This feeling of being cheated is reported by all the gifted adults with whom I have discussed giftedness . . . among gifted, the dropout rate is three times the national average."

Willings's findings were echoed in the interviews.

Mark, Trashing the Future

Jonathan was lucky. He was able at least to enter an intellectually stimulating college with motivation and transcript intact. As he

warned, rebellion against boredom in high school may produce a person who has read widely in theoretical physics "for fun" for four years; but that same person may have such a poor transcript that none of the schools where he belongs will admit him.

Mark, an underachiever and rebel since second grade, found himself at a poor-quality college where "I was the only physics major in the school. I had no one to talk to . . . the graduate students ignored me. I slept a lot." In his sophomore year, he was able to transfer to a very good school. Here, they made him repeat the work he had done in physics, because his As came from a place with a poor reputation. After one semester of repetition, his boredom erupted in a fraternity period where he majored in parties, lost his scholarship, and sorely tempted his worried parents to give up.

Another year, another major—this time, engineering—and another semester of hating it and failing. In his fifth year, he returned to his first love from childhood, math, and described his life as "quite pleasant." He took six years to earn an ordinary undergraduate degree and then worked in a supermarket and a clothing store while he made two tries at the actuarial exam. The job he found at an insurance company he hated.

The next move was a stint of high school teaching, then college teaching and graduate work in math—at two universities. Now, just over 30, he is a Ph.D. candidate in astrophysics, his lifelong dream. Over the years, he has said, "All I want is a chance to find out how good I really am."

Gifted at a University: A Very Mixed Blessing

Students like Jonathan and Mark constitute a powerful argument for more sophisticated counseling as well as greater flexibility for gifted students in college. Gone are the days when the gifted were the only ones who made it that far. Sidney L. Pressy of Ohio State University cited statistics from his landmark study to show that students who accelerated in college graduated in larger percentages than average

college students and had more notable careers. Those who also had special guidance showed an even higher graduation rate. In college, Pressy called for credit by examination, special programs of acceleration, and more special guidance so that young careers could be launched earlier and costs reduced. Such a program would prevent a student from "being conspicuous if his rate is not that of the average." Unfortunately, Pressy began calling for all of this in 1955.

In arguing for better counseling and greater tolerance of diversity at the university level, J. M. Tolliver says, "of all the disservice we do our students, perhaps the most critical is demanding that they 'fit' . . . We are intolerant of deviant discretions, expelling those who do not learn their (conformity) lessons well." Further, Tolliver suggests, "A cynicism develops concerning the generation of ideas. It rapidly becomes apparent to the creatively gifted that the central concern of a scholar should be, 'Will it sell?' and not, 'Is it right?' . . . each creative effort becomes an exercise in marketing."

In light of the shortage of talented Ph.D.s predicted for the late 1990s, perhaps the most depressing result of Willings's study was that, of the fifteen subjects he was able to follow, ten were so disillusioned they were not willing to go on to graduate schools, although they were eminently qualified to do so. Most of them had already published either literary or scholarly work. Fifteen months after graduation, all but one was a dissatisfied employee. One woman who had taken a position with an oil company wrote to Willings, "I've sold my soul, but I got a good price for it!" In subsequent years, "Radical career changes were frequently reported. Only one respondent has not experienced problems in personal relationships. Eight have felt the need for professional intervention." As Willings said, "To be gifted at university is not an unmixed blessing."

Marcelle, Mission Accomplished

Marcelle looks like a typical young mother on a hot summer afternoon as she arranges her baby in the car seat of a small car parked on a shady Washington, D.C., street. Marcelle has arrived at 30 with many aspects of her life sorted out, but "I'm not sure what effect the

baby will have on things when I return to work in a few months." In the passage from 18 to 30, she has acquired two degrees, married a fellow lawyer, had a child, and obtained a prestigious government job. Her ordinary clothes and unassuming manner give no indication of her degrees from Princeton and Yale or her position as an attorney for the United States Department of Justice.

She recalls, "The most liberating experience for me came in high school when I suddenly realized one day, 'It isn't me!' I finally decided that the world was run in certain ways; that human beings adjust or don't adjust their differences, and that none of this was my fault." She had no need to apologize for being bright.

"But you have to relearn that on every level. College and law school produced the pleasant shock of lots of people who were like me." It was still a smaller group within the university, but Marcelle recalls graduate school especially as "a kind of heaven, where everyone is bright and prepared. I had fun with people I really liked. It was an ideal time and place."

However, the larger world of educated professionals in the pressure cooker of working Washington made it necessary to learn "It isn't me" all over again. "What was valued in academia is not valued in the business world. Here the emphasis was on getting the job done. People who might not be a success academically are often well suited to the working world. You can often get the job done if you don't think too much."

Marcelle seems to have accomplished the major tasks of this arduous period. She was able to accept and understand her differences, both academically and personally. The second major task was that of allowing herself to meet her needs by more intense work, more school, a better job, trying new things when present ones did not provide satisfaction. Attendance at top universities and her present job seem to do that in fairly conventional (gifted) fashion.

The second major task is often complicated by a third element, which Marcelle seems to have escaped: the scattering of time and energy by multitalented young people. For many, the time from 18 to 30 is not a straight journey, but a winding and crooked one, full of detours and potholes, and things often don't settle down until the early

thirties—if then. Detours change the direction of many people's lives. The difference for the interview subjects seems to have been that the drive to learn remained constant through confusion, illness, rebellion, or drug abuse. The need to nourish the mind seems to be the factor determining whether a detour becomes a dead end.

Julio, the Search for Truth

Julio holds two master's degrees, but detours led him on several other paths before he became an educational administrator in charge of gifted programs. A philosophical concern with religious questions had led him, at an early age, to seek adults to whom he could talk about such things. One was the mother of the twins who were his best friends. "She was a hard-working, sloppy lady. I'd sit up late, talking to her after my friends went to bed . . . I even went to her fundamentalist church, and to see the famous evangelist, Kathryn Kuhlman, with her."

The search continued as he graduated from a high school he hated. He entered college, where he "spent more time in the library than on assignments. I failed several courses. At 18, I quit school and took off for San Francisco. I worked in a supermarket and had my own apartment. I roamed the city . . . I had more fun than I ever have had since then . . . even the cash registers were interesting, or seeing how fast I could memorize the prices . . . I cleaned a restaurant, and wound up helping the cook."

Trying college again, he took a course in religion taught by a Catholic priest and, "after pursuing the ideas to the nth degree," underwent a religious conversion and joined an order of teaching brothers at 21. The next years were spent studying and working in an orphanage, where "I saw too much suffering. I couldn't handle it"; later, he became a teacher.

The same relentless pursuit of truth which led Julio into the religious life led him out of it at 32. "I realized that there was no one answer." Now married and the father of two, Julio was a Ph.D. candidate but gave up because "I couldn't stand the courses. Too often, I knew more than the professors." He continues to pursue the study

of philosophy on his own, a continent and several lifetimes away from a San Francisco supermarket.

Adrian, Illness and Rebellion

Adrian's detours led through rebellion and illness. "I was accepted at Catholic University and quit after one semester. I couldn't handle that environment. I had been so stifled in high school and now here was college with all these rules: You can't sit on the grass. Men may smoke but not women . . .

"I went back to my Midwest hometown and got a civil service job with the city. It was awful! My parents were pressuring me to go back to college, but I developed tuberculosis. In the hospital I was out of the parochial school environment, away from my family, and among adults. I was actually happy during that year; people liked and respected me! When I went back to school, it was to the one I wanted, a city school and secular. I got Bs and never really studied; I didn't understand why some people seemed to work so hard.

"With an education degree, I taught until inner-city teaching became physically dangerous. I took a job working for a federal health services project and was instantly disliked just for being me. I talked about Shakespeare at work! A friend in personnel rescued me from the typing pool and in six months I was administrative assistant to the director. I was newly married, and during the next four years I held down a highly responsible job, helped my husband weather the difficulty of his decision to drop medical school, suffered a miscarriage, and gave birth to a son." In spite of all the evidence, it would be another eight years, when her son was in school, before Adrian would understand how bright she is. "What I had viewed as abnormality all my life was competence!"

Maureen, Giving Up on Yourself

Growing up in a small town in northern California, Maureen reports being a good little girl, painfully shy, who was bored in school and "hated it. I was the only person in my family who read. When I

was 12, the librarian called my mother because I was taking out books about Einstein's theory. I just wanted to see what all the fuss was about! One time, I decided to read the whole encyclopedia—and I did it. But I neglected my schoolwork. At 15, I just stopped bothering. Just before I quit at 16, I felt like a really stupid person, a loser. I had gotten low marks and disappointed my parents. I didn't know I was bored. I went to work in a factory."

There she met, fortunately, another gifted kid, who she decided "would do just fine." After marrying at 18, she left the mountains of California for thirteen years of raising a family in an eastern Levittown, "where you can't see the stars. I had always felt that people didn't understand me, and there I looked down my nose at the neighborhood ladies who were content with soaps and kids. I think I was even a little jealous that they could be content and I couldn't. Other times I tried to go along because I was tired of my kids being treated as if they were oddballs too. I felt all the time as though I was selling out just to make life easier for us.

"In my late twenties something began to happen. People around me didn't understand the change; I hardly understood it myself. I suddenly had the courage to express myself instead of trying not to rock the boat and offend anyone. I'd call the latest movie craze boring, if that's what I thought. 'No!' I'd say, 'I hate Tupperware parties; I'd rather stay home and read.' Finally, by the time I was 35, I realized how bored I was and went back and got my high school diploma. Then I took emergency medical technician and paramedic courses. I found that what I was missing was the simple joy of learning!"

Maureen has done emergency work for the Red Cross, and now that her children are older, she is hoping to find a permanent job. Looking back, she is still delighted with her fortunate choice of a husband. "I look at this man who has no education and he just sparkles. I can talk to him about anything!"

Fran, Questioning the Self

Fran recalls that she proceeded through this period in a series of moments, specific points when she looked around and asked herself,

"What am I doing here?" Not finding a satisfactory answer, she set off in another direction. Along the way, she has preserved those parts of her lifestyle and personality which she considers essential, but she has found a way to be accepted by society and even to accomplish something in the way of service to the world.

The first such moment came the summer before college. "I worked at a resort, as a waitress in a bar. I lived on my own, had a boyfriend in a rock band . . . went out every night . . . slept very little. I thought it was the life for me. I felt very glamorous, even though I still had braces on my teeth! By August I was bored. One night I looked at the bouncer in the bar. He was about 30, and going nowhere. 'What will I be like at 30 if I stay here?' I asked myself. Right then I knew I had to be in an academic atmosphere of some kind."

Fran found a haven in a Quaker-run college with an open atmosphere and curriculum. "I wasn't weird there. I could experiment. My clothes weren't considered strange. I could study things which interested me. At one point a group of us designed a light show and backed up a band . . . we toured other colleges."

Senior year was spent in England, and she graduated with departmental honors in literature. She traveled in France and Ireland, learning music and folklore as she went. Back home again and still without direction, she traveled and camped with a friend, until "One night I found myself sitting in a tent in the Adirondacks in the middle of a thunderstorm, while my friend went off to visit his latest girlfriend, and I decided, 'This is not the way I want to spend my time.'"

Returning to and marrying her longtime boyfriend, she tuned her life to his. He taught school, briefly. They picked potatoes. They lived in a remote cabin without running water for a year while he tried to write a book. He started a business that failed, and at that point so did the marriage. "I wanted to teach, so I worked as a waitress to get certification and a master's degree . . . Then I couldn't stand the confinement of a regular public school—all those bells!"

Her present job, running the educational facility of a juvenile detention center, provides daily challenge, variety, and the informal atmosphere in which Fran prefers to operate. Her position, plus an additional master's degree in criminal justice, allows her access to

people of stature in the community who can help her with the several volunteer projects which are always a part of her life.

"I'm still interested in the same things, the outdoors, social service, changing society . . . the forms have become more acceptable as I get older . . . It's easier to find acceptance than when I was a longhaired 20-year-old . . . people might think I'm peculiar, but they trust my seriousness of purpose . . . I do dress differently" (Fran is rarely seen wearing anything but jeans, a comfortable shirt, and sensible shoes), "but now I can talk to an official's wife and get support for a project.

"I can be myself and still feel that I have a place in this community. There has been lots of pain, lots of adjustments . . . times I did things I don't like about myself. But I have learned that if you don't allow ego to get in your way, you can get to do what you want . . . it is nice not to have to justify myself." Fran has finally constructed a lifestyle without compromising her values. A comfortable second marriage finds her emotionally secure also.

Colin, Tragic Possibilities

Colin's route to 30 could have taken many different turns, but he believes that his constant desire to learn may have saved his life. As he recounts it, "Until I finished high school I was a typical bright kid, bored with school, doing what he had to do to get by . . . In my senior year I began experimenting with the counterculture, hitchhiking and going off on my own . . . I thought I wanted to be a writer, that I had left science behind. I was going to write a sequel to *Catcher in the Rye*. I flunked out of Yale in one semester and then hitchhiked to New York. For six months I lived like a hobo, sleeping in subways, and eventually drifted back to California and went to live in Berkeley.

"The Sixties were in full swing. I became a part of the off-campus, nonstudent world of drugs. I was high every day . . . we lived in hovels, sharing food and rent. After a year, I was tired of living at the bottom, so I tried school again. I had been doing acid every day and was so bored with myself, I decided I had to 'cut the crap.' I would limit myself to being stoned only on weekends, so I could go to

school and read the books without my eyes twirling." He can laugh at himself now. Needless to say, it didn't work.

"I lived in Haight-Ashbury. I tried Santa Barbara. I kept going to schools, not finishing anything, but always seeking intellectual stimulation. Somehow, I always separated the drug-taking from school, and I think that saved me. I managed to avoid going to jail or going crazy . . . but it is a very hazy period . . . I wonder if I did mess up my brain . . .

"Finally I settled on a small junior college which was friendly and had small classes. I knew I had to give up drugs entirely, so I could study. I was swamped a little in the math for awhile, and still dealing with a 'hangover' from the drugs which affected my abstract reasoning ability. I dropped out with no degree and earned my living for two years as a freelance photographer. I lived on $100 a month and food stamps. Bored again, I tried filmmaking . . . I took the all-day test for an FCC license in two hours . . . I worked at Berkeley's TV station for a summer and finally realized that what I wanted to be was an electrical engineer. I did well at Berkeley; I stuck to one major for two whole years!

"By the time I got my degree, I had taken eight years, six colleges, and majors in English, math, physics, sculpture (yes, sculpture!) philosophy, psychology, and sociology—and that was just the officially declared ones. When I headed off to MIT and graduate work on a National Science Foundation fellowship, I was on top of the world." But the fellowship ran out long before the Ph.D. was completed, and the saga began again.

Teaching stints at several colleges have left Colin disillusioned about the possibility of teaching in the manner which he feels is most effective for true learning. "I want to teach people how to use their minds; I only happen to be doing it in courses in physics and computer science." Colin is still changing jobs and has turned to industry and research in artificial intelligence.

When last heard from, he was happy and challenged, working for one of the nation's largest companies. Along the way, he married a gifted woman who is patient with his needs and has two sons whose

education he worries about, even though they are only 2 and 5. He grins ruefully, "When the time comes, I will have some good first-hand advice to give them about drugs and rebellion . . . I only hope they will listen."

Why Some Gifted Grownups Don't Get Ph.D.s

Colin says frankly, "My attention span is about two years, and degrees take longer than that." His comment is not a facetious one. Many gifted adults do not complete advanced degrees for the same reason. The real world of graduate school often involves lockstep movement through a series of courses which go on long after the person has mastered the things he or she wanted to learn. And for many gifted grownups, learning takes precedence over a piece of paper. That may or may not be a foolish choice, but it is the way it happens for some gifted grownups.

Bernard, the Quintessential Gifted Person

As he enters the small restaurant where the interview is to take place, Bernard presents the image of a successful young man. He arrives in a shiny fast car. He is darkly good looking, beautifully dressed, and poised with the waitresses who come and go as we talk. His sense of humor bubbles up constantly, and he can speak knowledgeably about computer sales, auto racing, education, and the workings of his own mind.

Looked at during one of the phases he went through to arrive at being an assured 28-year-old, one might have seen a kid who appeared to be going nowhere. And yet for Bernard, it all fits together—he was simply busy growing. Attending a small but excellent college instead of twelfth grade, he "played" and "explored"—two of his favorite words. At one point, he went for a six-month visit to the artificial intelligence lab of a top university, when the lab was just being developed, and was allowed the run of the place. "I learned a lot." He spent time at another university on a National Science

Foundation grant. "I was one semester from a degree and I just got bored. People keep telling me that someday I'll be sorry."

Next, he spent a year as a counselor in a program for placing ghetto youth in good high schools so that they could go on to good colleges. "I was one of two live-in tutors . . . a very interesting experience. You don't learn anything really well until you try to teach it . . . a lot of things I thought I knew, I didn't! Part of the mental process which happens is that the way you explain something in this path, the person doesn't understand, so you start looking for alternate paths. Some of them you have never explored yourself, and it leads to an 'aha' discovery. It was lots of fun . . . I also found out that I had not grown up—these kids had lived in the South Bronx, Harlem, Atlanta!

"Next I got involved in racing. One of my college friends wanted to build a car and race it, and that sounded interesting. I was 20; I didn't even have a driver's license, but I learned how to design an automobile. We almost killed ourselves in it."

Going to work for his father's engineering firm "didn't work out. I was not too good about showing up regularly. So I raced a little, and went broke. Then I decided that perhaps I had better go out and get a job. So I did." In the meanwhile, he married a young woman who is "smart in different ways than I am. She knows how I operate, and Lord knows everyone thinks she's a saint for that!"

For two years now Bernard has been selling highly sophisticated computer systems. His sales are multimillion-dollar transactions that require both brains and finesse to close. "People get all excited about what I can do, and I'm just doing what I normally do." Recently, he was made sales manager for the company. "The people who work for me range in age from thirties to fifties and they tell me that I have gone from 'That intimidating kid' to the best manager we've ever had . . . Whatever it is, I'll learn it!"

Bernard expects the challenge to last "a couple of months at most. Then something will have to change." What's next? "I don't know . . . lately I've discovered reading." Although many gifted grownups are lifelong bookworms, Bernard is one of a number of highly successful people I interviewed who do not read very much, if

at all. In most cases, they explain it in terms of what educators would call learning style. The printed page is simply not their preferred route to information. A 17-year-old explains, "If I need technical information, and there is no other way to get it, I will resort to a book. But I prefer to learn by listening, watching, and trying things with my hands." Another says, "I learn best by listening, then by discussing, next by doing; reading runs a distant fourth." A senior citizen remarks, "I've never been a reader; there are so many other ways to learn things."

Bernard seems to have learned to live to the special rhythm of gifted lives. "I'm not sure I like stable environments; if it wasn't for racing I wouldn't be motivated to make much money. Racing has captivated me because it's so hard to be good at it; there is always something new to learn. It has matured me because it forces you to be honest with yourself; if you're not, you'll die . . . I am currently leading three lives: reading, racing, and selling computers. Who knows what's next?"

Cindy, Quiet Determination

There is a quietness about Cindy that makes one forget about the active life she lives. Soft-spoken, a determined wearer of casual clothes, her animated face shows no makeup and her long brown hair is pulled smoothly into a soft braid. She has learned to accept the reliability of change, to "concentrate on heading in the right direction in a series of moments." Perhaps her early study of Oriental philosophy and martial arts has contributed to her seeming ability to move through life serenely. The interview will reveal that she has her share of inner turmoil, much of it a result of her choice of vocation.

Photography and art were interests from junior high on. A quiet nonconformist, Cindy fit herself into a large state university by joining the photography staff of its daily paper. Becoming photography editor of the paper sent her off with its nationally ranked football team to "run up and down the field dodging the wheels of the TV cameras!"

Concern with fitness and health led to personal exploration of food and nutrition courses. Practical consideration of the job market led to a minor in economics because "editors like you to have some knowledge of a special field." An assignment making slides for a biology professor added medical photography to the list of things she could do with her photojournalism major.

Varied and intense interests left little time for social life. "I'd come home from covering, say, a basketball game and just be by myself. I'd have several parties to which I had been invited, and I might even feel a little lonely, but I would just choose to be lonely at that time. You get used to it." Cindy learned very early that "there will never be very many people who will like or approve of me. All I need is a small circle of friends with whom I can be myself." She began building that circle in seventh grade and it carried her through senior high school. One girl is still a special friend. "I knew that in college I'd have to build that circle again. I had three or four people with whom I could go out to dinner and not have to talk. That's a sure indication of good friends."

One of the things Cindy loves is travel, learning about a new part of the country. A summer job with the National Park Service awakened her photographer's eye for wildlife, both plant and animal. "The man I worked for was in his sixties. He had countless degrees, and he was very patient. When he looked out a window and began talking about the birds, I was all ears, I learned so much . . . We would have dinner and talk for hours . . . I began reading guidebooks on birds and animals . . . this field cannot be exhausted!"

In a series of careful and conscious decisions, Cindy has mapped out a life for herself. For part of the year, she works for the National Park Service in a part of Washington wild enough to accommodate her interest in skiing and hiking. In the winter, she waits tables in a small town in northern Washington. Meanwhile, she builds her professional portfolio one small photojournalism assignment at a time. "If I can have an established career as a photojournalist by the time I'm 40 or so, I'll be satisfied. If I fail, well, I can live on very little."

Constantly questioning, she continually reevaluates her freelance life. "I have very few possessions. My only 'home' is a room in the Park

Service headquarters. Sometimes I think I shouldn't depend so much on my creativity . . . get something nine-to-five-ish and do my photography in my free time. But I don't think I'd be happy. Leaving options open can be so unsettling . . . I can't tell what I'll be doing five years from now—except a seasonal job with the Park Service! I've seen my brother nail himself down to a conventional business life and I know I don't want to do that. I ask him if he's happy and he says, 'I'm busy.'"

A special companion along the way? "I always thought that intelligence in a mate didn't matter that much," she says softly. "I have learned that it does. I spent last winter with a man I truly loved. We shared many outdoor interests, and he loved music. But in the evening, when all the outdoor things were over and we sat across a table from one another, I found that we couldn't talk. He simply did not have any really intellectual interests, and he didn't read much. I also found myself consciously turning to others for conversation and sharing of ideas. It was sad, but I had to leave him. I could have done the whole husband and kids routine—he would have loved me to pieces, but I couldn't give up the intellectual life. Now I know that brains count in a relationship, at least for me they do . . .

"I am happiest studying new plants and animals, and working on prints in the darkroom. I hope to marry and have a family some day, but I never want to be forced to choose between my work and a family." In her own unspectacular way, Cindy is making a quiet success of her life. Her job yields new areas of learning all the time, and she is working toward the artistic goals she has set for herself. Since junior high, she has known how to create the circle she needs around her, for companionship and understanding. Her independence has cost her. But her independence is her strength. Like her life, it is an individual design of her own making.

Frank, Using It All

Frank is just 30. Dark-haired and slightly heavy, he arrives late for the interview, hurrying in the door of his attractive house in a dark business suit and carrying a briefcase. His pregnant wife talks about her banking career while their 3-year-old son plays nearby.

"I'll tell my story and weave in the things you want to know," he says, bypassing the interviewer's structure in favor of his own, and settling back on the sofa, comfortable and at ease. Four hours later, the interviewer emerges with the portrait of a happy man, one not without the usual anxieties that come with being highly gifted, but one who seems to have emerged from the struggle to set up a life for himself quite high on the scale of maximum use of potential and emotional satisfaction. In a few areas, he was just plain lucky, but mostly his needs were satisfied when they appeared, not allowed to die or be blunted by frustration.

Although pressured by his father to enter the medical profession, Frank also had the benefit of the pressure his father was willing to exert on schools and colleges to allow him to work at his own level. Thus he was able to go to a university part time at 15 and full time at 16. "In my first math class at Penn there was a little ego contest. It was almost two months before the professor could throw a problem at me that I couldn't do." Summers he had programming jobs, and the degree was completed at 19. Then it was on to Harvard for graduate work in math.

"Those years as an undergraduate were the happiest of my life. I met my wife there, and discovered classical music, which has had a big impact on me. Just about everything else in education has been wasted on me . . . when we moved I found an old ninth-grade history test—I could not answer a single question on it! I remember none of the meaningless facts; I just occupied my time waiting to grow. It made me philosophical about worrying about school. The good thing about Harvard was that they didn't make the Ph.D. thesis easy. You had to show some creativity, do something that had some real substance."

In spite of the challenge, Frank became disillusioned with math before he completed his thesis. "I realized that I might be one of the top fifty in the country, but I wasn't one of the top three or four who would get to do the really interesting new things, to break new ground. I tried the computer science department, but I was too late for a fellowship. I decided that I should work; school was over."

At 22, Frank accepted a position as a senior programmer for a federal research center. The job lasted for a year and a half, and then he

moved to a major communications firm, "where I was operating at a higher level than most of the senior people. They refused to promote me because I did not have the requisite years of experience. I started answering ads again after two years there."

Frank had come to graduate school as a married man—at 19. His gifted wife "transferred with me. She was 18. She has had the biggest influence on my career. When she went for her MBA, it looked interesting, so I took a job with a consulting firm run by an off-the-wall person who also happened to be brilliant, and went on to get my own MBA in corporate strategy. For two and a half years I worked in a very unstable environment. Eventually you outgrow that kind of thing.

"Job number four, what to do? I decided to pursue my interest in strategic planning, but the interviewers said, 'You've never had a job in it.' Product manager in computer software kept me happy for another year and a half, but I got no recognition for my work. I decided it was time to try to stick it out in a job. I am now a senior product planner for a large communications conglomerate.

"I have no complaints; the salary is very nice, but the challenge is going to run out soon. Right now I'm doing three completely different areas, one I was hired for and two others I volunteered for . . . you almost set yourself up to be disappointed; people don't know how to deal with someone doing all that stuff, and you don't receive much recognition. My boss is OK, though; he doesn't flinch when I remember things. He's glad I'm working so hard! I don't quite fit in with the system of who gets promotions. With all the grade-skipping I did, I did not develop the necessary social skills." Eventually, he admits, he will probably have to start his own company.

Social life for someone like Frank is rather limited. "Most people are not on my level, but it doesn't bother me that much any more. I have a few good friends. Once every couple of months we get together and talk about what is on our minds. My wife is really my best friend. We're married a long time; we are like the same person. I'm satisfied with the way my life turned out. I've been married ten years and have a happy family life, which has been a stabilizing influence. A lot of people think I'm 35 or so. I worry about my son; he's obviously

bright. I think he's going to be difficult to live with. Two of us in the house should be very interesting!"

Both in his own terms and in those of the outside world, Frank is what we call a success. But so are Cindy and Julio, and all the others whose lives have been described in this chapter; there are many ways to define success. For a gifted person, it would seem to involve mastering the tasks of the young adult period, but not in any prescribed way. Resolving the question of what you are good for, learning to live to the rhythmic cycle of a stimulus-seeking life, and avoiding the scattering or the frustration of your talent. It does not require an affluent lifestyle or a large circle of friends. It is long on inner satisfactions and constant growth.

How did these people do it? They learned, often painfully, to understand and value their special nature. They worked hard, and made sacrifices, to create the opportunities to allow their talents maximum use. So far, they have struck that crucial balance between making choices and being open to change.

Beyond 30: Midlife Choices and Changes

The twenties and thirties are a time of challenges and possibilities to young gifted grownups. Like their peers, many gifted people spend this time in their lives trying to define themselves, to carve out a professional path, and to find a mate. But always there is the using up of challenges, the desire for new knowledge, the adjustments to the intense emotional and moral levels at which many of the gifted live their lives. Tasks that others regard as "accomplished," such as a settled level of job achievement, often represent levels of stagnation to a gifted person.

Moving on into the forties and fifties, there are the challenges and satisfactions of family life, of raising one's own (very likely) gifted children. However, when observing the lives of gifted grownups, the stages seem to break down about here. They don't "settle in" like they are supposed to. They live to that special rhythm of challenge,

achievement, what's next? For many of those I interviewed, that cycle seems to last between eighteen months and three years. After that, the person usually needs some new stimulation: a new project, a new challenge, something new to learn, a new job, or even a whole new career.

But by now, most of them have also acquired responsibilities. Spouses, children, and employees or coworkers have come to expect a certain amount of stability. Psychologist Erik Erikson classified the midlife years as a time of choosing between generativity and stagnation. For a gifted grownup, there does not really seem to be a choice. For a person who is ever seeking new knowledge, new food for the accelerated brain/mind, generativity is a given. Marie Curie, a gifted grownup from another era, said it well: "Life is not easy for any of us. But what of that? We must have perseverance, and above all confidence in ourselves. We must believe that we are gifted for something, and that this thing, at whatever cost, must be attained."

Whether we call it a job, a career, or a lifework, "this thing" must both challenge and satisfy the accelerated perception system of a gifted grownup. It requires discovering the nature of the work we need to do and then placing ourselves in situations where that work can be carried out. But meanwhile, there is earning the daily bread . . .

Chapter Seven

Bored, Bored, Bored: The Quest for Challenging Work

If growing up means getting a job and then having to stay there . . . if it means a cessation of growth, then I don't ever want to grow up . . .

30-year-old

We are living in an age when the gifted are among the least likely to advance. Such people often run the risk of dismissal because, although their work is excellent, they do not fit in.
David Willings, "The Gifted at Work"

We have looked at the teens and twenties of gifted grownups, but what happens to the strivers, the superstars, the independents as they negotiate their way through corporate America from thirty-something into their sixties? Some of them do disappear into the Institute for Advanced Study or the groves of academe after college, but many of them do not even go to college. They take jobs in the real world, just like everyone else. But not quite like everyone else, as they soon find out.

Retail Salesman. "My brain works ten times as fast as my body. Nobody at work understands this . . . I haven't found anyone who understands this!"

Administrator. "I'm intense, opinionated. I'm always thinking about how I want to think and go—I assume the other person knows . . ."

130

Factory Worker.   "I've paid a price in terms of boredom and restlessness. If people perceive you as a threat, then you have all sorts of problems."

Scientist.   "Choices are limited by what people will pay for. You must mold yourself to a market, and that's not fun."

Nurse.   "The supervisor often feels threatened, so you have to hide your potential. I've done that a lot. You even get to be good at it after a while."

Office Worker.   "The worst kind of work is not the mechanical stuffing of envelopes; I don't have to use my mind at all for that. Checking references all day, I can't think my own thoughts . . . using *part* of your mind is awful!"

Psychologist.   "Giftedness is a two-edged sword, being at the mercy of a mind that just goes and goes . . . the turmoil, the restless need for new things. Some few manage this with a kind of contentment, but they are very rare. I wish I knew their secret."

In the interviews, I found that where employment is concerned, gifted adults exhibit an intensity, an insistence on the integrity to do the work at its best, as well as chronic impatience with shoddy work and slow thinkers. Gifted adults work too quickly, get bored, and show it. They raise the standards for everyone else, and that is always resented. They have odd approaches to things, which irritates their coworkers. They ask for more work and make enemies. The idealism seen in the younger person is still there, and can cause problems with authority figures or with fellow executives. In addition, the bright mind has difficulty accepting the illogical and may be very stubborn in expressing doubts about a project or in criticizing others. And yet, because of a heightened sensitivity, this same person may be unusually vulnerable to peer group rejection. College degree or not, gifted adults carry around in their feisty minds questions the boss can't answer. And sometimes they threaten the

boss, because that odd approach turns out to be better than the boss's idea.

As for the independents, the strivers, and the superstars, they do not seem to follow set career paths based on these categories; life is much more complicated than that. The superstars usually do continue on their successful trajectory to fame and/or fortune, but in some rare cases, the superstars are the suicides. The strivers may reach the corporate heights only to be displaced by someone more creative or younger. The independent may be a restless and rebellious job-changer whose career never develops, or the fortunate resident genius in a situation which welcomes creativity.

Executives Comment about Gifted Workers

Dr. David Willings, professor of personnel management at the University of New Brunswick, Canada, is one of the few academics who study gifted people in a variety of settings and in several different countries. In a paper presented at the 1981 World Conference on Gifted and Talented Children, he writes:

> I will quote just a few remarks addressed to me by senior managers, directors and vice presidents in England, Canada and America:

> "Why do we hire these intellectuals? They're no damned use. They don't fit in. They cause trouble."

> "We had a very gifted young chap. He came up with two ideas which we have unashamedly stolen. But he never learned to follow normal procedure. Couldn't fill out a PY34 form to save his life. He left us after seven months and I think it was for the best."

> "I would rather have twelve stable nonentities than one transient genius."

Why is it so important that a greater percentage of our smart kids find work in which they can realize their highest capabilities? One of Dr. Willings's executives replies, "The cold and brutal fact is that industry needs these people. If they cannot adjust to us, then I suppose we must adjust to them." Dr. Willings hastens to add, "He was not well received."

This phenomenon is not new. Over against the voices of resistance represented by the executives in Willings's study are the voices of economists, management consultants, industrial psychologists, academics, sociologists, CEOs, and popular writers. They have been calling for renewal and reform in the American workplace for more than twenty years.

What Researchers Say about Gifted Workers

As far back as 1971, D. C. Dauw, in "Use of Behavioral Science Consultants in Selected Industries," could say, "Industry can no longer afford such widespread inattention to the growth and development of human potential. The traditional company climate is killing more and more employees every day, not physically, but creatively." In *Creativity and Innovation in Organizations*, he added, "The real challenge facing most organizations is how to avoid giving most employees, creative and noncreative alike, some form of mental health problem. This is the result of meaningless work, poor supervision, inadequate communications, not providing proper motivation and the like."

In 1972, George Swope, in *Dissent—The Dynamic of Democracy*, characterized the workplace as "Stultifying . . . Some seem to be no more than a series of interconnected cages . . . the loss of talent is incalculable."

The voices calling for change have continued into the nineties. Robert Waterman joined them in his landmark book, *The Renewal Factor*, when he quoted John Gardner: "The only possible stability is stability in motion . . . There is a kind of rhythm to the process:

first, a constant search for standard ways of doing things. That makes life easier. Then the deliberate breaking of old rules, familiar patterns, past practice. That is the only way to respond to change. [Renewing companies] find and manage a delicate balance: enough security so that people will take risks, enough uncertainty so that people will strive."

The Job

Obviously, there is no single ideal job for a gifted person, any more than there is for anyone else. But based on what the research and interviews revealed, we can predict with some certainty that a gifted adult, at whatever stage of a career, will need:

- A day-to-day level of stimulation which provides challenge and newness
- To be able to communicate new ideas and to push ahead to new areas of work and learning as soon as the current area is exhausted
- To design his or her own environment, so that the first two needs can be satisfied

These are the elements which form the rhythm of a gifted adult's career. Item 3 is crucial. It needs to be present so that items 1 and 2 can be repeated endlessly, like the beat in a measure of music.

The Need for Stimulation

On the employment scene, gifted grownups do seem to be characterized by a low tolerance for limits, but the need for challenging work is only part of the story. If the challenge is simply to survive the day's aggravations, or to successfully smooth the same waters day after day, then it will not be enough. There must be something new in the challenge, not simply a fascination with endless novelty. Quite

the contrary: these people are more easily bored than others by mere novelty because they have the ability to see the underlying patterns very quickly and realize that it is all really the same.

We mean "new" in the sense of something new for the brain to work on, some new learning experience in which present knowledge comes into play, is placed over against the new situation; the gap between the two is crossed, and a synthesis takes place. This dynamic quality of the work is essential.

Wes: Medicine, The Endless Quest.   Wes is an emergency room physician in a small city in western New York, and he loves his work. A few minutes of conversation will reveal that he is already planning for the next stages, that he knows how to satisfy his need for an ever renewing cycle of learning. "I have been offered a job as head of an emergency room, and I would like to do that, but only for a year or two. In the meanwhile, I intend to become board certified in internal medicine . . . after that, perhaps a research job might be interesting." What may be viewed by others as restlessness or discontent is the norm for a gifted person. That understanding needs to be internalized by the person and accepted by those who share the same life space, be they lovers or employers.

Michelle: Business—The Hard Way.   Michelle is a telling example of a gifted woman who tackled the working world with energy, drive, originality, talent—but no Piece of Paper officially declaring that she was any of the above, and no clear understanding of how strong a bright woman's need for mental stimulation could be. In her third year of college, finances made it impossible to continue in school full time. The itch to be out of the classroom had also asserted itself, so she told herself she would be glad to have an excuse to be out in the world where people *do* things.

Her business major led to office jobs. The first one had been for an international development firm—typing and filing. It remained interesting while she learned how to run several types of duplicating equipment and how to type in Spanish without knowing the

language. But hours of typing and filing do not provide the necessary stimulation for an active mind.

The next job was for an executive search firm, where a perceptive boss realized that she could compose letters for him and run the office while the secretary with twenty years' experience was away. He wanted to make her a staff member, but the main office said not without a college degree. So it was back to the word processor.

Taking several college courses, she discovered that she had learned how to study and could earn As. Then the staff was cut. She changed jobs, twice. Money for college courses ran out. She barely made expenses. And her family wondered . . . How could someone with an IQ in excess of 155 be doing so poorly?

A new job seemed to point in the right direction. In the communications department of a large professional organization, she went through what was becoming a familiar routine. Step 1: Impress everyone with her mature approach to the job. She looked and acted at least five years older than her age (23 at the time). Step 2: Learn the office routine in record time. Step 3: Look around for more things to do. In this case, there was routine "monkey work" (her phrase) to do: typing, filing, Xeroxing, mailing the canned speeches the professional organization provides as a service to its members. But another perceptive supervisor realized that she could write speeches as well as type them. It wasn't in her low-level job description, but he allowed her to write them. She rewrote the company guide for making speeches and improved the layout and typography. Then her mentor was fired.

In the political shakeup that followed, her chief supervisor became a woman only a few years older, who bounced her right back to typing and filing. "I watch her take two days to do a speech I can write in two hours, and she is my boss! But she has a degree, and a title and an office, and I don't."

The arrival of a new supervisor suggests a new tack. "Try being a good little kid. Complete the monkey work posthaste. Cultivate a wonderful attitude. Then try to explain to the new person that you need more to do. The result? He listened very sympathetically and gave me more monkey work!"

An employment agency run by and for bright young women helped her to understand that most organizations have neither the understanding nor the motivation to provide the "more complex and faster, please," which a gifted woman requires. At the next place, she is hired after telling the interviewer frankly, "I plan on staying here a year, but I learn so fast that in that year you will have the best executive secretary that you have ever had. Once I get my feet under me, I will ask for more challenging things to do, and you will see that this can be a real advantage to you."

For the first time, she bluntly announced that she was highly intelligent and the environment said, "Fine." There was the usual amazement as she mastered the new word processor and completed a rush job in the first few days. When the "What's next?" stage arrived, she received more to do, but soon she bumped into the ceiling anyway. This time, no panic; she was prepared.

She moved to a new job with a high-status international law firm, where she discovered that law clerks worked half the night to impress their bosses, and secretaries were expected to do the same. "I had no life, and the work was a bore." She let her feelings show and was fired. At rock bottom at 26, she became an office temporary to pay the rent. Amazingly, she found that when moving from place to place with her considerable skills, she was welcomed and she found it diverting and interesting.

A temporary assignment led her to the youth projects director of a large international social service agency. Here, she was welcomed as "wonderful, because you are so smart!"; given an endless variety of jobs, from newsletter writing to preparing a proposal for an updated version of the Peace Corps; and surrounded by people who were devoted to helping others. Her self-esteem, stimulation, and caring needs were all satisfied in one ever-changing job. But there was still a catch. The fast track she said she wanted all those years terrified her! "I laughed at myself a lot. It took a year to get up to speed." She accepted a permanent job as administrative assistant to the director and can presently say, "For the first time in my life, I look forward to getting up and going to work. I love my job!"

Dora: Job Switching.   Sometimes, the gifted adult finds stimulation and variety only by making major career changes. After watching her spend all the time it took to arrive at a master's degree in home economics, it was obvious to her husband, Colin, that Dora was bored. "Colin convinced me to take computer courses with him. He pushed me into taking a job with a geographer at his university. There was one computer and no one else knew much about it, so I had to read the manuals and be in charge of things. My biggest accomplishment was writing a program for mapping using an electrostatic printer. I went to the library and did research on software. In a short time I had a program that did contour maps without making mistakes!

"At the point at which I left to have a baby, it was beginning to get boring. I was doing more of just processing data rather than writing programs. I hated that; I had no time to improve programs. My pregnancy was a good excuse to leave a job that was beginning to bore me. Besides, I was beginning to get resentment from one or two people because I knew too much."

Stacey: Banking—The Mainstream.   Stacey is a former music major who decided to earn a living by getting an M.B.A. She entered the world of banking, and in just two years has become a specialist in health care lending for a large national bank. Her friends and coworkers are bright at this level, but she recalls vividly what it was like to be "mainstreamed," working at a job requiring only ordinary skills. "In my first job I did documentation all day; I was worse than the low-level clerks who were just out of high school.

"Even now I find myself asking to be given more, wanting them to challenge me. This job does not give me the opportunity to see how far I can go on my own, to jump in over my head and dig myself out. That is what I miss. In music you are pushed to go beyond yourself all the time. I haven't been pushed that way since I entered the working world."

She explains, "Banking is fun because it is something that I don't know about. I like to be the one taught. But to be in the world of finance is not something I care about. I don't care if hospital XYZ gets a million dollar line of credit. I think when you don't really care

about something you may give it a good effort, but not 100%. I gave music my best shot; I'd like to be that devoted to something again."

The Need to Push Ahead

One characteristic that can easily get in the way on the job is the itch to "see what you can make out of it," beyond what everyone tells you that you are supposed to make out of it. Many frustrated gifted adults in the business world are doing what Stacey is doing, but they are 40 or 50 and restless in a job because they are not allowed to push on its top level. A journal article about gifted children called "Are There Tops on the Cages?" describes this situation aptly.

Those who find themselves, for whatever reasons, trapped in the mainstream of unchallenging jobs are a source of frustration to the people who must work with them. Often, they are unproductive, as Stacey was, in a "dumb" job. Supervisors wonder what is the matter with a person who behaves this way. Colleagues can't understand wanting to take everything higher, especially if one has already achieved a certain level of success.

Felice Kaufmann studied former Presidential Scholars. Here, she quotes one on the subject of growth in the employment scene: "One thing I've regretted about passing from the high school–college phase of my intellectual life to the graduate school–professional phase is that a lot of the sense of discovery and trying new things has been lost. I had a much stronger sense of continual intellectual growth . . . and opportunities for recognition."

Stacey agrees. "It is especially true in corporate structures where there are levels and approval processes. It is very hard to grow at your own pace in that environment. The game is the same. You are constrained by people who are not as smart as you are."

Bernard: Computers—Playing the Game. Articulate about so many aspects of being gifted, Bernard can explain how that game is played. Recently made sales manager of a data communications firm, he doesn't "see the challenge lasting more than a couple of months. It's a fact of

being intelligent that you get frustrated with people around you. You're waiting, and everyone else is discussing and trying to figure things out—the mind wanders. In school, my associates were bright but socially deviant people who were bored by school. Well, in business it's at least ten times as boring as it is in an educational environment! At least there the object, supposedly, was to learn. It can be disguised as learning, but here the primary factor is to be a breadwinner.

"What is alarming is how little time it takes to learn the framework and all the little nuances of a particular situation. I don't know how or why it happens, or if it is a formalized thought process. You see roadblocks coming and you attribute that to the strangeness of the people around you rather than the strangeness of yourself. Vice presidents and directors can seem interesting and you think, OK . . . but not OK! They are bright, or well-primed, but not intelligent.

"It really gets difficult when they jump to conclusions, as you are used to doing, but they jump to the wrong one and it's built on a flimsy structure. I can be a structured thinker, but usually the neurons fire and I end up "over there." If I have to, I can go back and lay out the path, but normally I don't. Frequently people are too obstinate for me to take them back and force them through the logic, so I just bury it. I've got this—some people call it a gift. I ask myself, is this how I use the gift—to become a sales manager?"

Tim: Quality Control—Playing to Win.   At 37, Tim and his wife Adrian are doing an outstanding job of raising their young gifted family, but they are also confronting the corporate "game" and finding that it can defeat a gifted person at any age. His brains and a chemical engineering degree led Tim up the technical ladder in industry; he was a vice president at 35. Fired at 36, he is presently in charge of quality control for a large corporation.

Her voice indicating her frustration and anger, Adrian asks, "How could my husband, who is so bright, have been without a job for months, and other people in much higher positions be really dumb? How could he have been fired while other less intelligent people remained, or were even promoted?!" Her husband smiles. The interviewer smiles. "Those are the first to go." Tim agrees.

Studies have shown that "Job performance is not a significant factor in promotability. Social acceptability, the ability to fit in, the
ability to think as the rest of management thinks, these are the factors which make a person promotable. The gifted employee is not
readily promotable. This idea that the gifted will get ahead anyway,
and if they do not, they were not really gifted, has no basis in fact."

Tim explains, "Being myself has led to conflict in terms of success.
You have to be careful. You can't go around offending people, but it is
inevitable that they will feel threatened anyway. There is a tremendous capacity in any system. I will push the system, take it as far as it
can go . . . take the people as far as they can go . . . see how quickly
they can grow, change. But I have to be able to get people to do what
I want. I have to walk a fine line between doing my job well and doing
too much; offering too many suggestions for improvement."

As Terman and others have shown, a smart kid often retains a
highly developed moral sense all his or her life. In his field, Tim is
challenged all the time. "It's my own integrity. When it's wrong, especially in quality control, I have to tell them . . . I am often told,
'Solve the problem; we don't want to know how you did it.'" He is
confronted with the less ethical as well as the less bright. Couple this
with his admission that there is always more to be gotten from any
system and you have someone who can, in the right situation, move
fast and far, all the way to a vice presidency. In a situation where
someone perceives him as a threat, he is ripe for being fired, as Tim
once was in a merger reorganization.

Tim is aware of the workings of his own machinery and, in typical
gifted fashion, is looking ahead for what is next. "One of the problems
I have suffered from is an awareness of my own abilities. I feel capable.
It is difficult to throw out an anchor and stick to one thing, to open
one door and shut others. What should I do? Teach? Write? Start my
own business? And by the time I get to any one of those, will it still be
what I want to do? I read a book on executives which asked what I
planned to be doing in three years—I don't know! I don't measure
success in dollar signs, although I know others do. I play the game in
industry more than I care to, but I have accepted the responsibility
for playing the game for now . . . the challenge is to play to win!"

Otto: Engineering—Fighting the System.   Otto is also an engineer. But he is farther along than either Stacey or Tim; his children are entering college, and behind him stretches a line of ten jobs, in which "I consciously test how far I can push. I use up jobs, get bored, get disgusted; I quit. If I'm too aggressive, I get fired before I find another one."

Otto's reasons for leaving jobs illustrate the disillusion and frustration found in many of those interviewed about their work. "In my first job, I wasn't prepared for what companies are really like. All the sitting around doing nothing, the fact that it was all so easy! It was a letdown, and then I was part of a 500-person layoff. I spent eighteen months in a boring temporary job, and then found a company where I was in charge of a new product development group. The challenge and responsibility were just right, but I quit because they were taken over by a large corporation. In another position I had a supervisory title, which I liked. But I would tell people how to do their jobs better, so when layoffs came, I was among the first.

"In my current job I am in charge of documenting project functions—I do some writing, some site visitations, some sales work. There is not enough to do, and no one to talk to. I work about 25% of the time. This is old-fashioned assignment-oriented management, and I find it hard to operate as a free agent. I like to be in charge and design my own way of doing things. That is the best way to use your creativity.

"I'm not that way now because it isn't appreciated; people get annoyed. I feel alienated. I really should be somewhere else. I am overqualified for some jobs and too old for others. I have learned to separate jobs from things which are important. Being a good father to my kids is important to me now. I don't mind daily living; it's functional, dynamic. Getting up and going to work—that I mind."

Eric: Electronics—Getting Fired.   Willings's particular area of study has been the creative person in the workplace. He reports that such people are strongly perfectionist and frequently perceived as undisciplined, moody, and aloof. They are often loners who cannot understand why everyone else is so stupid. In spite of their obvious talent,

they do not receive leadership positions and are viewed as a threat by both colleagues and supervisors. Many think of themselves as failures.

Eric is 53. A brilliant loner all his life, he did not have the advantage of acquiring good social skills, or the aggressive mentorship of an educated parent to propel him along. Behind him stretches a line of research jobs that disappeared in shakeouts of the economy and then industrial jobs, where he never quite understood what defeated him.

For the highly gifted person with a problem-solving mentality, negotiating the hazards of industrial employment can be a lot like going ahead in the workbook without the teacher's permission. In a job pattern that repeated itself many times, Eric worked his way up the ladder by getting fired. For years, he believed that he was hired because of the expertise he displayed in interviews. He would then proceed to solve the most pressing production problems in record time, answer questions from departments other than his own, gain a reputation as the company guru. That was always the good part.

Then, when everyone else was content, he would solve new problems, ones he had uncovered himself. Idealistic belief in the best possible job would cause him to push those in authority, who wouldn't see what was obvious to him. He always worked well with subordinates, but had trouble with authority figures—because most were "stupid," yet they controlled what he could accomplish. Of course, some of these authority figures were threatened by his ability. He would become restless and unhappy and let it show, and one way or another, the job would end.

After an interview in which he could feel the whole atmosphere "shut down," he knew he would not be offered a job for which he was eminently qualified. Amazed, he observed, "You know, I think that individual suddenly realized that if he hired me, I'd probably have his job in six months. I made him feel threatened!" It seems that, coming from a research field where brilliant display of one's knowledge is the path to success, he had blundered his way through ten years of jobs and interviews with no idea that in industry, knowing more that your boss can be fatal to your success.

In "Bridging the Creativity-Innovation Gap," industrial psychologists Dean Dauw and Alan Fredian discuss their study of people like Otto and Eric: "It is not clearly known whether these original thinkers have been able to actually effect any innovations . . . the most certain fact known about them is that their turnover rates are at least twice as high as their peers . . . they have had relatively little opportunity to perform much innovation."

Eric currently has a managerial position that requires making complex decisions very quickly. On a day-to-day basis, he is sufficiently challenged. An immediate boss who is bright and who understands how to utilize his talents has made things much easier. Learning to have patience with a company president who is not very intelligent has been more difficult, but it is paying off in respect rather than irritation when he makes a suggestion for improvement. Because no job has ever kept Eric amused for more than three years, he is already making plans for the next one. With retirement age coming closer, he hopes this move will be his last, a final chance to use the lessons he has spent a lifetime learning the hard way. "What I really needed all along," he says with a wry grin, "was a handbook for oddballs."

Designing Your Own Environment

The crucial third criterion—being able to design one's own environment—often seems to be more important than the first two. Or we might say, it makes it possible to adjust or even create the first two. This may be why so many gifted grownups are found in professions like teaching and law.

Teaching.   Teaching positions seem to be attractive because they provide stimulation, constant change, and the opportunity to design one's own environment. Of course, there are those situations where none of these is provided. It is those positions which the interview subjects report that they hate, and usually quit.

What Colin calls his "scatterbrained" approach to teaching science has made academic life a struggle for him. "I liked teaching. I

taught beginning programming at a large state school but finding that 5 people out of 500 were real students was depressing. I tried a small school which said it valued 'quality undergraduate teaching,' but I was considered subversive. I tried to be inspiring, do things differently, free students from structures by forcing them to define their own goals, basing their grade on what they learned rather than what they did.

"My attempt to free them from structures was regarded as threatening. I was trying to get students in a physics class to consider higher-level ideas, to find meaning in their lives. I taught my programming course straight, and there were no complaints, yet there was very little going on in the students' minds. In physics I made a few converts, but the more I did what was beneficial to those few, the more trouble I got from all the rest . . . 90% of students were threatened like crazy! I used to think I really wanted to be a teacher . . . I have doubts now."

The level must suit the individual, but all levels are represented in the kind of teaching which gifted adults find enjoyable. Delores reports, "In junior high every day is new . . . so much of their energy has not yet been spoiled by the uselessness of going to school. It is a challenge to get the kids to really remember things, not just to spit it back on a test. I am so pleased when they do well."

The structures, and strictures, of an ordinary public school prove to be too much for many, dedicated or not. Rita taught special education classes for a year or two and found, "I hated it. All those bells!" She and her husband, Rudy, run a successful tutoring service. "I need the constant stimulation of designing individual programs for all kinds of kids of all ages. I have complete control of what I do."

A veteran of the Peace Corps and social work in a riot-torn Los Angeles ghetto, Ned eventually returned to his hometown in Pennsylvania to teach in prison programs and public school. "A year of public school convinced me that I didn't want to teach in a public school. Ironically, I felt like a jailer! In my current job at the juvenile detention center I have a lot of freedom to choose curriculum and text. There are few enough kids that I can get to know them. The

fact that they are only here for a short time is a disadvantage, but here I can combine teaching and social work."

George speaks in almost lyrical terms of what he has been able to make of teaching literature in a small college. "There are two things which have made me extraordinarily happy. One is travel. The other is teaching a class, when everything works the way you always hope it will . . . often it's five minutes before the end, and a great light has dawned, and we have all done it together . . . we have achieved a kind of breakthrough as a group. It happens maybe once a semester. This job provides the opportunity for peak experiences, and gives me a way to help people using literature—it satisfies the need of the 'failed priest' in me. I get such a kick out of it that I often marvel that people would pay me to do this!"

Two Lady Lawyers.   Kate and Lauren are both vibrant women with law degrees from prestigious institutions, but the similarity ends there. Lauren is a sophisticated single woman working for a Wall Street law firm. Kate has a husband, two children, and a position tutoring law students at a Midwest university. However, both illustrate the need to design the environment, which follows a smart woman wherever she goes.

Helping others has always been a major goal for Kate; she began her career in law reform. "There are a lot of nonconformists in this field, which is the most hated; only 1% of lawyers will do it. I liked it. Preparing court materials was tedious but the initial solving of a complex problem I liked. I had a boss who was bright and appreciated my work. I did have a problem communicating with secretaries for a long time. I hate people who scream at secretaries, but it was very hard to be patient with people who didn't know how to do their job well . . . then I found a 50-year-old woman who could type 100 words per minute, *and* figure out all the mechanics of a Supreme Court brief by herself. She's a gifted grownup!

"Currently I work with a full professor and sixteen to eighteen law students. I get to do a lot of real teaching of the finest type of practice, and I go to court with them, too. It's fun. I'm helping. I want to do so many things well, but I am finally hitting some limits. I have

had to ask myself if the fine perfection I'm always after is possible, and does it matter? It scares me because my employers think I am a better litigator than I know I am. I tell myself: You could always take an easier job, one that you know you could do—but you wouldn't like it as much."

The drive to learn, learn, learn takes different form in Lauren. She rated the biggest problem of being gifted as "Being bored with your job." The government agency for which she worked in Washington was "driving me nuts! They put up with me because I contributed so much, but I wasn't learning and there was no one to teach me more. The only way to be promoted was to stop doing legal work and begin to decide who gets how many pencils and who sits where. I am impatient with people whose abilities are far below mine. I can be patient with subordinates, but a boss who makes more money, works fewer hours, and who runs your life? I was not very good about keeping that to myself!

"Now I work with two partners who are smart. They want me to grow. I do a lot of public speaking; they like to show me off. All the partners do legal work; I can stay here and grow professionally. Other places tried to hold me down. I am not a threat here. I hope I won't get bored. I want to make partner and keep expanding. This firm values my law skills, and as long as I don't lose original documents, nobody cares if my desk is messy!"

More, and Faster, Please

One can see this crucial third factor, being able to design one's own environment, applying in the arts, the helping professions, managerial positions of all sorts, even the choice of blue-collar employment to earn the daily bread.

Laura: Writing.   Doing more and doing it faster has been a problem for Laura all her life. A precocious, persecuted child and a rebellious adolescent, she has worked as an actress, writer, filmmaker; there was even a successful stint at a Wall Street brokerage firm. She has recently been the news director, first of a small newspaper in Upstate

New York and then a small radio station. Her college degree came at 40, via an independent study program.

"I have learned that more and faster may not always be appropriate. I did that as a kid and missed important knowledge. Where my economic well-being depends on it, I have had to learn to do more and faster only when it is nonthreatening. I suppose that is reasonable when not working on an independent project. When it's something I really love, it hurts just to fill a function, to know they just want you to do a job. It's just living in the real (money) world. If people don't want me to be smarter than they are—they're paying me!

"The radio station was a challenge only because I had to learn it. It didn't take long because there wasn't much to do. It was satisfying because it involved communication and because it was a bit complicated and mechanical. It was frustrating because it paid so little! I haven't found a way to make money at what I love. I earn a living and do what I love in the time left over. On the other hand, I'm glad I'm not a file clerk or a stock boy. I gotta be honest, being a radio newscaster is more interesting than most people get!"

In the "What's next?" mode so common to a gifted person at any age (Laura is 49), she has quit her job and embarked on a period of extensive travel to see what she wants to try next. Laughing, she explains, "I am trying to assemble a 'marketable package' to see if I can put something together that works in the world before I just retreat into a craziness which nobody can figure out but which makes me happy. I could easily become the mad recluse, sitting on a mountain!"

Janeen: Editing.   The mother of four highly successful people who are now in their thirties, Janeen admits that she, too, "wanted to write, to work in journalism." Instead, she has worked on the same scholarly journal for her entire career, first as assistant and now as the editor. A commuter from country to city while raising four children, she convinced the journal to locate its offices on her farm when she became editor. "The job satisfies me and it has always been interesting. I'm good at it. I'm my own boss. I never pushed myself. I stayed with this job and raised my family. I enjoyed the work of making a home for people I love. Once when I considered

out loud that I might quit, my son said, 'Mother, if you took the intensity that you give to that magazine and turned it on us, we'd all be vaporized!'"

Walter: Prison Warden.   Idealism often leads very bright people into the helping professions, but even here there must be the possibility for innovation and challenge. Walter is in charge of a large county prison system on the East Coast. He was led to the field of criminal justice after becoming disillusioned with the foreign service, where he stayed long enough to coauthor a text used in many colleges.

Walter is approaching a chronological age, 45, where he might be expected to enter one of the standard stages, but conversation finds him focused elsewhere, on his latest project. Stages come and go, but the rhythmic cycle continues.

"Being able to do things more quickly leaves time for more outside interests. My current project is helping a Cambodian family to find their grandmother. I had to learn the refugee laws, use my contacts in the foreign service to get help, and we found her! Now we have to go through all the legal business of getting her out of Cambodia. Right now there are many projects I want to do. I have all the stimulation and challenge that I can handle. In a year or two it will be time to move on, maybe to a whole new field."

Helen: Social Work.   However, moving on is not the way all bright people solve the problem of needing variety, stimulation, and independence. "I keep my jobs for ages," Helen declares. At 62, she is a psychiatric social worker with no thoughts of retirement. "If I feel myself getting bored, I go take a course, but I am energized by my clients; if not, I have to find out what is wrong, where I am going wrong. I love to run groups, to see people grow. I learn a lot from my clients . . . but I have a great many other interests—politics, art, music, documentary films.

"I went back to school because I want to be with people who explore and are excited about learning." The people who run the agency for whom Helen works do not provide that kind of stimulation. "I had to learn in my middle years that people don't like to

make changes. I got into trouble and alienated people until I met a man who taught me the more roundabout way."

"I am still learning, but I have gotten a bit more sophisticated. If I get all excited about a project, and if I have done my homework, people don't like that; they tend to glare. I get angry because people refuse to see the broader picture. I worry that the work won't get done. I fight for my clients because part of them is in all of us; and yes, I smile and put up with a lot of stuff."

Brad and Ian: Being in Charge.   Being in charge is one way to ensure that one can design the environment in ways that avoid too much of the type of frustration Helen describes. Ian and Brad come from very different backgrounds, but they are best friends. What they seem to have in common is their feisty minds and their love of philosophical disputation.

Quiet and humorous, Brad grew up in a blue-collar neighborhood, was the terror of his teachers because of his brightness, and went through college while holding down a full-time job. He got as far as the offer of a fellowship to complete a doctorate, but for personal reasons, which he does not share with the interviewer, he never accepted the offer. Currently, he is the automotive parts manager of a large department store in a national chain. Music is his hobby, and he spends his spare time working on his house, learning new instruments, and arguing with Ian.

"He's a hard hat," says Ian's wife, which belies her husband's private school background but is nonetheless true. Dropping out of college led him to a stint as a combat photographer in Vietnam. He is currently a manager of construction projects. His hobbies include ballet, listening to classical music, and arguing with Brad.

Each of these men illustrates many facets of gifted behavior in less-than-completely-challenging work situations. When I ask about boring jobs, Brad responds first. "When I first began working in the parts department, they called me 'professor' and 'hippie,' but they liked me. At lunch I didn't talk because I had a book to read. But I also went out bowling and drinking with them. Today, as a suit-and-tie person, I take my current instrument to work and play at lunchtime in

my office or on the patio. They thought it was kind of weird at first, but they're used to me by now.

"I'm smarter than my boss, but I still have a lot to learn from him. He knows more about the business, but I can grasp new things faster and I've taught him a lot. I appreciate his abilities, so I'm not arrogant. I try to make things better for the people who work for me."

Ian adds his perspective: "I'm not in a high-IQ business. I went very far very fast, and then sort of stagnated; without a degree you can't go a hell of a lot further. I intended to go to college when I got out of the Army. Three college courses later, I'm still in construction. I enjoy what I do because it's a combination of head, hands, and teaching. My company hires people who know nothing, and we're expected to get them to do mechanics' jobs. I'm getting the heebie-jeebies right now. I started with houses, got bored with houses and moved up to industrial. Now I want to move on to bigger industrial.

"People think it's strange that I enjoy the ballet so much, that I pay money to see these crazy people dance. I can also go out with my crew to see a stripper and enjoy that! I had one intelligent guy who worked for me who tried to play Joe Dumb, but there was always a different book on the front seat of his car. I never approached him about it, but after watching me read at lunchtime, he would sit down and read. I guess he figured, 'He's the boss, and he's reading!' Another guy who loves classical music would put on rock—until he worked for me—now it's OK to listen to a classical music station. Pompous college kids who come to make big bucks in construction? I let them spout off for about a week, and then I calmly tear them apart."

Calvin: Blue Collar.   Calvin is 40, and he is still looking for the answer to the question, "How do you decide what to do? I didn't have advice from anyone." Coming from a blue-collar background, he spent time in the Navy, then found that in college teachers couldn't answer his questions. He experimented with various majors, including biology and physics, ending with a degree in psychology. "I tried to figure out what I really needed to know. My first job was at a rehabilitation facility, preparing case histories which were filed in the basement and read by no one. I didn't look for another job of that

type, but there were always openings for machinists. I paid off my college loan in ten years. I always figured I could do my own stuff on the side."

Calvin's "stuff" includes playing numerous musical instruments, writing poetry, studying linguistics, and devising a computer program that allows the user to sort ideas and images while writing either prose or poetry. Calvin has exhausted the computer courses at his community college, and his program is being used there experimentally to help freshmen with composition courses. He hopes some day to be employed in writing and selling software.

Calvin has coped with his blue-collar jobs in various ways. "I once had a job machining artillery shells on an assembly line. Just in and out. I kept a tally of chalk marks on the machine to relieve the boredom. Then I began to draw elaborate scenes with the chalk marks—one night a snowflake, one time trees and houses. I'm not sure how that job affected me, but I know I'd avoid a similar one. I do have fond memories of the snowflakes and the houses, though."

He also manages to get a lot of reading done by using a system of his own devising. "When I buy a book I want to read at work, I buy two copies. One I keep and one I cut into small sections and stuff in my shirt. Periodically during the day, I sneak off to the men's room and read . . . then I can get back to work.

"My current job is like a playpen or a sandbox. I play with all these neat tools; I cut up shapes. The equipment I work with is obsolete. I am continually assigned jobs I have never done on equipment that was not designed to do that. I come up with inventions. I may work on a band saw but I make it do the job of a milling machine. That is how I maintain status in low-status work. If I were limited by the normal constraints of the business, I'd leave. They give me a lot of slack.

"One of my coworkers complained, 'You make things look too easy, and on top of that you do them quickly!' It's physically exhausting but it frees my mind to think. I worry about not being employed in using my best efforts for what I love."

In one of his poems, Calvin seems to speak for generations of gifted blue-collar workers:

Mules*

My father's father, Switcher Bill,
said that once a mule was in the mine
he'd never see the sun again:
they'd work him till he died.
Switcher Bill, the barn boss
who could calculate his pay
with a math of his own,
died of the black lung
just the same.

My other grandpa, Eddie, made
blacksmithing his trade,
spoke three languages
and carved a Swiss chalet.
My dad wrote sonnets to my mom
hand-built a TV set,
and worked an inspection job
on an assembly line.

Like some sort of crossbreed bred for work,
the men of my family
have pulled in the same trace,
cut off from the sunlight
by an unbidden "moral" voice
that tells us we are property.
I write songs
and computer programs,
but I work as a machinist.

If Calvin had known at an early age where to go with his brightness,
would the computer field be using his talents by now? Or if Calvin
worked for a forward-looking company, could he be making valuable
contributions to a manufacturing operation in a quality circle?

* Used with permission of Herb Perkins-Frederick.

How To Use Gifted Workers Properly

In *Developing Superior Work Teams*, Dennis Kinlaw writes, "Two realities are shaping organizational life in America today. The first reality is that all organizations are faced with the same challenge: they will either produce consistently superior services and products, or they will soon not be producing much at all. The second reality is that superior teamwork and developing superior work teams have been demonstrated to be the only consistent method for producing superior goods and services." In *In Search of Excellence*, Tom Peters and Robert Waterman emphasize that the successful companies they studied had specific qualities in common. One was the encouragement of worker contributions; another was a stubborn belief in quality; a third was continual innovation.

One adult comments, bitterly, that American business "knows only too well how to 'use' its gifted workers. Employers know that those are the people who won't say no. They give their all and burn themselves out. Duties are piled on; they are expected to do so much. I'll work seventeen or eighteen hours with something that interests me. If that coincides with my job, my employer gets a very good deal. I have seen it happening in lots of places. The person who cares enough to want to improve the system takes on too much."

In the search for maximum profit and efficiency, industrial America needs to pay more attention to information about how the most clever people really operate. Gifted people are restless. They tend to dive into something and learn all they can about it, and industrial employers need to understand this. Some cannot comprehend the sudden enthusiasms or the chronic boredom of a worker. Too often, employers regard gifted workers as unstable or troublesome and fail to utilize their innovative approaches to improve conditions in the workplace or to increase company profits.

Industrial psychologists could make use of the newest information on the brain to design work environments which maximize human potential on the employment scene. Integrated stimulation of sensory, motor, intellectual, and emotional functions is just as necessary

on the job as it is in school. The same information could be used by talented personnel directors to sort the incompetent from the merely underused. Work organized to meet human needs along with the organization's needs must surely produce the highest rate and quality of production.

It is interesting (and frustrating) to note that among the contributors to Dauw and Fredian's *Creativity and Innovations in Organizations*, written in the 1970s, were many names familiar to workers in gifted studies: Torrance on creativity, Parnes on problem solving, Maslow on human needs, and Guilford on the nature of intelligence! The information has been out there for a long, long time. Parnes's work in problem solving alone could be invaluable in the hands of gifted grownups in industry and business. These workers could be ideal agents for change, using the methods of fact finding, problem finding, idea finding, solution finding, and acceptance finding, which is familiar in gifted circles.

Allow for Worker Contributions

In his 1983 book, *Survival Strategies for American Business*, Alan M. Kantrow of Harvard University pointed out, "The companies best able to hold their own in domestic and international markets are those who have . . . integrated their people into production systems not by treating them as machines but by finding ways to enlist their eager cooperation in the work at hand . . . for of all forms of wealth, human capital is now rightly seen as by far the most precious." One method for enlisting that cooperation is the quality circle. A second but related concept is called by many names: work innovation, quality of work life, and work-life improvement. The terms indicate the purpose: to improve the bottom line by creating a humane and creative atmosphere in which all workers will do their best.

Richard E. Walton, in "How To Counter Alienation in the Plant," describes a situation in which a company gave work groups in a new plant complete control of how they ran each shift. Workers could receive more challenging job assignments and were able to engage in higher-order thinking skills, such as planning and diagnosing

problems, in the areas of jobs, maintenance of machines, wage increases, dealing with customers, and hiring new workers. Workers attended companywide meetings as equals with managers. They reported that they learned, had more social contact, and rated the operation a success with such remarks as, "I could make my own decisions about my work" and "I never got bored."

If the key to increased productivity is improvement of the quality and efficiency of work life, and if the key to that is to allow all workers to help with these improvements, then think how useful gifted workers could be on the assembly lines, in the offices—workers with little education, perhaps, whose innovative ideas are now being lost in the traditional mode of thinking that says managers give orders and solve problems and workers do as they are told.

The county prison system that Walter heads is a fine example of the benefits of using gifted workers' contributions properly in the public sector. The system is an outstanding one, with a humane rehabilitation program and a reputation for results. Two of its probation officers are very bright. They came to a job many would disdain from teaching and business. When asked why they liked their work, one said, "The job constantly changes and challenges me. I wear many hats each day. I can plan my own schedule. Administration is receptive to change, and new programs are initiated and designed by us, the staff." Regardless of which came first, talented employees or a system that can keep them happy, they feed each other in a continuing cycle, and society benefits.

Foster Creativity and Job Expansion

How many gifted grownups who would like to work with their hands *and* their brains are leading frustrated lives as salespeople or managers because they could not stand the stifling atmosphere of our industrial establishment? What if we could change the time-honored image of the factory as an undesirable place for the work of intelligent, independent, and resourceful people, by changes in the manufacturing and business sectors as vast as the changes unleashed in technology? A gifted adult's greater ability to handle complex thought systems, to

integrate and synthesize interconnected information is invaluable in making such changes.

Ways to get and keep the intelligent and creative people needed in American industry include job rotation and job enlargement (learning to repair, maintain, and use a machine, for example). As one worker said, "I like to use my brains."

Broader use of flextime and telecommuting could help to alleviate one of the major problems that exists for creative people in industry: the use of time. David Willings cites the example of Harvey Schwarz, one of the pioneers in the development of Decca Navigator in England, as one who successfully managed creative scientists and engineers by allowing "morning" people to leave in the early afternoon and "afternoon" and "evening" people to work during the times best for them.

Increased use of telecommuting may allow bright, unconventional workers to be more productive. Managers desiring to run profitable operations would do well to consider this as an alternative to firing a good contributor for being absent too much. Young computer professionals described companies where this kind of flexibility produces good results: "They give you a project, the equipment you need, and a key to the building. You are expected to report on your progress if asked, and of course to eventually produce results. Otherwise, they leave you alone. The company is small but quite successful."

The Bottom Line

In this chapter, we have seen that putting forth one's superior abilities can actually lead to sidetracked careers like those of Colin, Otto, and Eric. These gifted adults are employed, to be sure; they are even earning reasonable salaries and supporting their families. But industry, and thus society, has been deprived of the full benefit of their capabilities.

Employers need to stop using words like "overqualified" and find ways to use those who appear in their personnel offices with obviously superior abilities. They need to be able to recognize the symptoms of a

bored employee and allow him or her to contribute suggestions for job improvement. Increased profits accrue to those who know how to utilize the best and the brightest, whether they appear in the typing pool, on the assembly line, or in the boardroom.

Whether it is Waterman with the renewal factor or any of the other writers cited in this chapter, those whose field of study is the improvement of our economic life have been talking (for far too long) about some sort of reform/revolution in the way we work. Sure reform seems to embody the compacting of levels of authority and communication to allow more input from every level about how best to do the work, as well as flexibility, challenge, and constant innovation. Gifted adults, if recognized and utilized, are ideally suited to make important contributions in designing, planning, implementing, and working in such systems.

And yet, none of the writers quoted was consciously addressing the waste of gifted talent when they undertook their work. They were concerned, let's be honest, with the bottom line, productivity in American society, now and in the future. Part of the original premise of this book is the idea that addressing the needs of the gifted among us will be good for all of society. Nowhere more than in the workplace can we see that this is true.

Revisit the paragraph that begins this chapter in light of the information presented, and see if it does not seem more hopeful. If gifted adults are recognized and properly utilized, their intensity, integrity, and impatience with shoddy work could be channeled into the improvement in quality of items "Made in America." Working quickly and raising standards would be appreciated. Odd approaches to things? The coming century is already presenting us with a full supply of "odd" problems. The courage to express doubts about a project to coworkers or executives will be needed in the work groups of the future, courage that can be taught to others by someone sure of his or her own capabilities. How many more problems could we solve in a workplace where neither the boss nor one's job is threatened by a suggestion from an ordinary worker—one who just happens to be very bright?

Just the title of a Tom Peters book gives an idea of the pace and challenge which faces us, all of us: *Liberation Management: Necessary Disorganization for the Nanosecond Nineties*. He warns, "The only immutable competitive base a nation has, now that commercial operations can be shifted from here to there, is the *relative intelligence* [emphasis mine] of its work force."

Peters advocates "corporate investment tax credit aimed at brain enhancement rather than brick enhancement . . . support [and benefits] for job-hoppers." He adds, "brainwork increasingly dominates the creation of economic value." If that is the case, we cannot afford the waste of a single sharp mind; indeed, all minds are going to have to work at higher levels. Peters leaves us with this one-sentence advice: "Keep the competitive juices flowing and invest in brains."

Successful institutions, both public and private, need to learn to tolerate, even encourage, the messy genius, the crabby, cranky fanatic. "See if the system can bear them," Bernard said earlier. As we move into the high-tech twenty-first century, the system will have to learn to bear the gifted grownups, even encourage them, if it wishes to survive. The gifted among us have, more than anyone else, two qualities essential for that survival: their sophisticated thought processes allow them to grasp all the elements of a complex big picture, and they actually thrive on continual innovation and change. Society benefits from organizations that realize that making room for gifted workers can be the key to success.

We have an amazing opportunity here. The very changes we need to make to ensure our economic success as a nation turn out to be the same ones that provide the channel for the maximum development of our brightest people. If enough organizations could be convinced to accept really large-scale change, all workers would benefit. In particular, Michelle would not have to be driven crazy with "monkey work" and could move up in whatever organization needed her skills; Stacey could push for and receive as much challenge as she could handle; Eric and Otto could join the new breed of productive job-changers; Calvin could stop drawing snowflakes; and for Tim, the "game" would be a lot more fun to play. Productivity and

prosperity? According to both the experts and the gifted grownups, they would soar.

When the bright person learns to move to the beat of the constant need for renewal, independence, and growth, personal satisfaction can be found. But gifted workers face important choices as they confront the reality of the employment world. Armed with a thorough knowledge of how one's own machinery functions, one has the choice, even the obligation, to choose work that will provide necessary levels of newness, challenge, and independence. If you are a gifted grownup of any age, work which allows maximum use of your special gifts is a present you should give yourself. It may require the courage to take risks, change jobs, or even change lifestyles, but both you and society will benefit.

If, while you work toward a more satisfying job, you are stuck in an employment situation that is not sufficiently challenging, there are other ways to enrich your life. Look around at society's problems and volunteer to help solve them. Some gifted adults have discovered new careers that way. Pursuing the work you truly love on your own time is another option. Remember: Your job is what you do for money, and it can be taken away from you; your career is what you give to yourself by doing what you truly love, and no one can take that away. If you love music, theater, gardening, solving mathematical problems, or making maps, you can study and increase your skills on your own time.

There is an additional choice, which may be much more difficult. If your job matches your career, you may choose to remain where you are. But you must decide how to play the game: how much to push on the tops of the cages; how much to risk alienating authority figures; how cleverly you will thread your way through the maze of egos that may be threatened. By knowing both your needs and how the world perceives them, it is possible, as Tim advises, to "play to win."

PART THREE

GIFTED LIVES

The Dark Side

Idle hands are the devil's workshop.
Old Saying

Maybe the gifted person who turns to crime is really a broken person.
Probation Officer

In the coming chapters, we will look at gifted grownups as they face the crucial issues of relationships, the special problems of gifted women, and life as a gifted senior citizen. We will find them ignoring the conventional stages and following their own special rhythm. They will change jobs and careers, in spite of what it will cost them and their loved ones. They may leave those who cannot understand their needs. They may marry successfully at 19 or wait until 43. They may begin graduate school at 62 or take up mountain climbing at 65. One is beginning her first novel at 90.

But before we present the more conventional issues, we will devote a chapter to those for whom, sadly, the gift has gone awry. Through early neglect or frustration, or through later choices that trap them, some gifted people defy the society which does not seem to understand or accept them. They drop out, become criminals, or give up and end it all: a tragic waste of precious lives.

There are as many theories about why human beings become criminals as there are researchers who study them, but it seems particularly puzzling that a person with insight, ability, and talent of some sort would choose a life outside the areas accepted by society.

Gifted people are found in jail, just as they are everywhere else. However, they form a disproportionately larger portion of the prison population, perhaps as much as 20%. This is in contrast to the 3 to 5% of the general public who are gifted. Is the conflict created by being "different" connected to antisocial attitudes and behaviors? Do they get into trouble because it is fun? Or interesting? Or a clever game? Does crime have its roots in deep hurts?

When I meet Wendy, she is bent over a fat notebook filled with poetry and song lyrics for the rock band she dreams of having some day. She has large blue eyes that meet mine with a level gaze, brown hair that curls softly around her face. She is wearing jeans and an attractive pale blue sweater. We sit across the table from each other in a comfortably shabby room. "I see myself differently from other kids . . . I know I have talent, and I have never been allowed to use it."

Lee's features announce his Korean American background. His plaid shirt, jeans, and new sneakers bespeak a fairly affluent lifestyle. Warm afternoon sun shines over his shoulder as, seated at a student desk, he leans on a stack of books that contains calculus and advanced placement history texts. Bright-eyed and soft-spoken, he recalls, "I always wanted to be with older people because they knew more . . . whatever I study, it has to be in depth."

Ralph is aptly nicknamed "The Bear." He greets me in a booming voice, and we settle down at a sticky table in a dingy conference room with yellow cinder block walls. Dressed in jeans, a plaid shirt, and a cap set at a rakish angle, he tells me, "I am taking an electronics course, and I love it! I have always liked to learn new things. I tend to get 'wowed' when I contemplate something amazing, like the human body's ability to cool itself."

These three gifted people have never met, nor are they likely to. Wendy is 18; Lee is 16; Ralph is 34. What they have in common is their status as illustrations of the ultimate waste of giftedness—all three are criminals.

Wendy is waiting out the appeal process of her ten- to twenty-year sentence for murder and attempted murder. She doesn't elaborate. Verbally, she sticks to a positive attitude. "I may go to prison, but I can come out and go on with my life . . . I can't wait to do my time and get it over with."

The first time Lee encountered the law, he had taken a joyride in a tractor trailer and "I took out part of a building trying to brake." His latest adventure involved robbing a church, "For fun." He is awaiting transfer to a group home where he can continue his education. "If I wasn't smart, they'd send me to forestry camp."

Ralph describes his vocation: "I deal speed. Or I did. I haven't worked [at a conventional job] for ten years." Ralph has done time at Graterford, one of Pennsylvania's worst prisons. He is about to be released again, on probation for a bad check offense.

How Many Are There?

Are there large numbers of criminals who are gifted? "Of course," says Dr. Donald Dowd of the law faculty of Villanova University. "There are some crimes which you can't commit unless you are pretty intelligent—embezzlement is one." Most authorities seem to agree with Dr. Dowd's estimation that the most curious kind of criminal is the one who is highly intelligent, who has chosen a life of crime, and who is good at it. Sociopath is the term often used to describe such people.

Dowd's explanation for criminal behavior in intelligent people is Freudian. He explains that highly intelligent presidents and generals may be ruthless because they are lacking in a function which governs the morality of certain choices and actions. In Freudian terms, they have a weak superego. However, they generally have a very strong ego, which is the rational determiner of what can realistically be done. Thus, they stop short of overt actions that will cause them to be removed from their positions or charged with crimes. According to Dowd, the highly intelligent sociopath often has a weak superego combined with a weak ego, and does not sensibly sort out what can really be done. Carl Frankenstein, a psychologist, agrees, citing juvenile delinquents as having little or no control by or over the ego.

Gifted criminals commit big crimes, according to Al Levitt, a psychologist with the Temple University Division of Law and Psychiatry, who does presentencing evaluations for federal criminals. "They don't rob grocery stores; they rob banks, or skyjack an airplane—something

really dramatic. They often have control of a group of people, and they tend to be a little more ruthless. Terrorists tend to be bright."

When asked how he knows he is dealing with a gifted criminal, Levitt describes an eerily familiar set of characteristics:

They see things others don't see.
They read between the lines of statements made to them.
They don't test well.
The bright ones tend to be very bright.
They have a charismatic quality which allows them to dominate those with whom they come into contact.

Younger offenders, many of them one-time lawbreakers, can be spotted in much the same way. A juvenile probation officer explains, "They usually have more, and better, questions . . . are not awed by authority because they understand what I can and can't do. They can reason in the abstract, think through a problem, play the angles, challenge the book for loopholes. You can almost hear the wheels going around."

This seems to be a portrait of the same troublesome nonconformist whom teachers and employers encounter in the everyday world. But many troublesome nonconformists function fairly well, if painfully, without actually committing antisocial actions. How does a gifted person cross the line from just being difficult to being a criminal? Recall what has already been said about the need for stimulation, the heightened sensitivity of the gifted, the boredom and actual damage of school, and the negative reinforcement of some gifted children's childhoods.

The Mask of Sanity

In *The Mask of Sanity*, his classic study of the psychopathic (or sociopathic) personality, Hervey Cleckley presents a possible explanation for the waste of intelligent potential. Describing the psychopathic personality as a "rudderless and chartless facsimile of a human being," he explains that because they often have no identifiable clinical disease,

they are denied access to mental hospitals. They commit antisocial acts and are relegated to the criminal justice system, where they are clever enough to plead insanity. Often, after a brief time of hospitalization, they seem so sane that they are released to start again.

This type of criminal, according to Cleckley, "is often, if not usually, of superior intelligence when measured scientifically . . . has ability that is average or better . . . often gives the impression in conversation of an excellent intellect." Cleckley admits that some authorities make a strong case for saying that a parental background characterized by inconsistency (stern father, indulgent mother) can cause enough personality dislocation to distort the bright child's sense of right and wrong or to blunt that sense entirely. However, he says, "We must also consider the possibility that the psychopath may be born with a biologic defect that leaves him without the capacity to feel and appreciate the major issues of life or to react to them in a normal and adequate manner."

All of this would seem to indicate that, whether the emotional components of the bright child's personality are blunted and distorted or somehow not there to begin with, the brightness can be directed to antisocial acts. Cleckley concludes, "Perhaps the emptiness or the superficiality of life without major goals, or deep loyalties, or real love, would leave a person with high intelligence and other superior capacities so bored that he would eventually turn to hazardous, self-damaging, outlandish, antisocial, and even self-destructive exploits in order to find something fresh and stimulating in which to apply his relatively useless and unchallenged energies and talents."

What of the greater sense of right and wrong that the gifted are supposed to possess? Where do we find the antisocial element that turns pranks into repeated crimes?

Sean Ryan, a probation officer in Bucks County, Pennsylvania, says, "Look at it this way. It may be just an extension of the ability to circumvent the rules which a smart kid applied to parents and school, and may now apply to society. They think of it as something else—at least in the beginning. The computer hackers, for instance, don't start out to commit crimes; they start out with a challenge to their ability and the excitement of the game."

Psychologist Travis Hirschi explains, "Delinquents tend to be persons who have been led to expect opportunities because of their potential ability to meet formal, institutionally established criteria." Among students who expect to graduate from college, but who don't get very good grades, Hirschi has found that parental pressure is positively related to delinquent acts.

Don Crouthamel, another probation officer, agrees. "They attempt to be accepted; to fit in somewhere . . . often they commit crimes as the result of a dare . . . or their idea of 'special' means that the rules don't apply to them. Often, I think it's the kid who has been pressured to produce great things because he or she is bright, and who may fail to live up to those expectations. They look for a sense of identity somewhere else, even in getting into trouble. A fairly good percentage appear to have sociopathic personalities which exhibit no social conscience, little value orientation, little allegiance to anyone. I have to wonder if it is a product of their isolation."

Pranks which skirt the borderline of criminal behavior can be a danger signal. In repeated delinquent behavior, a troubled smart kid can travel some distance on the road that Cleckley's sociopath/psychopath follows to the end. Early intervention in the lives of young offenders is obviously essential.

A Key Combination

Levitt describes a key combination which, in his opinion, decides whether a bright nonconformist stays on the acceptable side of the law:

1. Is the identity correctly developed so that the person's view of the world is not distorted? (To one degree or another, all of these gifted young people who are in trouble with the law had some form of family conflict which affected their view of themselves as worthwhile persons.)
2. Has the intelligence/perception system received the level stimulation proper for that person's needs? (Lack of stimulation looms large in the lives of all of these young offenders.)

3. Has the maturity level progressed to the point of dealing realistically with consequences?

Crouthamel is optimistic about younger offenders who receive the advantage of early intervention in their criminal careers. "They are smart enough that at some point in time they begin to get pragmatic about it and stop doing what gets them into trouble." Of course, this assumes that factors 1 and 2 have not already done enough damage to defeat them.

Early Intervention Is Essential

Are all bright young delinquents doomed to become sociopaths or even psychopaths? Of course not. "It all depends on how they deal with their need for 'more,'" says Sean Ryan. "I honestly feel that most don't think they will ever be caught—and that's the challenge. They continue for the excitement and the challenge, weighing the penalties. As long as the penalties remain within acceptable limits, and two years probation may well be acceptable, they will continue to enjoy the excitement."

An Ideal Setting

If they are lucky, young offenders are sent to a juvenile detention facility, away from hardened criminals. If they are even luckier, it will be a well-run place where unusually bright kids' needs will be both recognized and dealt with. It is obvious that society will be better off if their talents can be directed to more positive ends. The center that shelters Lee and Wendy provides testing, continuing education, and counseling for all of its inmates. At this stage, many of them still have plans for a conventional future, including further education.

What they have already done was not a question I explored with these young people; under the terms of the interview, talking about it was optional. Rather, the goal was to see their similarities to non-criminal gifted teens and find clues to how and why these bright

people got themselves into trouble with the law. In these reasons may be the seeds of rehabilitation, even of prevention.

The metal strips on the windows and the constant locking and unlocking of doors do not allow one to forget that this is a jail. But there are brightly painted walls, things to do, classes to attend, and above all, a perceptive staff (mostly gifted themselves) who try to direct young offenders toward more positive goals.

What Are They Like?

Mostly, they look like kids anywhere. Personalities vary from voluble to quiet. They are clever in conversation, bright, and very self-aware. The dozen or so that I interviewed were interested in learning, but without exception, they hated school. They have dealt with their need for "more" in school with defiance and underachievement, but each one can point to accomplishments of some kind. There is a determination to go their own way at almost any cost, often expressed as being true to oneself. In spite of trouble with the law, they express concern for others. There is also a decided lack of realistic plans for the future. The consequences of GED diplomas and criminal records seem to be discounted.

Holding on to Dreams

There is energy and drive behind Wendy's words, which, in spite of the serious charges against her, one still hopes might be put to good use. That energy and her desire to show people what she could do caused trouble as far back as second grade. "The music teacher was trying to explain that each note was different, and the kids didn't understand. I knew about music even then, and I tried to say it in a way they could grasp. The teacher got mad and told me to stop trying to be teacher."

Her rock-oriented clothes and rebellious song lyrics, not to mention her attempts to organize an all-girl rock band, brought Wendy into conflict with her conservative stepfather. "He said I was going against society and forbid me to work on my songs in the house. He couldn't grasp the distinction between writing about something and

doing it. My only musical outlet was to play trumpet and be in the school marching band. I'd use my lunch hour to write music with the other girls in school."

As the appeals of her conviction drag on, Wendy has been at the detention center for over a year. During that time, she has written poetry, some of it rather good. She is working on her autobiography and, with borrowed equipment, was allowed to produce a video with several other women. The center staff worries about the intensity with which she attacks creative projects, and often tell her to slow down. "I don't need to slow down. I am consciously putting out all that energy; it isn't out of control. I push myself a lot, but it isn't just wanting my own way . . . I want to use my talent. I tried to get my parents to see that if I could do my music, I could also do better in school. At 14, when all this started, my grades just went. Now I believe: Don't listen to what others say, it will get in the way. Do what you have to do to get what you want, and if you have to hurt people's feelings, it's got to be done . . . I've never worried about acceptance . . . I've always been different."

Side by side with this ruthless streak runs an idealism and a belief that "I can come out of prison and do my dream. If I can write down something that another person is feeling, if I can share my feelings with others and make them feel that there is somebody else who has the same problems, that should be a way to help society."

What will become of Wendy's energy and drive? A good part of the answer will be determined by the success or failure of her appeal. But whether she spends ten years in a women's prison or is released next week, where and how and by what will all that cleverness and all that energy be directed?

Taking Risks

Of all those interviewed, Lee is perhaps most aware of the game he is playing with himself. "A smart kid may take risks because of a problem, but your mind won't let you get away with it. On one level I told myself that I robbed that church for fun, but on another level I know that I have problem, and getting into trouble would get me back in here where I can get help."

Bored and "disgusted" with school almost from the beginning, Lee designed his own electrical experiments at home. One involved hot-wiring the water dish of a bird feeder when he was about 10. "It was amazing; the birds somehow knew and wouldn't land on it." His parents tried military school, where he constantly flouted the rules. Public school was "more of the same. I'd get bored and get into trouble. They never went fast enough or deep enough for me."

His parents tried to explain his needs to teachers. "The teachers would always say, 'He isn't doing the work we give him now, why should we give him new work?' It was like being made to count the grains of sand in a bucket. There's nothing to work with, with sand. It's easy to do 1 + 1, then 5 + 8 . . . 18 + 5 isn't really any different; it's still 'sand'—the repetition of the same pattern. It would be different if they gave you new things. It could be like counting a bucket of diamonds. Hold them up to the light and you get different shapes, and glitters and shines."

The product of a stern father–indulgent mother type of family, Lee says he plans to go to college. The group home to which he has been sentenced for the second time should at least help him finish high school without getting into any more trouble. He explains, "It just doesn't work with me living at home . . . there is too much conflict with my father."

Lee says he is perfectly willing to cheat in this world, "If you're slick enough not to get caught." He would take another person's job: "I'd get him fired, but only if I knew I could do the job better." At the same time, he expresses a desire not to "hurt people." Lee would like to see society "work hard to bring everybody up to top mental level. Maybe that's just selfish on my part; it would mean there would be more people like me and I'd have company."

Crime as Reality Contact

But the misdirection of all this cleverness is still a puzzle. Dr. Levitt explains crime as a "reality contact." "If you commit robbery, the house is real; you take real things. If you hit someone, they are real,

and at that moment you are real." Who needs this kind of reality contact? Echoing Cleckley, Levitt says that it is someone "who doesn't derive appropriate satisfaction from life's ordinary activities." He reports criminals who speak of feeling "hollow" because of identity problems. He agrees that often they have overidentified with the parent of the opposite sex and have a distorted view of themselves as persons. "Committing crimes is too exciting for most people—robbing a house would scare the average person to death." But the stimulation of the crime allows the person to experience some of the feelings we consider "normal," to feel that they are living life as it really is, the way other people do.

If we combine lack of sufficient stimulation from the environment with maturity and self-image problems, we have a potential criminal, one who often has more than enough equipment to get away with crimes for a long time. If the opportunity to commit crime is not available, such persons may simply slip away into mental illness, withdrawing from reality in an internal way.

When highly intelligent people start thinking about crime, the consequences are so bad compared to what they will get, that Levitt thinks "something in the mental makeup is beginning to slide. They use crime as a reality contact to prevent them from slipping into a more pathological state." Perhaps they fear the feeling of being lost inside their own head.

Identity problems, because they depend so much on nurturance and acceptance at home, cannot be directly solved by collective action. But society can and does determine the amount of reality contact that is provided to gifted people of all ages, in school and employment environments.

Older Criminals

A Gifted Grownup in Prison: Bear

Bear informs me early in our interview that he enjoys being loud and obnoxious, but that he is actually a very easygoing and sensitive

person. There is a note of pride in his voice as he recounts how he ran an efficient drug operation for almost ten years. He claims that he was trusted with large amounts of drugs because he had a reputation for paying his bills on time. "I am not a mature person," he admits. "I require instant gratification; that's why I do drugs as well as sell them. I get into a lot of trouble because I don't deal with consequences." He certainly never expected to be caught and sentenced to prison.

A probation officer who has taught in prisons tells of meeting "streetwise people who border on genius in their ability to work whole systems out," and thus ensure their own survival. "In prison, gifted inmates tend to be runners for counselors, workers in the library. They sometimes have access to contraband others can't get. Sometimes they act 'crazy' so fellow prisoners will leave them alone; others will court solitary confinement to have time to themselves. Some will utilize the system to take college courses. In almost all cases, they have power of some sort, either the power to control other inmates, or the power to be left alone."

Bear recalls, "The judge said one to three and my knees buckled. I said to myself, this is not a joking matter. Two guys I knew went down with me. One was cool, but the other one I knew was a really bad character, experienced in prison ways. He could help me. Right there in the holding cell, I began to work to make this guy like me. I certainly had to hide myself as a gentle person in prison. For that to be known would be a disaster." His size helped him to survive Graterford. He also says that being a gifted grownup was a factor. "You've got to be clever enough to balance a lot of powers, to be in the middle and not get hurt."

Size is certainly an advantage on the outside. "My intelligence has never threatened anyone; my size does that." Bear entered school early, was placed in the highest groups, and says that he usually liked school and had "quite a few" teachers who seemed to understand him. Family life is something else, as he declines to enumerate his relations except to say, "I have an extended family composed of children from my parents' various marriages. Most of them are older and quite successful; I'm always in and out of jail . . . my father is

highly intelligent, but he does not know how to deal with emotions correctly. I am like him."

As we talk, Bear's life becomes more puzzling. Listening to the sophisticated vocabulary, the clever insights, the delight in learning evidenced in "I may become a professional student, I love it!"— somehow, it doesn't add up. Clues begin to emerge as he describes leaving school after eleventh grade because his summer job on a trash truck was more interesting and more lucrative than returning to school. Only in prison did he take the GED exam, and he claims to have scored quite high.

"I loved the trash truck. My ideal job is a physical one which you have to be alert to do, all the time, one which you can improve by doing it faster and better." Work on the truck yielded to a well-paid job in a steel mill. "I oiled a machine. That's all I did. I watched it, and waited until it needed oil, oiled it, and went back to waiting again. For four years. I hated it. I just couldn't do it anymore." In that offhand statement lies one clue to what might make an immature bright person into a criminal. How much more exciting, more stimulating would it be to manage a drug operation than to be an attendant at a machine all day? How much more of the system could be utilized, how much more cleverness and creativity required? If circumstances had made Ralph the foreman of a trash truck operation, how much different might his life have been?

Is Rehabilitation Possible?

Will his rehabilitation "take"? He speaks sadly of the lack of interesting conversation his sometime wife provides. "I get all excited about things, like how long a turtle can stay under water, and she says 'So what?' There is no one to get excited with me, so I'll just have to do without it. I fit in with almost no one socially; I never have. The only place I ever fit in was the Boy Scouts. The one thing I have is my intellect. I use it as a kind of home base, a rock-solid certainty that I can say to people, 'I'm better than you.'"

In some ways, Bear is like Cleckley's sociopath: immature, unable to face consequences, engaging in behavior which has embarrassed his

family and of which he claims to be ashamed, but behavior he has repeated. Perhaps the other category mentioned by Cleckley should be more carefully considered: the stern father–indulgent mother situation. What happens to a smart kid who identifies very closely with his mother, and who is not allowed by his father to express the more gentle emotions? Does that person become much like the type Cleckley studied, those who appear to have their feeling response somehow missing?

In spite of his behavior, Ralph says he is a Bible-believing Christian, and he introduces me to the leader of his Bible study group with a twinkle: "I snowed another one!" If he did, he is probably a sociopath. But if he wanted very much to be taken seriously as a person, then he confronts us with more questions about gifted criminals—questions that still do not have answers.

Probation officers describe the difficulty of dealing with gifted grownups who are being supervised by the courts. One describes successful criminals who seem to have consciously chosen a life of crime: "They commit economic crimes. They are good at welfare fraud. They are often the drug dealers who don't have a habit. They take risks, and are often not caught." A second officer adds, "They can be really friendly, present a good appearance to a sentencing judge, but push them a little and they get vicious. They seem bent on being successful criminals and they know the system as well or better than we do. Interviewing them can burn you out; if they realize that they can control the interview, you're lost. Five or ten of these in your caseload can make life really difficult."

Turning It Around: Lisa and Gary

Probation officers are not optimistic about the rehabilitation of the older smart criminal. "It's hard to change all those years of sophistication. We make the assumption that we are having an effect, but it isn't necessarily true." Gary and Lisa would seem to be exceptions, evidence that some can make it all the way back to functioning as nonconformists who are contributing to society.

Lisa

Lisa began, much like Goldy in Chapter 5, as a bright child with a terrifying energy level and a need to do things in her own way. She did not have the advantage of a special school, and her family, although loving, tended to be indulgent of her as a child. "I was always climbing mountains, getting lost. They took me to a doctor at 8 to see if there was anything wrong with me. Until sixth grade I was a pretty good little kid in school; I even had a penmanship medal."

Transferred to a strict private girls school in seventh grade, she rebelled. "For the first time, I felt as though I was learning something, but the name of the game in that place was 'Step on the old spirit.' Those nuns had no sense of humor!" She did learn other things. "Once the uniforms came off, those girls were much wilder than the ones I knew in public school!" She was asked to leave at the end of eighth grade.

Return to public school for ninth grade was a disaster. "They said I was opinionated, obnoxious, a troublemaker . . . I felt as though I was expected to be bad . . . my friends expected a show, that I'd be the one to stand up and scream about a problem or make everybody laugh. Speed intimidates people. Even if you do it well, the teacher will often give you horrible vibes for being finished so fast . . . I'd pull down 95s and cry because it was so easy . . . in my frustration, I wanted to get back at teachers . . . each one I could intimidate (and I could ask questions that would make them cringe) was another notch in my belt. The guidance counselor tried to talk to me, but when I told him that I had been reading physiology books to learn about my own liver ailment, and that I wanted to be a doctor, he laughed!"

Drugs.   At 14, Lisa visited the doctor again. "He gave me Valium . . . didn't even count them . . . just dumped a large quantity into an envelope and handed them to me. My mother made me give them to her, but not before I had acquired a supply. After that, taking pills or smoking a joint helped to get me through the day."

Lisa is willing to articulate why gifted kids often take drugs. "To dull themselves . . . there is so much of the wrong kind of stimulation

going on around you, being stoned makes it easier to block it out. I felt like an animal in school. I didn't like the way the drugs made me feel, but I didn't feel bored any more either."

Lisa quit school, "The moment I was 16," several weeks into tenth grade. "And no one, not even the principal, asked me why. The principal actually said to my mother that I was like a cancerous growth that had to be removed!

"My father forced me to take the GED exam. He just dumped me at the testing center. I also took a course or two at the community college." From then on, "I traveled; I partied. Opening a book was out of the question" for ten years. Working as a bartender or a waitress, Lisa saw much of the world. "The Andes . . . Macchu Picchu . . . Morocco . . . Spain . . . Russia . . . it was hard on my family . . . letters can take a month from some of the places I went to. And my friends would say, 'Lisa, slow down. Save something!' I'd laugh and say, 'I'm saving China.'"

Drifting home at 25, she met Gary at a party. "Everyone else was smashed. Gary wasn't. We talked until 3 A.M. It was so nice to find someone who respected brains. He was so bright and so different." He was also, by his own description, an outlaw. Thus began for Lisa a two-year descent into the nightmare world of users and dealers as she helped Gary sell LSD. She does not attempt to excuse her actions. "It was a conscious decision. I guess I felt as though in some way, society expected me to be bad, had almost given me permission to be bad. I decided to be really bad."

It ended with "a helicopter above my mother's house, very large men with very large guns . . . we were handcuffed together." Her mother allowed Lisa to spend several days in the county jail. "She wanted me to get a good look at it. When I came home, I weighed about ninety pounds. I lay on the floor of this (elegant) living room and my life was over. I was 27."

Gary

Gary is frank about his problems, disarmingly so. "I was no poverty-stricken loser from the slums of a big city. I didn't do drugs until I got

to college. I was a good kid from an upper-middle-class family who walked away and became an outlaw." Given a different set of circumstances, he could have had a career like Frank, with advanced degrees at a young age. Everybody knew he was precocious. From third grade, where he beat the janitor at chess after he finished his work, to skipping up to calculus in eighth grade, he was only sometimes given the stimulation he needed. The debilitating year described in Chapter 5 left him drained of all educational ambition, despite a merit scholarship and acceptance at a prestigious university. "I didn't know why I was there. I only knew I had to stay there, or I'd be in Vietnam."

The Sixties. "What happened to me happened to a whole generation. The government was in the hands of madmen, from my point of view. All over the country there were riots—on campuses, in ghettos. There were assassinations, the draft, the hypocrisy of an alcohol society. It was the first wave of the drug culture and it proposed values of peace and love and brotherhood. There was a feeling of being involved. I, who was the intellectual agnostic, ingested one dose of LSD and saw God. Everything became meaningful. In two weeks I had quit school and headed for California.

"When you have rejected what you consider a hypocritical value system and taken on an alternative life that has no legal or moral structure, drugs become OK. I like them. They woke me up and stimulated me. Gradually, they replaced the original idealistic defection from society and became the central point of my life." So, in his ten-year hiatus from his family and home, Gary traveled the world of California's drug and rebellion culture.

At the People's Park riot at Berkeley, he got bird shot in his head. "I remember the sheriffs weaving in and out shooting at the crowd." In prison in California, he had all the drugs he wanted. "I had seen people in pain, and at the time, it seemed wrong to put me in jail for giving them something which helped things to make sense." In or out of prison, the variety of drugs he ingested took their toll.

Drifting back to his home area, Gary recalls, "All I knew were other outlaws. Lisa was dragged into this. I was a monster. My life was a nightmare." It ended with the helicopter and the men with the

guns and the handcuffs. Gary had three months to get to know the inside of the county jail. While lawyers argued to reduce his bail, he was sure his life was over. He was 34.

Turning It All Around.   And yet, when I interviewed them, Lisa was curled up in a chair in a bright shift, looking both happy and healthy. Frank and humorous in expressing her views, she was halfway to a biology degree, a dean's list student intending to become a nurse practitioner. "It's as close as I'll get to doctor." Gary was stretched out on the floor reading the *New York Times*. He is older, but reminds one of a slender, solemn boy with piercing dark eyes, a soft voice, and a hesitant way of expressing himself. He has completed a master's degree in computer science at an Ivy League university and has a job with a small company run by people who are as bright as he is. They are creating a new product. "I'm director of software. We could grow. Things are moving quickly."

Family Support.   What made the difference? How did Gary and Lisa beat the odds that would have predicted that they were finished as contributing members of society—that their brains would be consigned to the scrap heap of prison or drugs? Levitt's three criteria appear to be a recipe for *un*making a criminal also. They had families who stood by them and offered them the space to try to reestablish their identity as persons. Lisa recalls, "My friend gave me a job in her restaurant. It meant that I had to get up and get dressed and go out of the house every day. That was a start."

Oddly enough, her three younger siblings, with successful academic careers, "set a good example for me. I was so moved at my brother's graduation when a distinguished professor asked if he could keep a paper that my brother had written. Somehow it gave me hope that if you stuck it out within the system, you could actually accomplish something."

Gary says flatly, "I was rescued by my family and came home to live with them . . . I realized that they were only able to rescue me because they had lived their lives according to very sound principles—ones I had rejected along with all the rest which I thought

was corrupt. I did a lot of work within myself [he still meditates every day], but it was easier in my parent's home. I'm lucky they were here."

Stimulation. While the wheels of justice ground through almost two years of hearings and a lengthy trial, Gary and Lisa undertook work that provided the high rate of stimulation their systems require. The first step on Gary's road back was winning the annual chess tournament in jail. "That convinced me that I might still have something up there to work with." Gary's parents were willing to go with their 34-year-old son and help convince the authorities to readmit him to the university he had abandoned ten years before. "Once you discover that you can still read, you can go on from there."

Lisa recounts, "I watched as Gary did wonderfully in college, and I guess I was a little jealous. I wanted some of what he had. He convinced me to enroll for just one course at the local community college and went with me to register. I had a panic attack in the registration line. I had climbed in the Andes, boated on the Amazon, but I was terrified of an algebra course. 'Schools are prisons!' I protested. Gary physically restrained me from leaving the line. Eventually I took two math courses."

When the time came for sentencing, they encountered an enlightened judge who believed them when they said that they had come to understand and regret the consequences of their actions, that they wished to become contributing members of society. The judge was convinced by a parade of witnesses which included two distinguished college professors, Gary's parents, fellow students, friends, and a lawyer for whom Gary had done some programming—here were two people who could best repay their debt to society by remaining a part of it. In a twenty-minute statement in his own defense, Gary articulated how a gifted person can go wrong and then can go right again. With a long and heavily restricted probation, as well as the obligation to pay restitution for the cost of the government's investigation, Gary and Lisa began a new life. They had convinced the judge that they could do it, but they had not yet convinced themselves.

A New Life.   Gary began graduate work in computer science at a prestigious Ivy League school. "I was scared to death. I knew I had to do this, or that would be it . . . my mind had to be exercised. I did seventy-eight semester hours of graduate work in two years with a 3.8 to 4.0 average, while earning $16,000. It was my first real job."

Lisa convinced the continuing education department of a nearby college to give her a chance. "They helped me to choose courses and said that if I could get Cs for two semesters, I could stay. The first semester was a brutal shock. Here was this 29-year-old woman who never went to high school, never brought home books, never studied, trying to learn how to do college. I'd stay up until 2 in the morning tearing my hair; get up at 6 and do it again. The first semester I made the dean's list. Second semester I got the hang of it and had straight As.

"And yet, I still lied about my grades . . . say I did OK when I got an A . . . I got caught at the end of a semester; a philosophy paper fell out of my notebook with 'excellent' written in big letters under the A. I heard someone mutter, 'You bitch.' When I got the highest grade in biochemistry second semester, the guy who had been first in the class said, 'Well, my father's not a doctor!' Neither is mine, but it didn't seem worth replying." There are differences and compensations. "Having teachers as friends was a new and shocking experience!"

Well aware that he is multitalented, Gary now has a more mellow view of how things work. "You have to make choices or you will never get anything done. I take one thing at a time now. I now know that projects can take weeks, or even months, and it feels good to get that far into something." His idealism has been tempered also. "The revolution we thought we were in as kids is really to establish institutions which will change the world—the governments will fall in line." Questions about his time in a California prison are dismissed with "It's over." Time lost can never be recaptured; damage done can never be repaired.

One cannot help but wonder what might have happened to Gary if he had been able to get to college early like Bernard and Frank; what might have happened to Lisa if the guidance counselor hadn't laughed. "It's so ironic," Lisa muses. "My Harvard superstar brother ran into that man in the supermarket recently. Know what he said

after all these years? 'I think I may have made a mistake with your sister—a big mistake.'"

Wondering how many Garys and Lisas are walking the halls of our schools and colleges, I recall the question I once saw a tired drug counselor address to the ceiling: "Why, oh why, is it so often the bright ones? Why?"

Mental Illness

One type of criminal worries probation officers: the one-time offender whom no one recognizes as bright. "The person gets the label of an isolate, a loner," says one officer. "People may see mental health problems and not see that this is really a very bright person. Maybe the gifted person who turns to crime is really a broken person." Their suggested solution? "Identify them, and at least treat them differently."

Bill

A loner, an isolate . . . No one would have suspected that the little kid growing up in south Florida had a very powerful mind. Small and quiet, picked on by other kids, Bill was tolerated by his family ("I think my mother wanted a girl") and wrapped up in his own world. "At an early age I knew I was different, but not bright . . . I spent a lot of time with me, my loneliness, and my dog. I was raised to worship the John Wayne ideal of the All-American family. My father forced me to wear a crewcut all through school."

Bored with school and only one credit short of graduation, Bill took a GED and joined the Navy. Not much for social life, he married the first girl he dated, at 19. In the Navy he began to notice that he could ace all the tests with ease and remember things no one else could. In the next ten years, he rose to become an expert in his field. He wrote manuals, supervised courses, instructed the instructors. Alternately bored and fascinated, he reenlisted five times and collected a wall full of commendations: "The perfect military guy." He was also a walking time bomb.

"My disorder," Bill explained haltingly, "was that I tried to be all intellect and suppress my feelings. That's how my doctors explained it to me. You can't separate your emotions from the rest of yourself like that, but I sure tried! I would think, 'It's time to cry' and let myself cry, or not cry, or laugh. I had a terrible fear of losing control. John Wayne was always in control—one slip and you are finished.

"My psychiatrist told me that, in Freudian terms, the id, the ego, and the superego were not communicating with each other, and that's dangerous. I was dangerous. I realize that now."

Bill recalls, "The first time I exploded, I had punched out a lieutenant and broken some windows before I came to my senses." The second time, "I don't want to talk about—I still can't remember it clearly . . . the charge was aggravated assault; the sentence one to four years in prison . . . one minute I was an ordinary guy with a wife, kids, a car, and a mortgage . . . the next minute I was a prison inmate."

Releasing a New Self.   The prison sentence may have saved his life. The nonstimulation of the prison environment affected him so badly that he became disoriented. His slurred speech caused him to be sent to several therapists who uncovered his disorder and in the process helped him to rediscover his own mind. Now, after eighteen months of intensive therapy, he is a resident of a rehabilitation facility that allows him to work in the community. In Bill's case, that means holding down a full-time job and carrying a full load of classes at a local university. He is majoring in physics and plans to go on for an advanced degree.

Bill is like a man reborn. "The kids I go to classes with think I'm old, but I feel young, like my life is just starting. The first book I ever read was *Ragtime*, in my freshman comp course—what a sense of power! A challenge is what makes a man live . . . I'm just finding my real self . . . I don't know exactly what makes me different."

The new self has been released at a high price. "My family is not backing me," is all he says. "My therapists are the only ones who are excited about my mind." His children are in another state and he misses his daughter especially. If he goes on for a degree when he is released, he will be alone. "That's one thing I always tried to do with my 10-year-old daughter, who is very bright. I always tried to keep her from feeling alone.

"I never knew what I wanted before, but now I have a goal . . . to go back and work for the government in the same field I worked in . . . I don't want to 'grow up,' that is, lose the feeling part of the little kid in me. He was repressed for so long; I'm just beginning to like him."

And again, one wonders how many more there are, how many kids with their loneliness and their dogs, and all that repressed energy ticking away . . .

Pushed to the Limit

As we said at the beginning of this chapter, there are many kinds of waste. Crime and mental illness are two. But in far too many cases, there is no overt criminality, little outward sign that the person is coming apart mentally. The repressed or misdirected energy has no place to go, and so, as Kerry explained in Chapter 5, it can be turned on the self. Shocking as the suicide statistics are, especially for our young people, they are also complex and confusing. None of the gifted researchers I consulted has been able to present definitive numbers of those who commit suicide who are also gifted. Again, we are confronted with the question of why someone who seems to have more than others would want to end it all. For those who wonder how that can be, we offer the following: a comparison and a fable. First, the comparison.

Let's face it, if you are a gifted person, you are, on the great highway of life, something like a Porsche. Whether you like it or not, you have a high-performance engine between your ears, and you don't have to be a car buff to know that an engine needs to run. It can be an exhilarating ride—but it can be dangerous.

First of all, you have to know what you are. Second, you need to be able to drive. Third, you must, at least most of the time, drive in traffic. Those exotic vehicles that can be operated only on specially designed tracks can be spotted by anyone, and they are in a class by themselves. No one expects them to do ordinary things. The Formula I people really do retreat into the Institute for Advanced Study or the Jet Propulsion Lab at Cal Tech.

But most gifted people are Porsches. They are street machines and look like all the others: same equipment (arms, legs, headlights) and same general configuration. They also operate in the same way, and are used to perform the same mundane tasks. They eat, sleep, and are multiplied by the same process of manufacture as all other humans. From the beginning—the very beginning, according to one researcher—they are programmed to perform at more intense levels. The engine is just capable of more.

Tool that new Porsche out on the highway and watch it go! A beautiful creation, it is the highest level of the maker's art, designed to go all the way. And it looks good, too. It can go farther, faster than almost anything on the road. The key: the sophistication of its design and structure, its efficient and rapid processing of fuel, and, above all, its speed. If it gets out on the freeway and can stay in the fast lane, it is a pleasure. Its engine purrs along. It can complete amazing journeys, taking tricky curves without a mishap. It can even slide into dangerous Ss and out again, if the driver is well versed in using the system and has had a chance to practice the necessary skills. The freeway is its element. Let it work there and it can do great things.

But take it off the four-lane and see what happens. If the local traffic is moving briskly, it will be fine. It doesn't even show much effect from slowing down for traffic lights. The driver can keep the engine happy if he or she has learned how to handle it. Besides, you know you can get back on the freeway. And if the driver only wants to go to the market for groceries, she knows she can't use the freeway for that. So she is philosophical as she makes her way through the temporary inconvenience of slower traffic.

However, if circumstances force the Porsche to operate in slow-moving traffic for too long, not only will the driver become upset and therefore less efficient, the machine itself will begin to malfunction. Tied up for many days in a row in the stop-and-go traffic of a metropolitan snowstorm, for instance, it may refuse to start one morning. No amount of skill on the part of the driver can cause a carbon-burdened engine to spark. It may be permanently damaged.

Solution? One method is to take it back on the freeway (after a difficult forced start) and let it run. It cleans out the engine in an amazing

way! And regular trips on the freeway can keep it going. However, long-term fighting of slow-moving traffic will take a toll, no matter how fine the machine, no matter how well trained the driver, no matter how skilled the mechanic who tries to help.

Making your way home one day, you find that the freeway is closed for repairs. You take the long way, winding for hours along secondary roads behind perfectly nice GEO-people who are not only being challenged by 40 mph, but having a good time doing it. You arrive home a wreck, nerves frazzled from the frustration of operating at half speed, of feeling the power you are never allowed to use. You check the engine. No damage . . . it didn't go on long enough.

What if it had? A frightening thought. What if the freeway was permanently closed or, worse yet, if for some reason you were not allowed on it? You remember the cop who yelled at you when he gave you that whopping fine for going too fast on a secondary road. What if the penalty had been to ban you from the freeway until you could prove that you would be a good driver and not exceed the limits set for the GEO-people? What if they made you drive at 40 mph for six months as punishment? At the end of that time, you would be a wreck, but so would the engine of your Porsche. A disturbing scenario begins to form in your mind . . .

The Porsche Fable

. . . The last day of your sentence had been served! Your Porsche coughs and spits, and getting it up to speed again is all but impossible. Perhaps a talented and understanding mechanic could help you to regain your former powers, but the damage to the mechanism from all that forced slow driving could be permanent. You try the freeway once again, and it is hopeless.

Sadly, you come to a big decision. You will get rid of the Porsche and get yourself a small, neat, efficient, conventional vehicle and drive like everybody else. You won't like it, but it beats getting into trouble with a Porsche. If you stick to the appropriate roads, you won't miss the freeway too much. You just won't be able to take the kinds of trips you used to take.

"Sorry," they tell you. "Changing vehicles is forbidden. It is against the nature of things. It is not our fault that you were born a Porsche person. You will just have to stop thinking of yourself as special and learn to drive like everyone else."

So you take your now-damaged Porsche and you try. Your nerves scream as you pick your way through the slow traffic. Sometimes, if you surge even a little ahead, the other drivers give you dirty looks or honk their horns at you. Sometimes they laugh. One day, a well-dressed woman in a shiny new Gutless Wonder backs right into you, viciously. "Think you're better than me because you've got a Porsche," she snarls.

The policeman who gives you another ticket is sympathetic. "I'm sorry. I know it's hard to have a Porsche and be stuck on the slower roads, but you must try to learn to drive like the rest. I really do sympathize. My sister almost became a Porsche person, but she just missed passing the special driver's test. She drives a GW, but you know. Sometimes I think she's pretty unhappy with it. I've never told anybody this, but I've always wondered what I might have been if I'd had one of those."

You smile sadly, grateful for his kindness, and say, "You'd be getting tickets instead of giving them."

Another six months of being banned from the freeway! For a while, you don't drive at all. You just sit and stagnate. The engine is in such bad shape, you can barely get it going. But there are only the secondary roads, and you do have to live, go to work, get the groceries.

Then you hear about a very good mechanic on the other side of town. Understands Porsche people, they say, so you set out to see him. Can he help you to learn to drive differently until you can get on the freeway? Can he show you how to run at half speed until your ticket time is up? You have to drive; you can't just sit still. And you know that if you could just survive the time in between, he might be able to help you to get your engine in shape for the freeway again.

He turns out to be a she. Older and obviously very experienced, she talks with you for a while, and then runs various tests. She smiles sadly. "I can't teach you how to run at half speed; no one can. Your engine needs the freeway. You'll have to hang on until they let you

back on it again, and your engine, well, it does need a lot of work. Once they let you drive the way you were meant to, I can help you a lot. Until then, well, I hope there isn't too much damage. Come by and we'll talk. Maybe I can devise a course or two along the back roads where you can open it up a little. We'd have to be very careful. If I am caught encouraging fast driving, I could lose my own license." She looks away. "I'm a Porsche person, too."

"Thanks for trying." She knows what it's like. She, too, has probably been punished.

You start the engine for the nerve-wracking trek home, and you know. You can feel it. It is losing more and more all the time. Wait, she said. Settle for crumbs. One or two little chances to open it up, but mostly poking along with the GWs, knowing you have a super engine and are a good driver, and knowing that the freeway is there but they won't let you on it because you haven't conformed to the rules. Knowing that life for the foreseeable future will be slow traffic and frazzled nerves while you can feel your engine dying . . .

You are a Porsche person. You have known it all your life. You couldn't drive a GW if they gave you one, and they won't even do that. If only you could shut yourself off: no more feeling the power you are never allowed to use, watching it drain away from frustration and disuse, no more punishments for racing your engine, no more longing for the straightaway where you could open it up.

In spite of the damage, the engine begins to race, faster and faster. It's right in the middle of Main Street, but you don't care anymore. You have been pushed to the limit. But at that limit, you know that you have a choice. You are valuable. Too valuable to waste. There is a mechanic who understands. That means there must be others. "Come by and talk," she said. She can help you. The engine slows. Tickets and all, you'll make it.

We seem to understand that when machinery is not properly used, it breaks down, and it must be repaired or assigned to the junkyard. Manufacturers exhort us to understand how the machine works and give it proper care. Good advice, it seems, for avoiding the waste of all kinds of national resources.

Chapter Nine

_____

Finding the Others:
Friends and Lovers

*Touch my intellect and you touch my emotions, because you
have touched my "sacred space"—the essential part of me.*
                                                        Laura

*If you are a gifted person . . . working out your life is a very
private tightrope . . . contact with others can make a difference.*
            Linda Moore, *Does This Mean My Kid's a Genius?*

There is more to life than work. In addition to struggling to
find a satisfactory method of earning the daily bread, many gifted
grownups encounter difficulties with interpersonal connections. As
we saw in Chapter 2, a gifted adult has a brain/mind that works
faster than 95% of the population. That complicates relationships
with the rest of the human race. Many people may not understand a
somewhat peculiar way of operating or odd interests, and loneliness
can be the result. The problem of friendships is sometimes solved by
keeping to a small circle of people who understand and accept, or in
having different sets of friends for different activities. Meeting a
kindred soul can be a moment of joy. Given the mental and emotional capabilities of those involved, long-term friendships can lead
to a deep, almost mystical closeness. Cross-generational friendships

190

are a part of many gifted grownups' lives. Dating can be a problem, and, as one person put it, "Marriage is a real tricky business." Is a bright person doomed to life as a lonely misfit? Not at all, as the people in this chapter will show.

Certainly, lack of understanding is experienced by people at all levels of intelligence, but they have a larger pool from which to draw companions who understand.

Both the speed and complexity of a gifted person's thought process can make for barriers to communication and connection. Those barriers can be created by other people who don't understand, or they can be created by the gifted person, deliberately. Some people screen out the pain of rejection; some simply prefer their own company. Some people find it very difficult to explain their difference to anyone, and in a kind of defeated way, they settle for isolation. This difference is the key to understanding the problems many gifted people encounter in relationships of all kinds.

Explaining the Difference

"I can put more things on my mental blackboard," is the way Calvin describes the difference between himself and others. "I have spent a lot of time learning to drive my own machinery; there's no owner's manual!"

Rudy speaks of "acuity and speed of perception. Everything is connected to everything else like a giant puzzle. How crazy that mystical vision is! My parents often thought I needed a psychiatrist! It's a hard thing to explain. I don't know what you call it, but that's what I do. Most people don't think it's a reasonable way to explore everyday life." His wife, Rita, adds, "Every statement leads to a question which leads to a statement which leads back to another question, and I am never satisfied with my own answers! What is light? What is color? Watching Jupiter in my telescope knocks me out! I question everything. I want to know. Yet when I know it, it prompts the next question."

Lee is a teenager, and it is easy to hear in his conversation at the juvenile shelter that he has not come to terms with his difference. It may be a factor in his difficulties with the law. "Ideas just pop into my head and I say them. Connection is so fast and so complex that nobody else sees it. I can get wild ideas. I have to be alone to argue things out in my head because my mind goes so fast. Most people have to follow what's going on; I have a kind of 'mental sleep' I use. I can tune in and out. That's why I come up with so many weird ideas in classes. I have to have something always going on in my mind to do."

Bill comments, "I am not a genius, but when I look at a situation, I run all the possibilities through my head in an instant and know the only way it can be done. Nobody has ever understood me; I'm still trying!"

Audrey probably is a genius, and says, "I try to create a normal mental image for myself by seeing my abilities as a tool and telling myself, 'It's a skill; just use it.' I get the big picture quickly in a lot of situations: artistic judgment, math computation, a social event, the bottom line in everything. I can create unusual responses to situations which are interesting and catch me by surprise. When I am emotionally threatened, I become hyperintellectual."

Limiting the Input

Paradoxically, a number of interviewees report that it is often necessary to learn how to limit the amount of input which an extremely sensitive brain/mind receives. "I have a problem with being overwhelmed with sensory details," is how Meg describes it. "I live in a world of visual images; I catalogue what I see. Things like malls cause me to shut down. I need simple walls, plain colors. My mind has to have a place to rest. I can 'do' cocktail parties by accepting people one image at a time, then I need a blank. I have a different sense of pacing."

The artist's approach is evident in Pearl's lyrical description of how this takes place. "It is almost as if whatever holes perception comes through, the holes are bigger for a gifted brain/mind. Stuff just pours

in. So many things make a difference! Little details on things, a person, a rock . . . you look differently . . . how color changes. I get drunk on shapes and smells, on empty air. I get so flooded, so beautiful! You have to stop and do something stilling, something physical . . . and yet, you keep stretching to open."

Leisl, also an artist, needs "a lot of time to myself, large periods as well as one time each day to digest. My sister can rush from one thing to another and not go crazy, but I can't. I can push myself for long periods, but then I must rest and digest."

Loneliness

Is loneliness a problem of greater proportions for gifted adults? Answers to that question ranged all the way from "No! Loneliness is part of the human condition" to "Yes, it's like being on an island with no one to talk to." Slightly more than half of the respondents felt that loneliness was also a problem for other people as well. Most also found that they had positive ways of coping with the fact of loneliness. Alix says, "If you can't find someone who wants to do what you want to do, you do it by yourself. You are lonely for a little while, but then you get involved in what you are doing and you're not lonely anymore."

Inner resources may be larger for a gifted person, many of them seem to think. However, the frustration of trying to relate to people who are not interested in the same areas is more uncomfortable than the loneliness. Colin explains, "I *crave* the companionship of others who get excited about the same things, but social companionship? No, I don't miss that too much."

Age is a factor. Many of the those interviewed recall being lonely in high school or college. As careers develop, more mature understanding of loneliness as a state of mind comes about, as well as the realization that many other types of persons are lonely. Some emphasized that they cherished time alone and did not consider that it defined them as lonely. Many also seemed to view time alone, lonely or otherwise, simply as time necessary for growth. In Mark's opinion, "As long as you have Beethoven and Wagner, you are never really lonely."

Learning to Give and Receive

The intensity of a bright person's desire to *know* may extend to his or her manner of getting acquainted with people. There is a depth in personal relations which a gifted adult seems to need and which can lead to much confusion. Intense interest expressed in body language, tone of voice, or sharp probing questions may be interpreted as aggressive. LaVerna describes this trait in a coworker: "I try to remember that it's just his way of expressing sincere interest, but when he asks you about your weekend, it's like being interrogated!"

Trying to make contact with persons who cannot match the necessary level of intensity can be painful for both parties. Many bright people project a kind of attractive energy, which might be called charisma; others, reacting to the charisma, may be initially attracted to them on a very intense level. Sometimes the gifted person, mistakenly thinking that an "other" has been discovered, responds with the full force of high energy and intensity of emotion. Whereupon, the object of this force field becomes completely overwhelmed and backs away, often abruptly.

Other gifted adults report the opposite problem: a feeling that people want too much from them. The attraction of the high energy level bright people project again seems to be the difficulty. Certain individuals are able to make others feel good about themselves, to bring out the best in them, and to offer moments of deep sharing. They may invest too much of themselves in a friendship or love affair with one who has little to offer in return. The result is often a bright person who is torn and confused about how to conduct successful social relations.

Psychologist Dierdre Lovecky describes possible disadvantages to being unusually perceptive: "The intuition and ability to see several layers of a person or a situation simultaneously can allow the person to cut through social facades and sense real thoughts and feelings." This presents difficulties because others, unaware of what the gifted person sees so clearly, may feel both vulnerable and threatened. He or she is then faced with the dilemma of whether "to hide the insights and respond to the social facade, or use the gift and risk rejection."

Struggling to Make Friends

Heather tries to be realistic about college. "You have to have some friends, but you have to face the fact that there might not be enough people in the world to satisfy your intellectual needs." Faced with this fact of life, gifted people deal with it in one of several ways. Most report that they have learned, sometimes painfully, to function with a very small and select group of friends who understand and are usually gifted themselves. Some describe having different sets of friends for different activities. Farah relates, "I have this wonderful friend with whom I love to play tennis . . . God forbid I should try to have an intellectual conversation with her!" A third solution is the one suggested by Will: "Solitude can be a friend."

After her difficult childhood, described in Chapter 5, Goldy can now say quietly, "I like being accepted by people . . . one way I have learned to compensate for my individuality is to select friends who like that quality in me. My niche right now is a Science Fiction Club at my university."

In "Friendship and the Intellectually Gifted Child," Harriet O'Shea describes the situation of a child forced to associate only with age-mates whose mental age is much lower, she could be describing the lives of gifted grownups as well: "An isolated individual for whom activities tend to drop dead, and for whom there is malnutrition in the area of rich, constructive, developing, rewarding experience of close friendship."

The struggle to find compatible people is ongoing. Julio occupies an administrative position in a suburban county filled with affluent people; he says, "My wife and I are suffering through this. We went to the home of another couple a few weeks ago. I was pleasant and tried to make conversation about the trees, the property. There were no books in that house that I could see. The people didn't talk about anything but the mechanics of living. If you even allude to anything literary it's not the style. I have a few deep friends from my days as a member of a religious order, but where will I meet these people now?"

Tim would agree. He finds few peers in his work as an executive of a paint company, and envies his son, who seems to have made friends

through his school's gifted program. "His mother and I have a limited range to choose from. We seem to find a lack of sensitivity. I want to use my mind, to develop information, but our neighbors are concerned with football and new drapes. It's kind of lonely."

Cross-Generational Friendships

For many gifted people, a unique solution to the problem of friendship is cross-generational friendships. Helen is working on her Ph.D. at 62 and says, "My friends include my 95-year-old cousin and an 80-year-old rabbi's wife. I also love all the younger kids at school." Nina, who is 19, reports, "My friends right now are women who are 20, 36, 55, and 60. They all have families, or I could spend more time with them." Scott, who is 30, says, "My best friend currently is a woman 60 years old. Her son was my best friend, but we outgrew each other."

Liesl describes "close friendships with people who are seven or eight years older. There is a woman in the nursing home where I work [who has] a creative mind. I love to talk to her. I also have an aunt I admire. Whenever I see her we have the most interesting conversations. She reads metaphysics and philosophy. A lot of times my parents' friends interest me as much as my friends. The parents become my friends and the ones my age break off. Interestingly, my parents' closest friends are a couple in their twenties."

"When I was very little I wanted to be with older people," Julio recalls. "There was an old lady on my street, who had a son in prison. I would empty her trash and help move furniture in her boarding house. She'd make me lunch and talk to me like an adult. Another lady had the grocery in our neighborhood. I helped her, too. She had this interesting little desk at the back of the store where she would let me sit and read her *Reader's Digest*. She was Jewish and I can remember reading aloud with her an article about Auschwitz, and how she cried, 'When will they leave us alone?' She talked to me like an adult, too . . . I guess I kind of was. Even then there was an interest in complexities that I didn't find in people my own age."

"I always wanted to play with the big kids," Michelle says. "I date older guys. One reason I like to be around older people is to pick their brains—they simply know more things. I can just suck up data like a sponge—and they never know. People like it if they can talk to you."

In Cecile's case, "I tend to be drawn to those older or younger. The only friends among my peers are two college friends whom I've carried for long years. I am 56 and my two best women friends are 39 and 35. My two favorite male friends are 60 and 12!"

"I pick friends from an oddball collection," Georgia smiles. "One of my dearest friends is a librarian who was the highlight of my childhood. I visit her in a nursing home and we have the same friendship now that we had years ago. I used to clean and dust for her—now I manage her wheelchair."

However, Ned seems to feel that managing such friendships isn't quite that easy. "I wish I could do it more. I wish society were more open to people twenty or thirty years apart being friends."

Meeting an "Other"

Some gifted adults, like Lillian, insist that loneliness doesn't have to be a problem. "Everyone has something that you can be interested in. Some of my friends are not smart, but they have other redeeming qualities, like kindness, or even being a good listener." Jean agrees. "I try hard to find that quality in each person to which I can relate. I once had a good friend who was a construction worker; I could talk to him about all kinds of things." Lisa is even more vehement "It is absolutely not a problem! I love people!"

But in spite of the disclaimers, one does notice a change in voice when gifted persons describe those all-too-rare occasions when they meet someone with whom they can communicate. Artist Frederick Franck describes it well: "Communication is possible, indeed, but it is limited to those of one's contemporaries whose interest, degree of awareness, and especially, whose capacity for experience is rather

close to one's own. To meet such a person is always a rare, moving event, an exhilarating surprise, as if one suddenly spotted a long-lost brother in the faceless crowd."

Pearl describes "meeting another gifted person's eyes and your needle goes 'bink.' You start to talk and someone understands where you are going and gives you a phrase just a little beyond where you are so you can jump over that and get to the next thing, and the conversation triples in speed. Or you are asked a question that is so pertinent and intelligent and you can answer with such pleasure—a joy to answer."

Joy. The word is used over and over. "It is a joy, a relief, refreshing and exciting . . . a wonderful thing . . . a joy to meet someone who is 'simpatico' . . . serendipity, utter joy . . . the thrill of the year; real joy . . . It's a joy to find someone exploring, questioning, looking for answers . . . There are few out there who understand . . . this person at school . . . it feels so great to talk to someone who doesn't say 'Uh huh, uh huh'. . . when you find someone who can operate on your level, it's like finding an oasis . . . When things 'hit' like that, I could go on forever . . . I feel an instant connection, because I don't have to explain myself so much . . . It's almost as wonderful as getting a really good book!"

Liesl admits, "You work all your life and you are basically happy, but the high points are very few. We live for those few moments when we do have people to communicate with. I think of people I hardly know and yet they understand; there is no need to bring it into words."

Getting in Touch with Another Mind

According to the interviews, thinking and learning is what keeps you alive rather than existing. Ideas and things of the mind are almost sacred, in the broad sense of that word, to a gifted grownup. Getting in touch with someone else's mind can be an almost overwhelming emotional experience. Discovering that someone thinks the way you

do provides a closeness that is like no other feeling, difficult to understand unless one experiences it. In *Illusions*, Richard Bach says, "You are led through your lifetime by the inner learning creature, the playful spiritual being that is your real self."

But not your whole self. Your whole self lives in the real world and has all sorts of labels that classify you according to age, sex, race, occupation, social status, religious (or nonreligious) preference, political bias, and nationality. We choose some of those labels ourselves; others are dictated by accident of birth or forced on us before we are old enough to fight back. And so, even though we may be directed by this inner playful spiritual being, we live a larger life, and it is in that wider arena where we must work out our lives. The closer one can come to matching inner and outer, the better off one will be. It is not often the easier path. My own theory is that the playful being is unusually active in gifted grownups.

Some highly gifted people, those at the far end of the scale, choose to follow this inner being almost exclusively. They can tolerate a lot of banging and crashing in the outer rooms of their lives because the inner self is the most important part of their universe and the material world is very unimportant. We often call these people saints or lunatics . . . or great artists or world-changing scientists.

In many gifted grownups, this playful inner being can be satisfied only in that outer world of organizations and labels, and to keep it happy, these gifted people become writers, singers, politicians, scientists. They choose active lives in the outer world, possibly driven by that inner learning creature. It seems that we often let it push us around, drive our careers, just to provide it with something new to play with.

Sadly, some gifted people have been conditioned to fear the mysterious energy that pushes from inside. They worry about what the neighbors, society, the church, their teachers, their parents, their bosses will think and never develop the courage to listen to the voice of the real self. If, in the midst of all the noise from the authority figures, the being gets a word in edgewise, the upheaval can be enormous, and it can happen at any age. These people may make drastic

changes in their lives, or they may weather the storm so quietly that no one ever knows what they have been through.

Saddest of all are those who, knowing all along that the being is there, ignore its cries. They settle for the outer world's estimate of who they are and go on with their lives as if the being didn't exist. Eventually, it no longer does.

What does this have to do with the emotional impact of getting in touch with another person's mind? When a gifted person discovers another gifted person, the beings can often be seen peeking out of their eyes. Sometimes, they get together and talk among themselves! It is fun, joyful, playful, and ultimately a kind of spiritual high. It is rare and precious and definitely not for the fainthearted. While communicating on that kind of level, one is working on a platform in midair, with no railings; one slip and it's back to the world of labels.

The painful part is that this kind of communication happens where there are barriers of age, sex, race, social status, religion. It can, in spite of such boundaries, create a lifelong bond, a friendship that can only be described as spiritual, although most people would smile and say "intellectual." Such friendship can yield a tremendous feeling satisfaction, accomplishment, and understanding of both inner and outer selves.

Wider Dimensions?

In the 1983 edition of her book, *Growing Up Gifted*, noted gifted researcher Barbara Clark devoted the last chapter to speculation about the possibilities of further development of all human beings. Dr. Clark is a past president of the National Association for Gifted Children. She makes it clear in this chapter that, in her view, if we are to understand and foster the development of gifted persons, we need to take serious interest in modern studies of brain function and higher levels of consciousness.

The late John Gowan was another respected educator and researcher in gifted studies. Based on a lifetime of research, he believed that the greatest minds have always been attuned to the forces around them, the Zeitgeist of their particular era. He wrote extensively about

developing connections between the accomplishments of famous gifted minds from Mozart to Einstein, great moments of creativity, and increased levels of consciousness.

Dierdre Lovecky is a clinical psychologist who has studied gifted people. In an article in the *Journal of Counseling and Development* titled "Can You Hear the Flowers Singing?" (which has become a much-reprinted classic in the field), she details some of the special social sensitivities which seem to be part of the experience of a highly developed brain/mind.

At a conference on the gifted several years ago, I asked Barbara Clark if she thought that behaviors that indicate possible access to expanded levels of energy and perception were in fact normal behavior for gifted people. "Getting more normal all the time," she replied with a smile.

Repeatedly, I encountered this type of information in reading the work of these and other authorities on the gifted. I came to believe that the possibility of such special sensitivity forms an essential part of the backdrop against which gifted people work out their stance toward reality, as well as their adult relationships. I decided to try to compose an item for the interview cards that would allow the gifted adults to talk about this controversial subject if they wished. I finally selected a well-known quote from William James, the psychologist and philosopher. "Our normal waking consciousness . . . is but one special type of consciousness, whilst all about it, parted by the flimsiest of screens, there lie potential forms of consciousness entirely different. We may go through life without suspecting their existence, but apply the requisite stimulus, and at a touch, they are there in all their completeness . . . how to regard them is a question."

The quote provoked many thoughtful silences. When they finally spoke, the gifted adults didn't say much, but comments like "Of course" and "Yes, that is so" were frequent. Some replied with amazing casualness. "Oh, you mean knowing about things before they happen, stuff like that? Sure, but you can't tell anybody about it!" Others seemed to regard it as a part of normal living.

According to Laura, "Gifted people do have a special kind of perception. In some ways it's a handicap. I realize now that there are

some things I perceive that would be considered 'psychic,' but they are not psychic to me. I have simply linked things and come to a correct conclusion."

Maureen says, "You just know. You feel an instant connection. There is no way to explain it that sounds rational to anyone who hasn't experienced it."

Meg explains, "I believe in the beyond limits of the mind. I run my life that way. It's not strange. It's just there. All things are in tune with it. When I moved into this house, I could still sense the energy of the people who had lived here. It's why I have no problem with dying, which is just a transfer of energy."

Jean says, "I feel I have a real sense of this sort of thing . . . there is no way to explain the basis of these feelings."

Adrian is matter of fact as she says, "Yes, I always knew the sex of my baby before it was born. I usually know that about all my friends too, but I keep quiet. I know in advance if we are having company; I know if my husband is upset when he's away on business. This has always just been a part of my life. I will teach my children to accept it when it appears in them, as I am sure it will."

Nina, Margo, and Paul agreed that it is difficult to talk to just anyone about this subject. As Margo said, "They think you're a little crazy, just because you're smart!" These are the comments gifted people made about the possibility of a wider scope of human awareness. As William James said, "How to regard them is a question."

Dating

Against the backdrop of all that we have discussed so far in this chapter, dating and social life take place as part of a larger search (among a small population) for another person with whom to build a permanent relationship. Starting out in the social scene can be especially difficult for the young adult who begins dating only in the later teens or even early twenties. Colin laughs as he remembers being forced to go the senior prom. "It was my first date. In junior high they sent me to dancing school for three years because they were afraid I'd never

find out about girls! I never related to the dances and football games crowd. Fortunately, I find I fit very well into the computer subculture, where my wife and I are not considered weird."

Social Connections

How does one spot another gifted adult? This is how Michelle explains it: "If I am, let us say, attending a meeting, and the whole thing begins to suddenly seem ludicrous to me. If I glance around the room and I see someone who looks as though he is suppressing a grin, it is probably a smart person. We tend to find the same weird things funny!"

"At a party, the bright person will have his back to the people—he'll be reading the bookshelves," says one young woman. "You listen," says another. "A bright person will speak intelligently. Sometimes vocabulary is a clue."

Paul has discovered a provocative way to save time discovering whether a new female acquaintance "has any brains. When you first meet a person, don't talk about the weather. Start right out with a serious question, like 'Do you approve of the death penalty?' A less bright person will look at you funny, and probably walk away. An intelligent person's eyes will light up and, even if you get into an argument, at least it won't be boring!"

"Something about the eyes" is how it was phrased, over and over, in the interviews. Cindy declares emphatically, "Gifted people have sparkly eyes." She goes on to relate how she used her belief to sort out people in college. "Walking into a room full of strangers was always difficult for me. I'd look around, and if I spotted someone with those shiny eyes, I would know that before the evening was over, I might not find a new lifelong friend, but at least I'd have an interesting conversation. In fact, I did meet one very good friend just that way."

Confusion about Feelings

Drawn to someone by mutual attraction or mutual interest, the gifted person may explore another person just as he or she examines anything else: not in a consciously cold way—it is simply in the nature of

being gifted to seek more and more levels of anything. As long as there is an "answer" on each level explored, a good relationship can grow. This is true for friends as well as lovers. If interesting responses are found on only one or two levels, the other person may be hurt and confused when the gifted person just ends the relationship.

In a 10-year study by Canadian researcher David Willings, former college students reported on their broken relationships, engagements, and marriages. Several explained the causes as "exhaustion" on the part of the other person. One man was told by his fiancée, "I just can't keep up with you. You are the most exhausting person I know!"

Bernard agrees that an acutely active mind can lead to difficulties with romantic relationships. "When I was dating, I was always looking for something that interested me. God forbid it was a skill I could master quickly; it would be a very short-lived relationship! I dated an artist for six years. She fascinated me because I can't draw. In other cases, I'd observe and absorb and go on to something—and someone—else. I didn't know how to tell a person, 'You don't interest me. What interests you doesn't interest me. It used to, but that was ten minutes ago.' That can cause a lot of social problems! There are women I'd like to write to and apologize and try to explain that I'm not a monster."

On the other hand, it may be the bright person who is deeply hurt at realizing that there is no answering voice, except on a superficial level. Sadly, some people, especially women, see the discrepancy and decide that they can live without that answering voice in the most intimate relationship of their lives. Many live to regret it. Sometimes, it takes them twenty years to find out why they are unhappy.

Other gifted grownups, ones who remain single, adopt a screening function which they don't like but may feel is necessary. "One date to check out the brains," is one young woman's method. "Isn't that awful? But I'm tired of hurt feelings—mine and other people's. I can't afford to let something begin that doesn't have a chance. I need a mind to match my own or I can't be happy."

Goldy tries to be realistic about one issue that is very delicate: competition with the beloved. "The person I'm seeing now is bio and art—I'm the better biologist; he's the better artist. I'm somewhat jealous of his artistic ability and somewhat uncomfortable with

the fact that I am a better biologist. It's a funny situation because we are both bright."

Even Emilia, a senior citizen, can exclaim, "It's terrible. I've met many men since I was widowed at 46. Blow one my way who is halfway intelligent! It is awful to have a man ask you out and the conversation is so boring that you are thinking 'I have to have an excuse if this one calls again!'"

Marriage

Gifted people marry, but they may choose mates who don't understand them if they aren't careful. In the present world of multiple marriage, or no marriage, do gifted grownups fare any better than the general population? (The old Terman studies showed that they had a lower divorce rate.) Is an intellectually compatible mate essential for a happy marriage? Most of the people interviewed seemed to think so.

A young teacher confides, "I feel like such a rat. I broke it off three weeks before the wedding. She is a very dear girl and I hurt her badly. I will feel guilty for the rest of my life. But she didn't read! When I got all excited and tried to tell her about a book, she would say that she thought reading was boring. I couldn't live with that for the rest of my life. How can you tell people that you broke your engagement because your fiancée didn't read? They would look at you like you were crazy!"

They get divorced for odd reasons, too: "She didn't understand my need to be alone." Sometimes they stay married for similar reasons: "He's the only person I know who understands my need for intellectual stimulation."

If two people can share the outer world of labels and the larger society as well as the inner, it can be a marriage of very special dimensions. Frank explains, "Most people are not at my level but it doesn't bother me that much any more. My best friend is my wife. We're married a long time-ten years [he married at 19]. We are like the same person."

Daniel, the retired headmaster of a private school, thinks, "It makes an awful difference who you marry," agreeing that an intellectually compatible mate is essential for a happy marriage. My impression from the interviews, that women have a harder time sustaining a marriage, seems to be borne out by an informal poll of the interview subjects. Of twenty-three married men, five had been married twice. Of twenty-nine married women, eleven had been married twice, and two had been married three times.

If such a small sample can be used as a judge, the men marry later, perhaps a reflection of the pressure still exerted by society on women to "get a man" and worry about the brains "after the children are grown." But man or woman, intellectual compatibility and friendship are key elements in gifted marriages.

Bernard makes a careful distinction between "compatible" and "alike" in describing his four-year marriage to another gifted adult. "Certainly, intellectual compatibility is more important than physical attractiveness—at the very least, you can buy that if you choose. My wife is very different . . . her thought processes work in baffling ways. Her way of drawing conclusions fascinates me. She has a lot of knowledge I don't have. It was quite spontaneous; we knew each other for three weeks and we've been married for four years!"

The happily married men often expressed admiration for their wives' talents and brains, perhaps a large factor in keeping them happily married. Married for the first time in his early forties, Walter says, "I had a terrible time sustaining relationships at all. I'd analyze the books they read, make bets with myself about what would be on their bookshelves. Other than college texts, they never bought university titles after they finished college. I was afraid growth would stop, so I'd break off the relationship." No longer concerned about limiting his own growth, Walter describes his marriage as "expanding horizons, willingness to change, to leave a comfortable situation. We give each other time alone." His wife, Fran, responds, "I have the security of going away to explore and knowing I don't have to worry. He wants me to learn and grow."

The extremes of emotion and action to which gifted people of all ages are prone can find a balance for some women in a mate who un-

derstands her needs and allows for them as part of the marriage. Laura and her late husband had careers which separated them for periods of time, but Laura declares, "I learned from my husband a long time ago: 'human, human, touch, feel.' Intellectual sharing was not our strong point. I need, more than anything else, someone who balances my intellect by pulling out the feeling side of me. His realization of my needs kept us from splitting apart. We were so compatible on a human level that when difficulties cropped up, he realized that I had needs for mental pleasure. He made adjustments. He didn't like it, but he accepted that I got wound up in things and ignored him for a while. I had to have time alone; nose to nose twenty-four hours a day would have made me crazy!"

Lisa would agree. "Gary understands it better than I do. He will say, 'You're getting restless; go study something.' With his encouragement, I studied karate for four years; I have wanted a black belt since I was a kid!" But the balance is there, because Gary is brilliant. "I'm used to winning," Lisa smiles, "but I don't get away with much around here. It is nice to be with someone I can't manipulate."

Establishing and living with that balance is not always easy for two strong-minded (in both senses) people. Marcelle and her husband are both lawyers. "We are alike in terms of things we like to do, but we can't talk to each other about the law! We have different styles. His is the classic one of discussion/debate. I am more collaborative; I don't like being attacked. We like to read and talk and it's hard for us. But this marriage is the nicest part of my life. There is so much equality."

Marriage Is for Growth

Spouses who not only complement each other but who push each other to learn and grow, who see talents to be developed in each other, seem to have a good chance at a lasting union. They also need to frankly recognize their differences. Colin and Dora are starting a family in their late thirties, after a rather rocky beginning. Colin explains, "We've really gotten to like each other. We did all of our fighting when we lived together, off and on, before we decided to marry, and it has worked out well. We realize that if we didn't have

each other, who else would we ever find? We're both weird in a lot of ways, and recognizing that holds us together pretty well.

"Our needs are alike. She was obviously bored with her field, even though she had a master's degree. I convinced her to join me in computer science. I could see that she had the ability, but it took a while to convince her that she was smarter than she realized in math. We can talk, and she has great ideas. We get all excited about starting our own company some day! While she is raising the kids it is hard for her, but once they are a little older, she will be able to move right back into the field."

There are, of course, exceptions to the match in intelligence, but the understanding a gifted spouse needs is ongoing. Lillian is in her sixties, a partner in a satisfying long-term marriage to a nongifted man. "At first, my husband thought my wanting to go to college at my age was a bit peculiar. He kept asking me what I was going to do with it. I am not going for the reasons that younger people go; I don't expect it to get me a better job. I just like learning. Now he only worries that I may be doing too much and exhausting myself. He cooks dinner on the nights I have class and picks up books at the library for me."

George grins as he recalls getting to know his wife while commiserating over a sadistic graduate professor. "In *Parade's End*, Ford Maddox Ford said a great true line: 'The only reason for getting married is so you can finish your conversations.' We can read books and poems together, and talk. [He is a college professor, she a poet.] She's Dionysian; I'm Apollonian. She has a talent for the creative leap and I have a talent for analysis, and they work very well together. The two kinds of insight combine for something better than we could develop separately."

Joan responds, "I have a lot of friends, but they are partial relationships. Marriage provides a much fuller relationship. Here I can share all aspects of myself. I would agree wholeheartedly that an intellectually compatible mate is essential for a happy marriage."

George adds, "I feel so incredibly lucky that I have someone I can talk to about literature, about peak experiences . . . One of the things which has always fascinated me about Joan is that she seems

to have another level of awareness, almost mystical . . . I can be talking to her and have an awareness that she is not quite 'here,' that she may be in some other dimension." Joan smiles quietly, as if she knew that she is one of the lucky ones who have found a mate who understands and admires that "other dimension," the special sensitivity Dabrowski describes as "overexcitibility." Dealing with the special aspects of your own sensitivity can be very lonely, even with a mate who tries.

Finding the Others

A gifted adult's capacities may differ from the average person, and basic emotional needs may be satisfied in a more intense and slightly different way. And yet, we all need companionship. From early childhood, a bright person needs companions who can share on special levels. At any age, friends and lovers who can both absorb and return the intensity will make the most satisfying relationships. Marriage remains, as stated earlier, a very tricky business. Both emotional and intellectual mating may be difficult to achieve, but it is probably worth the struggle. Gifted friendships and loving relationships can reach across many barriers.

If you are a bright person, you should know that intensity in feelings and in relationships is, for you, the norm. Along with your quick mind, you have a greater capacity for communication and feeling; it needs to be acknowledged and provided for without apology. There are others who function on similar levels. The work of locating them is worthwhile, but be prepared to find them in both odd and familiar places.

If you have not already done so, set about to assemble around yourself a small circle of supportive people. Cindy, who is currently living in a rather remote area of the country, explains how this can be done: "I learned very early that there will never be very many people who like or approve of me." Cindy built a circle in seventh grade which carried her through high school. "I knew that in college I'd have to

build the circle again. I eventually found three or four people with whom I could go out to dinner and not have to talk—a sure sign of friends!" Working for the National Park Service, she has built the circle a third time; it includes two coworkers and an elderly woman who shares her interest in photography.

Realize that the difference in the way your machinery operates may explain why you do not get the responses you expect from other people. Consider their point of view and plan new strategies for sustaining relationships. Seeking out compatible persons by locating places and activities which attract people who like to learn is probably a present you should give yourself. Following your own recreational interests while keeping a lookout for those "sparkly eyes" is another strategy you might want to try. You could even begin by contacting Mensa, a national organization for gifted adults. They can help you to locate members in your area.

If you are feeling lonely, understand that it is part of the human condition and can be dealt with. Learn to cherish time alone as an opportunity for renewal and growth. If you enjoy reading, three books that might provide both inspiration and consolation are Maslow's *The Farther Reaches of Human Nature*, Miller's *The Drama of the Gifted Child* and Gowan's *Development of the Creative Individual*. This last is out of print, but well worth a search through interlibrary loan.

Advice from gifted people themselves tends to be rather frank. Nina says simply, "It's OK to be the way you are." Amy cautions, "You don't have to conform, but you do have to live in society." Theresa states, "You are a human being like everyone else, and everyone has value. It is your job to discover what is valuable in you." Scott is blunt: "Find things to get fascinated about—you'll live longer." Liesl less blunt, as she suggests, "Work your smartness into the flow of things. Make that intelligence a part of your whole being so that you can enjoy life."

My own advice would be to adopt an attitude which will allow you to savor the following statement by Gail Sheehy: "The prizes of our society are reserved for outer, not inner achievements. Scant are the trophies given for reconciling all the forces that compete to direct development, although working toward such reconciliation, hour by

demanding hour, day by triumphant day, year by exacting year, is what underlies all growth of the personality."

Be on the alert for "others," of whatever age or station, who will appear in your life; you can both give and receive validation and support. Most of all, do not hesitate to savor the special joy of sharing knowledge and feelings with such a one, whether your encounter lasts a moment or a lifetime.

Chapter Ten

Gifted Women

We don't have the advantage of being told we are human beings when we are younger; we have to discover it for ourselves.
Meg, gifted woman, forties

Few questions can be raised about whether or not the underachievement of bright women exists; the fact remains that in almost all professional fields and occupations, men overwhelmingly surpass women in both the professional accomplishments they achieve and the financial benefits they reap.
Sally Reis, "We Can't Change What We Don't Recognize: Understanding the Special Needs of Gifted Females"

As we have seen throughout this book, the problems and pleasures of being smarter than 95% of the population are encountered by both men and women throughout their lives. Why, then, devote a chapter to gifted women? Are their difficulties unique? Are their issues any different than those faced by gifted men? The answer to both questions is an unequivocal Yes.

To show how this is so, we could begin with a statement by Linda Kreger Silverman, director of the Institute for Advanced Development, an institute devoted to the study of gifted adults. She says, "Most gifted women are unaware of their giftedness; they are only aware of their pain—the pain of being different from the way women

are supposed to be." We could begin with the damage done by the conflicting messages modern women receive about accomplishment versus caretaking and the fear of success that holds back so many. We could even begin by noting the large numbers of books on gifted education which feature not only chapters but whole sections devoted to the special needs of gifted girls, or the journals and conferences which focus entirely on this subject.

But let us begin with the women I interviewed. The various phases of *any* woman's life take place against the same background: the struggle to know and to value what she is and to learn the mechanisms for making the most of her potential in a society where the models for accomplishment are still male. As I interviewed them, bright women of varied ages and economic backgrounds expressed the same concerns as their sisters with home and family, relationships with men, and the difficulties of the working world. However, gifted women worry about the need for mental stimulation and the management of a high energy level. They express impatience with the slowness of the world. By far the largest category of concern revealed in their interviews could be titled "Self-Worth."

Audrey, a college professor, recalls, "In kindergarten we had these magnetic fish, and as a class we built a boat out of blocks. A newspaper came to do a story on us, and the reporter said that the boys would sit in the boat and fish. I was outraged, and I spoke up, 'Why just the boys? We all built it!' And so my picture appeared in the paper as 'the little girl who asked, Why just boys?'"

"In parochial school, I asked my fifth grade teacher why the boys always got to line up first," Michelle reports. "'Because that is the way it is done in the church,' the nun replied. 'Why?' I persisted. 'Because Christ was a man.' Then she told me to stop asking questions."

Catherine, a physician, admits, "I wanted to be an engineer, but my mother said that wasn't ladylike. I chose medicine because I knew it was something my father would approve of."

Pearl is now a poet and photographer. Here she describes herself as a young wife: "The vacuum cleaner has not been taken out. I've got a big roll of shelf paper stretched out on the floor and I am drawing a long and twining tree on it in watercolors. I hang up the tree; it is

eight feet tall. I feel so excited to look at it, but I also feel guilty, because there is a voice in my head which says, 'That is very nice, but you should have done it after the vacuuming. One should not do something for oneself until all the necessary things are done.' Vacuuming was necessary . . . it never occurred to me that an eight-foot tree which gave me private pleasure could be necessary."

How does the early promise of a feisty little Audrey give way to a brainwashed Pearl, denigrating her own talent? Barbara Kerr of the University of Arizona is among those psychologists who have shed light on important aspects of being "a person with a fine intellect and extraordinary talents, who also happens to have the cultural 'disability' of being female." Indeed, after attending a class reunion, Kerr was so dismayed at what did *not* happen to the girls with whom she graduated from a high school for the academically talented that she changed her career focus and made the study of such women her field of work.

Kerr sees the pressures of society dampening a bright girl's aspirations from early adolescence through adulthood, encouraging her to adjust, adapt, and ultimately abandon her dreams. In *Smart Girls/Gifted Women*, she described "pressures to conform to the group, act dumb, or await information passively." Kerr emphasizes that better counseling in schools and the nurturing of a smart girl's gifts can help to ensure her full development into a gifted woman. Her views are echoed by others who are studying the problems of gifted women in our society, including the 1992 report by the American Association of University Women, which describes "How Schools Shortchange Women."

Kerr found that the choices about their lives made by the gifted women she studied were partly dependent on personality, but she sees the cultural pattern as still forcing women into either the single, career-oriented lifestyle, or that of family-oriented homemaker who may have a part-time job but not a career. Kerr makes a case for what she calls the "integrator," who combines career and family, as a healthy third choice for many bright women. A 1993 study of women executives with children found them happy and successful, in spite of the many claims on their time and energy. *Answers to the Mommy Track*, the result of a ten-year study of high-powered women (judges,

governors, vice presidents of General Motors), stresses that both women and society would be better served by utilizing the qualities that make women successful in both personal nurturing and professional achievement.

A Woman's Different Voice

Carol Gilligan of Harvard University and a number of others see a deeper, more pervasive problem, which is connected to a woman's feeling of self-worth. Gilligan's work has its detractors and defenders, but it seems to have helped many women view themselves in a more positive light. It also pushes us a little farther on the path toward rethinking what constitutes "success" for women.

It seems logical to believe that girl babies are born with the capacity for high achievement in the same numbers as boy babies, but that they develop in different ways and possess different strengths as adults. In human relations, all too often, "different" means "inferior." Gilligan explains how she believes this comes about: "Girls, in identifying themselves as female, experience themselves as like their mothers," thus imprinting the idea of fusion with the caregiver as a strengthening of identity. Women develop more in terms of relationships for this reason. They are not as legalistic and show more willingness to make exceptions, even in childish play. Because of women's experience of likeness and unity with the caregiver at an early stage of development, Gilligan's survey of the literature shows women with a much more highly developed sense of "other" than men. Gilligan sees women arriving at maturity through a process of responsible care and attachment, where the self is eventually included in the circle of those to be cared for.

On the other hand, to define their selves and grow into healthy males, boys must separate themselves from their mothers. According to Gilligan, boys learn to regard intimacy and close relationships with suspicion because this works against their inner definition of themselves as male. Gilligan sees this separation as causing men to

develop a much weaker sense of "other," to work by rules, and to have a greater concern for legality and justice. She concludes that the male moves toward maturity along a route that eventually shows that the achievements of the self must be broadened to include a circle of others to be cared for responsibly.

Even though each child's ego strength has a different basis, both sexes arrive, by different routes, at what Gilligan terms "a reality common to both sexes." A problem arises because most psychologists have defined progress toward maturity in terms of the male separation model. Girls, quite naturally, acquire a basis for defining self that shows itself in empathy and sensitivity to the feelings of others, and this has caused some psychologists to define the feminine ego as "weak." This misperception, which relegates a woman's intelligence and her moral development to a less mature status, has been possible because most of the developmental literature has been based on studies of *males only*.

Gilligan's book, *In a Different Voice*, exposed this masculine bias in psychology. For example, in Piaget's study, *The Moral Development of the Child*, "child" is assumed to be male. Even Kohlberg's landmark work on the six stages of moral development, a work heavily used (and highly respected) in educational circles, was based on a twenty-year study of eighty-four subjects—all male. If the standard for growth is male, then anything nonmale may easily, and mistakenly, be labeled "immature." Here is where different becomes inferior.

"It changed my life," is how one bright woman described Gilligan's work. "I had always measured myself on a male scale, and come up short. All the female perceptions, which I had discounted, I was able to perceive as valuable and useful. The 'different voice' in which I speak about the world is just that: different, not inferior."

Given the male bias in psychology until now, the following observation by psychologist Elizabeth Drews becomes understandable, and alarming. "Mental health studies in the 1960s showed far fewer girls than boys in guidance clinics as children and adolescents, but more women than men neurotic by age 40. Talents stultified are reflected in deteriorating mental health."

Delores comments bitterly on what she sees as a cultural pattern, one still faced by older bright women. "In our generation, you went

to college, fine, but then you got married, you worked for a while, and then you stayed home and had kids. You did all this volunteer stuff and then maybe, after the kids were in college, maybe, you could go and do something. Too many women never did."

Feminist Betty Freidan cited later mental health studies which showed a correlation between improving mental health for women and the improved opportunities they began to realize in the 1970s and 1980s. However, even in 1993, Linda Schierse Leonard's *Meeting the Madwoman*, a study of how women come to terms with the various forms of creative energy, warns that if this energy is not expressed in a healthy way, it will take form in what she calls "madness."

Changing the Cultural Pattern for Women

Interestingly, even a strong feminist like Friedan warned that we abandon the traditional pattern completely at our peril. "There's a whole evolution of the family, no longer based on women as housewives. [But] people need the family . . . it will take a new shape . . . it would be terrible if we defined ourselves in such narrow ways that these impulses [for family and children] which are very powerful in women are denied because feminism tells them that somehow they're going to have to fulfill themselves, as opposed to having children, or as opposed to marriage."

Is a bright woman trapped by her own psychology, by her drive for accomplishment and her desire for nurturing? Not necessarily. Her challenge is learning to understand and enjoy the true sense of her own capabilities, in defiance of anyone's pattern. The Mommy pattern, the Superwoman pattern, the masculine Career pattern, the Books-or-Babies pattern, even the Goddess pattern are among the predetermined life choices which confront all modern women. Being a gifted woman just makes it more complicated, but more joyful, if you play it right. "A woman with a sense of autonomy has the capacity to cope with being perceived as unconventional, is not dependent on others for what she thinks and feels, and is capable of reinforcing her actions with positive feedback of her own."

The different voices that Gilligan highlighted are beginning to speak out on their own behalf, and they are suggesting, not abandonment, but profound changes in the way we view our cultural pattern. Not only do researchers view the forced choice of books-or-babies as a myth, they view the concept of the career woman as a myth also.

As more of these different voices speak out, the message emerges that a bright woman is not obligated to seek to "have it all" if "all" is defined as a male, career-driven model for successful living. Sally Reis, an educator and psychologist who is an expert on underachievement in females, says, "The realization of giftedness in women may need to be redefined to include the nurturance of one's children and family . . . the joy of accomplishment from the pursuit of a career which still allows time for a satisfying personal life."

In "Why Doesn't Jane Run?" Jacquelynn Eccles of the University of Michigan suggests that if we are accepting the "different voice" that women bring to life, then we must not simply settle for advocating more career opportunities, we must also become advocates for valuing the intelligence, creativity, and caring that bright women, like Adrian, bring to the raising of healthy children. She advocates allowing for less than full-time careers in business, law, medicine—all the high-status jobs. She says we must honor bright women as teachers by giving that profession more status, and we must honor motherhood as a profession worthy of the time and talent of a smart woman.

The two accomplished authors of *The Mommy Track* remind us quite bluntly, "If we want educated and well trained women to have children in this society, then we must support the needs of these women *and their husbands* [italics mine] to take care of training, developing and educating these children." Because giftedness is partly inherited, there would seem to be no "if" about it.

How Do Confident Women Evolve?

In terms of the needs of gifted women, how should an evolution (revolution?) in our cultural pattern for success take place? Certain clues

emerge from the early years of the women whose talents have been realized. Regardless of the era in which they were born, these women report a rich childhood and a sense of being able to do whatever they set their minds to as factors in their success.

Rhonda remembers an Irish immigrant household in Boston early in the century and a mother who had her own millinery business. With little education, her father acquired a responsible position with a shipping company. "We had marvelous music . . . Red Seal records with Caruso and Galli-Curci! Father read us poetry, and every Friday night we went to the theater. I saw Shakespeare, Chekhov, Shaw. At 12, I was allowed to become a student at the theater, and in high school I acted professionally." By age 18 she was appearing on the New York stage.

"My mother didn't do housework," reports Jenny, who at 70 has had several different careers. "We had to find our own way ourselves. My father told us, 'You can do exactly what you want to do; just find out what that is.' No one suggested there was anything I couldn't do because I was a woman. My parents were always 'on my side.' Children were important. Being yourself was important."

Family Support

Lauren had no difficulty with the academic discipline which carried her through to a position with a prestigious New York law firm. Although she received a fine education, pressures existed to discourage her from using it. Her family was an important source of support.

"In the high schools of suburban Virginia, you didn't even get to talk to anyone who wasn't bright except in gym. Class ranks were posted on the bulletin boards. My brother's friend killed himself over a D in math. And yet, the attitude was very 'Southern'; men dominated the classroom. They were called on more than women, who had the idea that you shouldn't do better than a guy. Some admitted to doing less well for social acceptance. I'm very proud of myself that I didn't do that. I was first in the class. My family never felt that my learning wasn't important. Now a date for the prom— that wasn't important!"

Theresa contrasts her early life with her mother's and explains that it has determined what each was able to do with her life. "My mother and her sisters were immigrants who grew up ashamed of their heritage. She didn't know about scholarships and things like that, and she had no one to help her. You were supposed to find an Anglo-Saxon husband and get married, but my aunts did not do that. Many family troubles stemmed from very intelligent unmarried women who had no other outlet for their frustrations but the manipulation of people.

"My mother did marry a doctor, so I was able to go to a demanding private school, and I entered Vassar at 15, and went on to medical school and a residency at top institutions. My mother does not consider herself as bright as I, but the only difference between us is that she was stopped short. I didn't grow up with any limitations. I was always encouraged to be me."

In "Guiding the Career Development of Gifted Females," Patricia Wolleat poses the question: "How many African American, Native American or Hispanic girls have the potential to become scientists, writers, artists or musicians, but will not, because [like Theresa's mother] they never believe it to be within their reach?" Minority women who, for whatever reason, have not had the support of an understanding family, can spend most of their energy struggling toward self-worth instead of developing their talents.

Barriers and Choices

In thinking about the needs of gifted women, the operative word seems to be "choice." There are decisions about mates, marriage, children, and career, and each choice colors and directs what follows. The second important word is "barriers." Both begin early.

As a young gifted woman begins to reach out into the career world, she has many difficulties to overcome. First, there is the difficulty many gifted adults of both sexes face: finding a career that fits. Then, there is the prejudice that still bars women from areas where

they have the same talents as men. Finally, there is the pressure that society and the self exert to find a personal relationship. The place where one will fit is not always clearly evident, and the barriers can be discouraging.

After successfully emerging from the pressure cooker of a suburban Virginia high school, Lauren recalls, "My law school was only 10 to 20% women, but we were in the top of the class. The politicians and lawyers whom I knew from some political work I did considered my going to law school a big joke; they were sure I would fail. On the other hand, when I was successful I was told that I was taking the place of a man who really needed that place in law school. It was assumed that I would get married and not use my education.

"The women's lounge in law school had a bulletin board with disgusting comments from interviewers like, 'What kind of contraceptive do you use?' I was in the top 5% of my class, but the men went to law firms and we women went to government agencies, because by then there were antidiscrimination quotas to be filled. The official who gave me my first job actually said, 'Discrimination is great! We get all these terrific women because the law firms won't have you!'"

Jean, career-building in her forties, is blunt about her prospects: "As a woman, I have to compete in a man's world, run a home in a woman's world, and prove myself to *me* by always being better." One of a team of visiting nurses in a large suburban county, Jean finds, "Bosses often feel threatened and you have to hide your potential; this is the first job I've had where I can be myself. However, among my fellow RNs I see a lot of brains but a great lack of self-confidence. We had a woman with a lot of confidence who held a difficult job in our department. When she left, no one was willing to take that same level of challenge. Somewhere along the line we haven't taught our women to be assertive. I can only attribute my own self-confidence to my divorce—that was a great learning experience."

Male Authority Figures

On the job, whether fresh from school or more mature, the typical gifted push for "more, faster, better" can present additional problems

if you are female. Lillian reports, "There is a woman in my office who could be so much help to her boss if he would let her, but he gets threatened and says, 'I run this office, not you.' And she could do it!" Of her own situation as a personnel secretary of some years experience, Lillian says, "If I say a job is simple, they simply don't understand. It's hard to know how to deal with people who resent you for being able to do something better than a man."

Even when success is within reach, problems may arise. Audrey relates, "I am at the top of my field, and it feels good! I just gave a talk to one thousand psychiatrists. I am at the point of telling others in my field that their work is wrong. I am writing a book. This is *it*. But recently at a conference in Washington, I was part of a panel of experts trying to make decisions about how to obtain a grant, and I could see that all these men were missing the point. Do I stand up and tell them? I did, and they got the money, but they were told, 'If Audrey hadn't spoken up, you would have lost the whole grant.' When I presented a paper later the same day, I was savagely attacked by the same men I had helped. I want to be part of the group, but now I am resented for solving problems which others couldn't solve."

Choosing Men

As troublesome as male-female relations can be in the workplace, a gifted woman is not an exception, by reason of her brains, to the need for a person with whom to create a satisfying relationship. Choosing men, as friends, lovers, or husbands, presents special problems for a person whose intellect forms an essential part of her integrity as an individual. In discussing social relationships, comments from both married and single women included "I was isolated and lonely in high school; disappointed in my few dates because they weren't too bright. I never felt comfortable with boys in high school as boyfriends; I had boys as friends." One adds, "I grew up in an enriched atmosphere with girls who were all like me, so I didn't know any better than to make guys feel threatened in college." For some, there is a different problem in college. "You finally find people who are like you, but you lack experience in socializing with anybody . . . most of my friends in college had inactive social lives."

At 40, Fran sees that smart women may make foolish choices when it comes to men. "There was a time in my life when I didn't know any smart guys who were eligible and *alive*—happy, committed to their work, able to share with others. Let's face it, a charming scoundrel is often more interesting and more fun than an ordinary guy, and then there is the curiosity which a gifted person has about other people, other lifestyles. There was a time when I was attracted to people who were different intellectually also. There is something magical and dangerous about playing with that. I suffered for it. The alternatives they offered were not dull, and I guess that was the attraction."

Single Women

Many bright women are skeptical of entering into a marriage; they observe, wait, choose carefully, and then may opt not to marry at all. Regardless of age, they seem to consider the whole process a dynamic one, admitting to moments of loneliness but maintaining their determination to grow and be whole persons above all else.

At 56, Cecile is the successful head of a college department and sees things changing for younger women. "It is no longer unusual to combine education and a family. Women are able to speak out for what women want, but it was different for me. My parents wanted me to have an education. My high school teachers said that I was imaginative and creative and suggested Bennington, but my parents said 'Oh, no, she must stay close to home,' so I went to a small state college and lived at home. When I began work on a master's degree they were very nervous. Their hope was that I would meet a man, and combine teaching and a family.

"Then I became engaged to Gavin. We were very compatible, but he was ten years older and anxious to start a family. I wanted to finish my degree, he wanted me to put it aside, and we broke off because of it. I am strong enough to tune into my own felt needs and to act on them—even if it means leaving someone I love. I love me, in the best sense of that word. I have come past having to play dumb in social situations. Why would any self-respecting woman be drawn to a man with whom she has to play that game? I've been spared in my career, encountering very little in the way of male disdain, and I've never

been romantically involved with someone I worked with. I have always had to be my own person. I do go through periods of mixed feelings about never having had children."

Stacey is exploring the corporate world and is looking at her options carefully. "I am in the process of using this job up, and for a woman there is always that Critical Question, and you try to use your smarts to make it as creative a decision as possible. In my opinion, you have to be in a field you can get in and out of. Is there prejudicial treatment? Well, you are eyed a bit more closely, and despite the current laws, they always find ways to ask if you are planning on getting married or pregnant and leaving your job.

"I couldn't have the job I have now and have a family. I get home at 7, and sometimes bring work home. I have to travel. I have been thinking about how I would choose, if I want to marry, about whether I choose against a career, against a project I want to do. I have to wonder what would be left of me to share with a family."

Choosing Marriage

Many of the women I interviewed were happily married, but often it was the result of a second try after a failed first marriage. The failures are often connected to the husband's acceptance of a bright woman's need to use her intellect. So are the successful second marriages.

Failed Marriages.   Georgia recalls, "I was a smart kid and a rebel who refused to go to college, to the horror of my parents and teachers . . . I got myself into 'such a condition' that I could marry. I had a child at 19. In my small house back in the woods, with poor heat, I cried for days and weeks. I didn't recognize postpartum depression. I began to write poetry. My husband regarded it as part of my 'illness.' He had many problems, among them the fact that he was threatened by my need to use my mind at all! Why did I want to read books? Poetry writing was neurotic, why couldn't I watch TV and be happy? When he died, I pushed the poetry aside and set about to raise my three daughters, but my second husband has read all my poetry; he goes to poetry workshops with me. He is not intellectual. We share interests

in health and running, but he is there for me when I need him . . . he is my friend."

Delores speaks about her first marriage in a soft, sad voice. "I was 22 when I married. I am so sorry now that I did that. I should have been something more. It ended because I could not have an honest, intelligent discussion with someone who supposedly loved me. I lived in a loveless marriage for eight years because of my children; I stayed for them. During that time I read every book I could to improve myself as a wife, a mother, and a woman. I was always smarter than my husband, but he was the one making sixty thousand a year! You play a role. You use your intelligence to create a person who can keep a situation stable until you can get out of it. My second husband is nowhere near me in IQ, but he is a success at what he does; and he is a caring person."

Helen became what others dream of: the wife of a corporate executive, living in one of the most expensive suburbs in the nation. "I can remember being in magnificent houses and sneaking away from the smoke and the sexual flirtations to find the library. I remember once hearing two women whispering about me: 'What is she doing in there? She appears to be reading the books!' . . . In my forties, it became a choice between suicide and divorce, and a wonderful therapist helped me choose divorce." A Ph.D. candidate at 62, Helen is now happily residing in a very modest house in the country. Married to a local government official, she can say, "I have been married now for five years and this man is a jewel. There is nothing he doesn't understand . . . there is nothing I can't talk to him about!"

Successful Marriages.   Alison and Mike met at a church social when they were 17; they have been together for thirty years. "You have to be friends. Sometimes it's the two of you against the world! But your mate needs to be a person in his own right. You don't want an intellectual yes-person, or someone who will only enhance your own ego. I am fortunate to have a mate who is smart and weird; a real deep down friend—those are hard to come by!"

Knowing what you need and want and speaking up for it seems to be one of the keys to a successful marriage for a smart woman. Gaile,

a retired psychologist, describes her twenty-five-year marriage: "One of my criteria for marrying David was that he would have the capacity not to interfere in my need for doing the crazy things I do with my hands and my head. For the most part he stands back and lets me move along. He doesn't necessarily give me a lot of support, but he doesn't interfere, so it's OK."

From a thirty-year perspective, Morgan can say, "You'll have a problem if you don't at least pick a husband who has enough self-confidence to let you do what you like. My husband doesn't understand me much any more. I am so much more tolerant of bizarre people, but he tolerates me! He encourages me in school. If he didn't, I might be gone by now. He doesn't really share it, but you can't have someone who says 'Stay home and do the wash.'"

In contrast to Morgan, Maureen says, "One of the most delightful things about this marriage is that we can have the most wonderful discussions. He is the only one I can be like this with . . . our personality inventories are even alike! I am a lot of things that I don't realize I am, and I need a good kick in the butt sometimes. He is marvelous! I look at this bright man who never had an education and he just sparkles! He will say 'You are smarter than I am, why don't you do something about it?'" It is little wonder that when she met him at 18, at the factory where they both worked, Maureen decided, "He would do just fine."

Adrian has a most whimsical way of describing the linking of minds which fuels her thirteen-year marriage to another gifted grownup. "I married at 25, to Tim, who was 23, after many long talks about all kinds of things. He was my best friend. I wouldn't even have minded if I couldn't have married him—I just wanted to live next door to him for the rest of my life so we could talk!"

Choosing Children

Once the decision to marry has been made, a bright woman who chooses to work at home, nurturing her own bright children, faces special challenges and rewards. (I recently heard this choice referred to as "The counterculture of the nineties.") Even today, there is a price to be paid by bright women who live in America's isolated

suburbs. Whether the ordinary or the affluent, their daily lives are often limited to the company of other wives and focused on endless carpooling and activities designed for children.

Margo is an older gifted woman who describes her experience: "There were a lot of things I liked about being home . . . being a writer helps. I honestly felt when I married that I could cause enough things to go on, that I'd be happy for some time while my children grew up. A bright woman, if she wants to be at home while she is raising a family, can stop short of actually having an outside job, but she must order her life to take care of the crucial question of contact: with college courses, meeting other bright women. Living in suburbia is very difficult. In a city there are interesting activities and people at your doorstep if you are willing to seek them out, but out here you get bogged down in the car pool. I could never stand to get really involved . . . two coffee klatches and I'd want to run screaming back to my books. I could satisfy my need for more learning that way, and I do have a smart husband to talk about what I learned, but I desperately missed the company of other intellectually alive women."

Younger women are reporting a change in this situation. As more women refuse to accept society's male-oriented definition of what constitutes a successful career path, they are taking time out to raise children. Younger professional women are finding that their suburban neighbors may also be stopping out from substantial careers and that the conversation over coffee is becoming networking in the suburbs. While the babies play, these gifted women are discussing graduate school and where they will place their maturity and special skills.

Dale and Sylvia are two young suburban mothers who seem to be working this out well. As neighbors, they provide support for each other, and their children are friends. Dale has converted her cellar to a darkroom so that she can improve her photography skills while she is at home. She is also taking courses at a nearby college; she has a history degree, but has decided not to use it. Sylvia says, "I want to be ready to step into a nursing career as soon as the kids are on their own. I'm taking it one course at a time and it's fun!" She also does volunteer work at a local women's shelter, which adds to her knowledge of the health care field.

A particularly poignant example of a gifted woman's dilemma comes from Marcia, a young African American writer, who started out doing the "expected" thing: working at her career and raising her 4-year-old. Her husband shared all chores, to the detriment of his own career, because he was unable to travel. "One morning," she related, "my child became ill at day care. Some reference was made to his clothing, and I realized that I was so busy that I had no idea what clothes I had put on my child that day. That night, we sat down and reordered our lives." Marcia quit her job to become a full-time mother and part-time graduate student and writer. As a fortunate bonus, the freedom to travel landed her husband a promotion and a salary increase.

However, when we first met, this talented woman apologized as she described herself as "only" being at home with her son. My reply that she was doing the most important work in the world— giving emotional stability to the society of the future—took her by surprise. Before we parted, she was feeling a little better about her "job."

Opting for a full-time career while your children are still small presents the most formidable challenge of all. Kate, a lawyer, describes it this way: "It's a great job; I almost didn't take it because of my second pregnancy, but they wanted me anyway. I can bring the baby to work with me if I need to. I have a sitter at home for Jeffrey. I juggle a lot of things, but I realized that I couldn't just stay home. My husband shares everything. I play so many roles, I sometimes wonder which one is real. I jam so many things into my life."

Audrey is a successful person, an upcoming authority in her field; she voices similar concerns. "I don't have time to sit and think. When I do, it's very productive. I try to arrange time away from intrusions of job and children. Then I feel bad because I shouldn't want this just for myself, because my husband and kids are needy, too."

Researcher Jacquelynn Eccles validates the choices these gifted women are making:

Educational and occupational training systems are now designed to mesh well with the life-patterns of men. They also tend to operate

on the implicit assumption that (1) late entry into such professions as medicine, law, or the sciences and (2) less than complete devotion to one's profession, are bad ideas. [Are they not, in reality, simply different ideas?] Both of these assumptions need to be evaluated . . . In addition, educational and occupational support programs that are specifically designed for gifted women, who have different life patterns from those of gifted men, need to be developed . . . many gifted women are influenced by their desire to spend significant amounts of time raising their children . . . the assumption that late entry signifies lack of commitment should not be made.

What others may have found problematical, Morgan has found zestful. She married young and was kept busy with the raising of five children. But she filled her do-it-yourself lifestyle with artistic and musical accomplishments. "It's quite an experience going to college at 40. Sometimes I come home from school after learning something new, on a real high that lasts all day." Morgan admits, "I don't daydream; I'm too busy. I'm going to be dying and saying, 'Wait, I haven't tried enough things!' I don't agree that a woman necessarily needs an outside job." Meg, who has tried it both ways, doesn't think it matters which choice one makes. "I am a functioning member of a household whose talents are used, regardless of whether I work outside the home or not."

Having It All

So she survives through childhood and education, even the hassles of making a career in what is still a man's world, and arrives at a stage that embodies, supposedly, all the best of a satisfying marriage, children, and career. She finds that being Superwoman is no easier than being Superkid—it is only for rare individuals indeed. Even while encouraging women to consider this option, psychologist Barbara Kerr admits, "It is difficult to adapt to this combination and great mental stability is needed."

This parceling out of the many facets of her admittedly talented person often leaves Mrs. Gifted Grownup feeling "constant ever-widening guilt," as Alison describes it. Raising five bright children with a man who has been her best friend since they were both 17, and then earning a doctorate while working full time, can result in a feeling that you are "shortchanging your duties to others . . . if you take time to pursue what you are interested in, then someone is suffering because of your selfishness." Alison seems to be an example of the older role model just described. "The only way you seem to be able to handle it is to take it out of your own hide, and do your own creative and exciting things after everything else is done. Then you give up sleep. So you feel guilty because you give your husband less, and he married you for the physical and intellectual sharing . . . and you can't seem to find a way to fit all that into one life! My husband understands, but he has needs for support and if I'm already harried and frazzled, then I am causing another person's needs not to be met . . . No wonder there are so many divorces!"

In *Answers to the Mommy Track*, the authors paint an optimistic picture of how Superwoman can actually manage the marriage, the children, and the major career. They offer advice from Debbie Smith, who is a vice president at Xerox: "Get good help and use it. Delegate at office and at home. You have to be very organized . . . know your priorities . . . know what you are going to do about the inevitable conflicts that arise . . . I've taken the red-eye across the country to have lunch with my kids or attend a school function. Not everyone has the physical stamina or the desire to balance things in this way."

Again, gifted researcher Sally Reis has a different view. She suggests that it is time to reexamine these older role models in which women strive not only for success but for the "Jane Fonda body, a house that could be on the cover of *Better Homes and Gardens* and perfect children." The authors of *What Smart Women Know* describe this situation in a bit more realistic, if whimsical, way: "Women with children and paying jobs fantasize about finding a clean blouse, an hour to themselves, and a decent night's sleep." It would seem that, realistically, most modern smart women fall somewhere between the two extremes.

Self-Discovery

Unlike the younger women, many of the older women I interviewed reported going through much of their lives not even knowing that their struggles with marriages, careers, and lifestyles could be tied to their valuable minds, their high intelligence. (Again, in the case of disadvantaged and minority women, I am fearful that the situation has not really changed.)

In a number of interviews, the exhilaration of a mature woman's self-discovery was evident. After thirty-seven years, it can be heard in Adrian's voice: "It's like being unbound after being kidnapped and stuck in a closet. There is new energy, a new view of life. My husband always told me I was smart, but I thought that it was like telling me I was pretty. My son's teacher helped me to see that I could do anything I want to do. People who know all this early are more disciplined; they know how to use their intelligence efficiently. When you come to it so late, you have a lot of baggage to lose."

"I was 35 when I discovered my own intelligence," Meg explains. "I didn't realize my potential until I taught an advanced course in our school. Something was clicking inside me . . . I could systematize knowledge. I could complete a Ph.D. I had never perceived myself as capable of that! Being female and 40, now is a critical time. It's like coming out of the closet. Now that I am 'out here,' I am finding out how to connect logical intelligence to my female insights and I find it a great source of strength."

Georgia, a grandmother, exclaims, "Thank God it has finally come! Finally, how to be yourself, like yourself, and decide what is important to you. It is not easy to do. It's like a quiet little inner revolution. The layers fell away, and I decided I was myself. What I want matters."

And with maturity may come new insight, even for those who have always been aware of their own gifts. Delores explains, "I spent too many years being intellectual and it didn't feed my soul. Intellectual is easy. Emotion is what counts; it makes a human being human." Laura agrees. "I have concluded from studying Jung, that a woman

whose intellect dominates her can get caught in its games, and that can be devastating. I used to think intellect was all I needed. Not true. You must give attention to feelings or they will waste energy and wreck the accomplishments of the mind. If one function dominates, you thwart your own growth."

Gaile says frankly, "I adore being an oddball. I am odd, and I don't find anything wrong with it. I have been trying, as I entered my sixties, to find out how good I really am. It is fun and scary. In pushing myself beyond the usual limit, I've broken through and found myself in arenas where I never thought I'd be able to operate. It is discouraging that people, especially women, are horrified when they hear all the things I do."

Challenging the Status Quo

We can acknowledge that women are not encouraged to develop their potential in the way that men are, and we can acknowledge that women are underrepresented in the upper reaches of almost all organizations, but the different voices of a variety of researchers are pushing us into newer and bolder considerations.

Why should we push our bright girls into a male-configured model for their lives—we who argue for their right to a different voice? asks Barbara Ehrenreich in "Strategies of Corporate Women." "We accept society's definition of the problem . . . rather than tackle the real problem—that our economic structure is incompatible with raising children."

Why should the words "achievement" and "success" be defined only by the salaried workplace and not by the raising of healthy children and service to society—for men as well as women? Why can we not create a female life-model, based on time for those nurturing functions? In *The Mismeasure of Woman*, Carol Tavris reports the kinds of questions women psychologists have begun to ask:

> Why, they wondered, is it so desirable for an academic career to be uninterrupted by experience, family, outside work? So what if

women's life paths were less linear than men's? Wasn't this way of structuring one's life as logical as, and more humanly beneficial than, the straight-up-the-ladder model? Shouldn't administrators be worrying about the deficient education of male students, so woefully un-weathered for real life? And why, as psychologist Carol Gilligan argued to great acclaim, do we focus so much on the importance of separation from parents, instead of on the continuing affectionate bond that is the norm almost everywhere in the world, the bond that females promote?

In fact, as we move into a twenty-first century where constant change will be the norm, it may be that the more open female life-pattern finds women *better* prepared to manage our corporations than men who are products of the current career-driven model. In *American Spirit: Visions of a New Corporate Culture*, Lawrence Miller writes, "The style of corporations is often the macho, quick-draw variety, which is destined for extinction." He encourages women to resist the effort to make them adopt male characteristics in order to move into top corporate positions. In explaining why women must legitimize their more feminine style of management, he declares that the integration of women into corporations should be viewed as "enrichment of the repertoire and talents of human capital."

What Gifted Women Can Do

If you are the parent of a gifted girl, remember that she needs a sense of her own value and power from her earliest years. It is never too early for her to read about or even meet accomplished women. Middle school is not too early to help her discover that any career she wants could be an option, and that taking the most challenging academic programs is a "smart" thing to do. Her intellect must be taken seriously and nourished, at the same time that she learns to accept herself as a woman—through the crucial period of adolescence. And no matter what your own achievements, believe that you can do this. Research has shown that among highly successful women, most cite

their own mothers as powerful role models, whether they were homemakers or had their own careers.

In addition, see to it that your bright daughter receives careful guidance and counseling in her high school and college years. Kevin Kelly at Purdue University has shown that young smart kids, especially if they are female, need to *believe* that they can be successful in the most demanding occupations before they can actually be successful. Ways to encourage this belief include challenging them with the most rigorous academic programs and making sure that they are aware of the women who are already successful in their chosen field. These additional role models are crucial for your daughter's belief in herself. Be sure that she is aware of the importance of mentors and networks in the advancement of her career goals.

A caution: Try not to assume that your daughter is a superkid just because she has brains. Prepare to accept nonconformity and uneven progress in her development. As she matures, help her to avoid the false idea that she must, or must not, have a marriage and a family. Support and actively encourage her to be all that she can be, because the pressure from society to do otherwise is very real. In this way, she will be able to choose what is best for her from among all the options available. There is no ideal way to choose, but over and over in the interviews, one statement appears from those women who have accomplished something great or small with their lives: "I was always told that I could do anything I wanted, if I worked hard enough and I believed in myself." Remember Marie Curie, who achieved two Nobel Prizes and produced two outstanding children.

If you are attempting to deal with a loving relationship with a gifted woman of any age, understand that she needs a great deal of room in which to move around and grow. Especially for a younger woman, the world is an opening place filled with new and delightful opportunities. If you find yourself feeling threatened, perhaps you should consider ending the relationship. It might be better for both of you.

If you are a gifted woman, and you are bored and restless, take the responsibility for your own growth with more meaningful work,

further education, or systematically seeking out other bright women. Reading the work of Kerr, Gilligan, Reis, Silverman, Tavris, Ferguson, and Eccles can widen your perspective and increase your self-esteem. To the degree that you are able, insist that society make room for what you have to offer: competence in your work and the nurturing, creative, life-giving functions which our society needs in positions of authority.

On the employment scene, do not accept, except as a stepping stone, work that does not challenge you to stretch and grow. As the outer barriers of discrimination fall, beware that inner barriers do not keep you from seeking work that you know you can do. Remember that your "different voice" is just that: different, not inferior. Value yourself as an intelligent person. Highly successful women have confirmed that being forthrightly feminine in the business world is an asset if used intelligently. Caring, friendliness, cooperation with others, and intuition were all cited by these women as keys to success.

What does it take to develop a strong gifted grownup who knows who she is and what she can do; who does not let society's attitudes about her sex or her brains deter her; who can decide to take on the enormous challenge of children and career and manage it well; who has the fortitude to work at home with her children and prepare for a later career, if that is what she really likes doing; in short, who has confidence in her own style and who makes choices for herself? It depends on many things. The era in which you were born is one—we know that our younger women have bigger and better chances. It depends on the recognition, acceptance, and encouragement of a loving family—and we have seen how important that can be. It depends on finding work you love and being accepted in that field—and those barriers are falling, slowly. It depends on sorting out the personal decisions: finding the generous, egalitarian marriage; having the strength to go it alone and finding it rich; or, more painfully, being able to walk away from a bond that is stifling. More than anything else, it depends on hanging onto and believing in yourself—all the way.

Chapter Eleven

Young in Mind: The Later Years

Grandmothers are supposed to worry about the grandchildren getting into their knitting—I have to worry about them getting into my dissertation!

62-year-old graduate student

Least attention has been paid to the needs of, and society's need for, the gifted senior citizen . . . those older gifted who may not have made Who's Who *but who can still make a significant contribution to society.*

Ernest Newland, *The Gifted in a Socioeducational Perspective*

The high-powered brain/mind that drives a gifted person's life does not switch to low gear simply because the body ages or some chronological milestone has been reached. The persistence of curiosity, the need for stimulation, and the drive to *do* things does not fade. It cannot be satisfied by a steady diet of bridge, bingo, or bus trips, which well-meaning programs seek to provide. Whether superstars, strivers, or independents, gifted senior citizens must continue, in their own way, to move to the rhythm of the ever-renewing cycle of a gifted life.

True, the steps may move more slowly, and a hearing aid may peek from beneath stylish gray curls, but one can spend an entire afternoon with an older gifted person and never hear the word "retire." In at least two cases, the person who answered the door when I arrived for the interview appeared to be so young that I thought I had come to the

236

wrong house. These people do not behave in terms of endings. What they seem to do at a certain point is simply start on another lifetime.

After a writing and publishing career, Bennett started his own small printing shop and does fine, hand-set type only. After a lifetime of boring jobs, Henriette discovered, in her late fifties, that she loved to help people learn, so she became a tutor for immigrants and prisoners. Denied the chance for higher education in her youth, Emilia took up the study of literature after retiring from the retail clothing business. Discovering running along with everyone else, Lewis entered and won his first marathon at 61. He went on to climb his first mountain at 63.

Always, there are new things to learn; always, there is the endless curiosity, the continuing urge to *do*. The acting career is over, but in study and discussion groups, Rhonda continues her lifelong quest for answers to the Great Questions: "Why are we here? Where are we going?" Mechanical skills were sidetracked, but only sidetracked, as a police career took Liam through traffic duty, managing school safety programs and directing the K-9 Corps in a large city. Along the way, he rebuilt an entire colonial farmhouse and furnished it in period style. After ten years working at the UN, Jenny used the psychology courses she took to enable her to have another career as a counselor.

Some people never bother to pause at all, simply continuing the same career. At 67, Janeen has no intention of giving up her job as editor of a scholarly journal. Helen continues her job as a social worker and has begun doctoral studies at 62. Lewis still teaches history.

As in other age groups, the superstars certainly have been recognized. Musicians from Andrés Segovia to Eubie Blake have performed into their ninth decades. Piaget was still making contributions in psychology in his eighties. Maggie Kuhn, founder of the Gray Panthers, continued to be an advocate for older Americans in her nineties. However, less well-known senior citizens are also making a difference in their families and in society as they enhance the quality of their own lives. As the future arrives at an ever-faster pace and the talents of every person must be utilized, many more gifted senior citizens must have the opportunity to follow the example of the gifted seniors interviewed for this chapter.

Each of these people has had to deal with illness, death, loneliness, broken marriages, and unrealized dreams. For the most part, they have accepted physical aging gracefully, and each has some way of keeping fit. What they have not accepted is the myth that learning and growing become less possible as one ages. These older smart kids have given free rein to their drive to learn and grow and have created for themselves rich and satisfying lives. They seem to validate Terman's connection of good health to giftedness, but knowledge of and belief in your own special capabilities is still the key.

As friends and spouses disappear, these active people spend time with younger generations: children, grandchildren, even much younger friends. Some are partners in happy second marriages. Rather than loneliness, most of them spoke of relishing time alone after the pressures of work and family. All have maintained independent living arrangements. In light of the current emphasis on interest in life as a factor in elderly health, one might speculate that the active brain/mind of a gifted person gives one an edge as old age approaches.

Those gifted grownups who have moved out of the day-to-day routine of full-time employment and look back on their careers with satisfaction find that they did involve variety, stimulation, and the opportunity to design their own environment. They enjoyed moving from one job to another, welcoming challenge and change. One remarks that the only job he ever hated was the stable one: "All predictable, day after day. But I kept it for ten years because I had a family to raise."

A Printing Business

When Bennett ushers a visitor into the small building behind his farmhouse, he looks like a typical suburban retiree, in plaid shirt and tweed jacket. At 75, he moves slowly, "but I haven't been sick since I started this place." The building is filled with hand presses, some of them valuable antiques. "I bought my first little press when I was 12," he smiles. He prints what interests him: books of poetry, local

history. All set in carefully chosen typefaces and lovingly hand printed, they are small works of art.

The shelves around us are lined with the memorabilia of a career in words, in languages from Sanskrit to Norwegian. Bennett has taught classics in a college, taken a degree from the University of Salamanca, had a try at fiction writing and editing small magazines. A six-year period as office manager of a large national magazine was followed by a fascination with hand weaving. "For four years I did hand-woven fabrics for coats and skirts. I finished them in the bathtub and put them out on the lawn to dry. The looms are still upstairs. I was working for an advertising firm when my first wife died. I thought I'd write books to keep busy, but writing is too hard, so I started the press. I do only what interests me, and I make a tidy amount each year."

One has the sense that Bennett has always done what he wanted to do, in his own way. "In school, I used to get into terrible trouble for correcting my teachers, but I don't feel very smart to myself sometimes. The more I read, the more ordinary I feel, and I read a great deal! It helps to keep the languages up. Languages actually get easier the more you learn of them. I have picked up enough Arabic to get along in Morocco; I can get by in Greece. One thing I have learned in recent years about myself is that I like to work alone, to compete with myself to beat my own deadlines. Apprentices (and I have had a few here) sometimes annoy me. I have to stop, slow down, and tell them what to do without hurting their feelings."

Discussing what constitutes a gifted person, Bennett compares a person's knowledge to a ball: "The inside of a ball is what you know. The outside is your contacts with the unknown. An ordinary person is like a golf ball; someone a bit smarter, like a baseball. But the really smart person is like a basketball—and every contact with the unknown is a challenge, of course. The only sin is a closed mind."

Tutoring Immigrants

The arrival of Bennett's second wife, Henriette, interrupts our talk. Tall and elegant, her manner bespeaks the socialite background of

her youth. She is hesitant about being interviewed, claiming that she possesses no special talents, let alone special intelligence. As the conversation progresses, however, the traits of a gifted grownup emerge.

"I only went to high school for two years . . . my parents were always taking us off to Europe. I went to a junior college at 16. I don't really know why they took me. I spent time on probation and felt very stupid. I loathed the social scene. I did two years at Barnard, but I dropped out because it was so impersonal. I got a job as a trilingual [French, German, English] secretary and I liked that. Then I joined the foreign service and worked my way up to clerk of immigration at the embassy in Mexico City. I quit when they told me I would have to agree not to marry if I wished to take exams for higher positions! Can you imagine such a thing now?"

A husband who was always being fired led to a series of secretarial jobs, "supposedly intelligent jobs which bored me to extinction." Divorced and looking for something worthwhile to do, Henriette took a position as a teacher's aide in a poor school in Miami and discovered that she liked to teach. Currently, she works through various social agencies tutoring adults in English. Now she speaks about having, "an Iranian, a Cambodian, a Cuban, and a couple of prisoners. I see myself as giving a chance to someone who never had a chance."

On the subject of wanting to do more and do it faster, she laughs, "Oh yes! I hurl myself into things—things which other people are usually glad to get rid of." An avid reader, Henriette does recordings for the blind in French and German and likes people who "can talk intelligently about politics." A neck problem that causes her to don a special collar at home does not seem to slow her down. "I don't see how some women can stand it dithering around shopping all day when there are so many important things to do!"

Marathons and Mountains

Dithering around is certainly not on Lewis's agenda. He is busy catching up on the athletics he missed as a boy. A former minister

who holds a doctorate in religion, he can speak about a "dissertation with footnotes in Greek and Hebrew," but seems proudest in showing me his medals, won in several marathons, and the scrapbook from his mountain climbing and backpacking expedition in the Rockies two years ago. "I wrote an account of it; I guess I'll give anything a try!"

Some of his stamina is used to commute to a job teaching social studies in a special magnet school in a nearby large city. He runs from the train to his school; his frail-looking figure with a backpack has become a neighborhood fixture. "People speak to me along the way now; I've been doing it for several years." What does he teach? "I try to help students to think better of themselves, regardless of their inherent potential. Our school draws students from the whole spectrum of the urban scene. Some people object to my teaching, but I remain independent. I do political philosophy with the tenth-graders, ethics with the eleventh-, and metaphysics with the seniors. They tell me I am doing what is now called 'affective education.'"

Lewis's future plans include another try at climbing. "After my first trip, I am inclined to say that the Sherpas are the greatest athletes in the world. You know, I don't get to read as much as I'd like, I don't seem to have the time. Sometimes I guess I am a little impatient with others, especially teachers who don't do a good job, but I would never resent being considered an oddball—if you are, you are."

The Great Questions

Rhonda never really considered herself odd, just self-conscious about her lack of reading ability. Today, we might suspect dyslexia from what she describes, but in the early part of the century, she simply used her cleverness to compensate in very creative ways. "I had one or two wonderful teachers; they told me I had a beautiful voice, even when I stumbled." The personality, the talent, the tall good looks, and the voice helped carry her to Broadway and a career on the stage that spanned forty years.

Now she sits, still graceful at 84, in the elegant stone-walled living room of the barn she and her husband remodeled into a house. A

hearing problem is taken care of by a hearing aid. Over the years, she has developed her own strategies and has become an avid reader.

"I have a wonderful life and I know it. I can do readings for fun, study for First Day school [Rhonda is a member of the Society of Friends] and read the books for my discussion group. There is time to relish visits from family and friends, time to do what I want, to please myself." There is even a long-standing marriage. Rhonda's husband is a retired set designer, so they share an interest in the theater. He continues to work in a studio that is part of their home.

A committed worker for peace, Rhonda no longer attends rallies and marches but continues to "support those groups I can with my dollars and my heart." Her voice is full of energy as she says, "You know, the most wonderful aspect of life is that things change. New things become old things, and old things aren't as true as they once were. I feel that we are here to learn all we can about the great questions of human existence."

A Curious Boy

Visiting Liam, the man who answers the door appears too young to have graduated from high school in 1929, with high grades and a scholarship to a technical college. Liam's immigrant mother had no understanding of such things and said to her tall, shy son, "What would a great thing like you do in school? They'd laugh at you!" He explains quietly, as if it were yesterday, "I took the scholarship back the next day and went to work on a farm."

Several years later, a friend told him about the police exam for a large nearby city. It looked interesting, so he took it, even though he was technically two years below the required age of 23. Without explaining, those in charge asked him to take another special test, and at 21 he became a policeman. He is still not sure what the second test proved.

Seven years of traffic duty was "awfully boring," even though he managed one of the city's busiest intersections. Then came the chance to help develop a school safety program. Liam became a public

speaker, visiting schools, turning nursery rhymes into safety slogans so small children could understand them, training kids for the Safety Patrol, a new concept at that time. He can still cite the statistics on reduced deaths and injuries among schoolchildren, which were the results of his program.

Organizing a K-9 division came next, and he still acts as a consultant on dog training. All the while, remodeling work on his farmhouse proceeded, a mechanical challenge always to be met. During this time, Liam was widowed and then remarried. At his so-called retirement, he simply went out and got another job, as maintenance supervisor for an industrial plant. Finally, at 70, he consented to "join Uncle Sam's payroll," and since then, work on the house has continued.

"Since I have been all these things, I have no concept of what I can and can't do. I don't read much. When I do, the boy in me comes out—adventure and sea stories. In my later years I have found more things to understand, though. On a cruise to Mexico, I became fascinated with the motion of the ship. Did you know that the engines run at a constant rpm and to change speed, you change the pitch of the propeller? I was so disappointed that they wouldn't let me in the engine room. Last cruise I was on, I talked them into letting me in the engine room!" The curious boy is indeed evident.

Seeing things faster than others is still a problem. "I have been fighting to get this through my head for fifty years. I want to blow my top and yell, 'Where are your eyes?' at slow people . . . but it's always you who are wrong, you who are called impatient." The edge in Liam's voice as he says this bespeaks countless rounds of holding, or not holding, his tongue. He has "exchanged words" with little old ladies and powerful mayors, recounting these stories with a mixture of impatience and wry humor.

Counseling

A bit more diplomacy was required for success in Jenny's work, but she also appears to relish the outspoken opinion. "I admire people

who live their lives as they see they should." Seated in the shade of the patio of her tiny house in the country, wearing a cotton tunic, her long hair tied back in a ponytail, Jenny's lively blue eyes and outspoken opinions belie her age. The patio adjoins a pool where she swims daily. Devoted to the natural world, she has just returned from a trip to a nature preserve to drop off the raccoon she trapped this week behind her garage. "They are such pests, getting into my garbage, but it would be a shame to kill them."

At 70, she can look back on a series of careers, each of which provided challenge and stimulation. She managed bookstores, sold real estate, managed the entertaining for her second husband, a foreign service officer. When her husband's job took him to New York, she found employment as the head of a hospitality committee for foreign delegations at the United Nations, a post she held for ten years. "I guess I met the whole world," she recalls. Along the way, she had taken enough courses for "probably two graduate degrees; I have no piece of paper that says so, though."

"When my marriage broke up I sought something I could do on my own." Courses in hand analysis and in Jungian analysis have led to her current work as a counselor and hand reader. Always concerned about helping others, she now says, "I think of the local prison as my 'parish.' I try to tell the people I counsel, 'Stretch! Try something different! You can be anything you want; just figure out what that is' . . . that is what I was told as I was growing up."

"Self-acceptance is number one on my list. Tell the truth and accept the consequences of your actions." Jenny admits to still experiencing the "innate restlessness" so common in smart kids of all ages. Boredom? "Oh, no. People enchant me." Stimulation? She answers with a slow, serious smile, "One can be very stimulated by the repetition of spring."

Jenny has maintained enough contacts from her UN days to periodically embark on several months of world travel, staying with old friends as she goes. When I interviewed her she was planning a move to Cape Cod to manage a rental property owned by her daughter. "I always wanted to end my days by the sea," she smiles. "When they

asked me to do this, champagne bubbles went off inside me. I am so excited about this new place!"

Challenge and Change

Will and Daniel have never met, but they serve to illustrate the special qualities of gifted adults which continue into old age, regardless of early background. They spent their formative years on opposite sides of the Atlantic Ocean. Daniel came from a middle-class English family and took his degree at Oxford. Will is a product of a quiet Midwest town and an American university. Their professional paths have not crossed, even though they share the same field, education. Neither one considers himself "retired."

Moving to the rhythm of challenge and change is apparent in both their careers. After several years of teaching in England, Daniel accepted a position in an American college. He taught at several schools, serving as dean at various times. Then he became headmaster of a private secondary school on the East Coast. Along the way, "of course I've always read a lot, and been involved with music, although I don't know it academically. I did lots of drama, light opera, recitals, at least one or two a year.

"I have always lived on the campus wherever I worked. I believe that teaching should take place in a community; this leads to knowledge and to wisdom . . . I think perhaps the British system favors the bright person a bit more, especially in the universities. You are expected to gain broad areas of knowledge outside your field." Currently, Daniel and his wife of many years live in a converted schoolhouse. The rooms are not conventionally placed: the front door opens into a huge kitchen; the living room is in back. Its white walls are lined with paintings and antiques.

Small of build but sprightly and physically fit due to daily swimming, Daniel is currently involved with volunteer work at a nearby retirement community. "So many people don't drive. I have found

that I can be of service in a very simple way because I have a car, and Quakers have always believed in works as well as faith."

In discussing his American career, Will reports, "I guess I changed jobs about every five years. I started out as a classroom teacher, then became a high school counselor, then a principal. I worked as a curriculum director and then as the head of a private school. In the fifties, I had a Ford Foundation grant to visit gifted programs all over the country." He laughs, "I became an 'expert'! Finally I took a position as director of gifted education for a large suburban county in Pennsylvania. I feel very strongly that the things we are giving to children should be those which increase their humanity, not their salary."

Will explains, "What I am doing is called being retired, but I have no intention of letting it be boring. I have had other men ask me, sadly, 'How do you fill your time?'" Will smiles as he reels off a list of the activities that fill his days. He serves as an officer of his state association for the gifted, does volunteer work at a local hospital, and belongs to several literary societies in a nearby city. Widowed and childless himself, he has become a surrogate grandparent to the gifted daughters of the younger man who inherited his job. He laughs as he gestures toward the dollhouse nestled under a table in his elegant living room. "I never explain that. It tickles me to think that someone may wonder if I'm a senile old man who has taken to playing with dolls!"

Daniel and Will are both in their seventies and willing to speculate about the mysteries of life which intrigue them still. "I'm not a psychic enough person; I'm a little too cold and rational," says Daniel. "I'm not highly sensitive, but I am not critical of that approach. I like William James; I'm keen on his comments about life being a struggle, a struggle which should be meaningful . . . choose life rather than death. You know, any bright person must have a streak of the agnostic in them, to take things beyond doubt and partial understanding. I don't think of this as being irreligious."

Will shares Daniel's rather open view about religion, but "I do belong to a church. I meet in a discussion group for ministers. I am the

only layman there. I admire those who believe wholeheartedly and get great comfort from that . . . It is a real dilemma to handle all the levels of experience . . . I still think kids should have some sort of religious background."

Getting to 90

At 91, Emilia is the oldest person I interviewed for this book. We sat in the spacious living room of the Victorian house in which she maintains an apartment. Her widowed daughter spends part of each week with her, and friends help with shopping and errands, but in a very real way, she is on her own. She provides a good example of a gifted person of truly advanced age who has used her "smarts" to create a satisfying life for herself.

To begin, she has very little patience with her peers. "When people get to be my age all they seem to want to talk about is their doctors and soap operas." Emilia would rather spend time with her bright grandchildren. "Their conversations are more stimulating— and with them, I'm allowed to be smart. When I try to talk about serious things with people my age, they just stare at me."

Emilia has been "different" all her life. The middle child of a large immigrant family, she loved school while her siblings resisted it. She was skipped ahead "until my mother put a stop to it. I was too small for the desks!" As was the custom then, she left school at 16 to take a job as a sales clerk, then a secretary, and finally manager of a hotel coffee shop—unusual for her age (21) and the year (1928). Marriage and three children precluded any return to education.

Her salesman husband's job difficulties (he was a gifted man with no patience with slow people) repeatedly led her back to the work world until she decided to have a real career. "I was living the same life as today's young mothers, but it was the 1950s!" Intelligence, drive, and, "let's face it, a crazy kind of *nerve*" culminated in managing a women's clothing store for a national chain. "I was one of only

six women managers in the nation. For twenty years I operated successfully in a man's world. They were sure I would fail; I showed them." She grins. "Not bad for a high school dropout. They tell me that now that same job requires a college degree!"

Widowed at 46, Emilia finished raising her third daughter and retired at 62. Determined to "catch up on what I missed," she borrowed textbooks from the daughter who was a teacher and shared reading projects with her college-age grandchildren. They watched as she discovered e. e. cummings, then Thoreau—"How could I have lived this long and not known about *him?*"

Sometimes, the results of this drive to learn were hilarious. The tenacity of a smart kid who wants to learn something is illustrated in what happened when her daughter innocently presented her with a copy of Henry James's *Wings of the Dove.* Momentarily taken aback by the complexity of James's style, she demanded, "What have you done to me? I can't put this down! I must understand this man's style because I feel there is something wonderful here." She then proceeded through two readings of the novel in order to be sure she got it all.

With the freedom of retirement, she traveled, had an active social life, and even experienced a brief second marriage. She advises tersely, "Never get married because you are lonely." Striking out on her own in her seventies, she redecorated a new apartment and took up designing afghans, producing original ones for most of her extended family. She also did what many senior citizens do, and renewed ties with siblings and her oldest daughter. Death took the siblings, one by one, and it also took her daughter, a cancer victim at 49. A much-loved son-in-law followed in a traffic accident. Emilia describes her method for dealing with life's tragedies. "I lay there in bed and said to myself, 'If I get out of this bed, I will have to go on with my life.' I took a very long time to decide to get up."

The sensitivity and empathy of a gifted person is illustrated in Emilia's place as the family sounding board. Children, grandchildren, great-grandchildren, nieces, and nephews—all know that they can unload on "Aunt Emilia." But as one of them

warns, "You'd better be prepared for the truth. She may sympathize and cry with you, but if she thinks you need it, she will read you the riot act."

On the process of physical aging Emilia is blunt. "I hate getting old! But you have to accept it, and slow down to preserve your health. Be active but don't push yourself. Eat right. I still cook for myself every day. I take a short walk, but I always take my cane. If the weather is bad, I walk ten times the length of my apartment. Boy, is that boring!" She has survived a broken ankle and two cataract operations by doing exactly as one doctor said and by refusing to continue treatment with another, who "treated me like a senile old lady and refused to answer my questions!"

Loneliness cannot be denied, but Emilia copes with it in typical gifted grownup fashion: she finds younger friends. Currently, she spends time with a photographer in her thirties. These two women find each other interesting and spend hours in satisfying conversation. Long phone calls from her adult grandchildren are a special treat. "We always laugh a lot. I guess that's why they call."

She has also taken up writing. A journal-keeper for a number of years, Emilia has attended a week-long writers' conference with her daughter for the past two years and now wants to write a mystery novel. She will pass up the conference this year because she has an offer of an extended vacation on the northern coast of Maine. "I have never been there. It will be interesting to see."

Emilia has used her drive and intelligence to cope with the inevitable consequences of aging. She gets help with chores and shopping, makes careful selection of food to keep up nutrition, takes regular exercise to stimulate mind and body, has reading, writing, friendships, and travel to keep learning something new, and as she says, "laughing—lots of laughing." Visitors to this spacious Victorian living room can expect to be asked about their views on current issues, especially as they pertain to women. "We women have always been able to run the world. It's time we got credit for it." They will also likely hear, sometime during the visit, Emilia's favorite questions: "What have you been reading?" "How does that work?" "Why

do you suppose people are so dumb? If I can figure it out, anybody can" and "How's your love life?"

What Senior Citizens Can Do

The wide range of activities seen in this chapter confirm that, whether high school dropouts or professionals with advanced degrees, bright senior citizens continue to have both the capacity and the desire to learn and grow. The need for mental stimulation does not diminish as the body ages. Can a senior citizen center help? One retired gifted man belonged to a group that raised funds by selling pastries. He presided over their marathon baking sessions and organized a delivery system to local stores. He seemed to be having a very good time using his skills. However, like so many other things which satisfy a majority of people, programs like these may fall short in satisfying a gifted senior's very real need for intellectual companionship.

Recognizing this, caring families can help. As gifts, elderly parents could be treated to theater tickets and the transportation older persons often require. A great-aunt living on a tiny budget could be sent a subscription to a journal such as *American Scholar*. Renting a wheelchair to make possible a tour of a museum or gallery, buying two copies of a book and asking a gifted relative to read and discuss it with you—these encourage the older person to follow the instinct for learning. An entire family could pool resources to provide a computer and a window on the world. Providing stimulating conversation, transportation to cultural activities, recognition of valuable skills, and encouragement to try new activities will not only enhance the dignity of the elderly gifted, but can prevent these valuable citizens from becoming isolated. Often, their contemporaries may very well have ceased being active.

Communities and social agencies need to become aware of the valuable resource that exists in older gifted adults. They can serve society as they satisfy their own needs, as the people in this

chapter have done. For example, the extensive use of older gifted persons as mentors for gifted students could add a vital element to hard-pressed educational programs. Grandparenting programs, if keyed to the special abilities of certain individuals, could provide the crucial element of recognition that a tiny smart kid may require. The larger degree of empathy found in many gifted persons could be combined with their capacity to learn quickly and allow them to be trained as counselors in the criminal justice and mental health fields. By the simple act of engaging an older gifted person in intelligent conversation, any individual may tap into a wellspring of not only accumulated wisdom, but new knowledge as well.

Notice that those interviewed for this chapter seem to have struck out on their own for new experiences. They organized reading groups, volunteered to help at the hospital, took courses, and climbed mountains. If you are an older gifted grownup, take one of the people in this chapter as your model and do not let anyone deter you from following your interests. Whether it is physical activity, catching up on your education, or helping others, you have much to offer, much to learn. Increasingly, college and university campuses offer specially designed noncredit courses and lectures where you can meet other gifted seniors. Many communities have transportation services for older people, so don't stay at home. If you have serious physical limitations, make creative use of the telephone and the mail. If you can afford it, acquiring a home computer could transform your life! If you can travel, look into the Elderhostel program, which is both challenging and inexpensive.

As was said in the beginning of this chapter, gifted grownups in their seventh, eighth, and ninth decades do not operate in terms of endings. And just as one can spend a whole afternoon without talking about retirement, one can interview all of these people without talking about dying. They appear to be too busy to worry about it!

The speculation about death that follows on page 252 seems to embody many of the qualities of a typical gifted mind: the curiosity, the sensitivity, the desire to *know* right up to the final second of consciousness. However, the person who composed it is only in her fifties.

Final Observation*

I want to watch when I die,
to be aware when death comes,
to be there with senses sharp enough
to test the air,
to hear its approach,
mouth open to taste and see
if it has taste and how much.
Fingers wide, palms up and out to
catch and feel the shape, and hold it back
just a little more, to be sure
nothing's missed:
does time slow, or just the heartbeat?
Does thinking become thin and crisp,
drawn taut and fine,
or does it spread wider,
lose its edges, melt,
become reflecting surface?
I want no unsuspected nuance
to pass unobserved.
I want a clear look as it comes,
to watch and FEEL as I'm leaving,
this single
chance to understand.

* Used with permission of Pamela M. Perkins-Frederick.

Chapter Twelve

The Value of the Gift

*A great gift is futile when its owner is not appropriately connected
to the world.*
Howard Gruber, *Giftedness and Moral Responsibility*

*Especially must we learn how to transcend our foolish tendency to
let our compassion for the weak generate hatred for the strong.*
Abraham Maslow, *The Psychology of Being*

I conducted almost three hundred hours of interviews in
writing this book, in living rooms, in offices, under trees, in restau-
rants. As I realized the depth and variety of what these nonfamous,
everyday people have to offer, listened to their accounts of misunderstanding, rejection, and frustration, shared in their stories of success
and communication, my own view was enlarged dramatically. A new
perspective on my own life emerged, as well as new insights into my
job, American society, and its leaders. It is my hope that readers have
also experienced some of these new insights and may be developing
ideas for changing things.

This study of gifted people has helped me to acknowledge and appreciate the value of my own gifts, as well as the gifts around me. I
have been able to view my own history with new eyes, seeing where
my parents and I fit into the dynamic that created our extended family of gifted people. My grandparents were immigrants making their

way in a new world; their successes, and their failures, are better understood in light of my research.

Because they have been a part of this project, I have seen my own four children acquire new ways of looking at themselves and other adults. This has been helpful to them in personal and professional relationships. My children's spouses are more easily understood as I view them in their variety as gifted grownups.

And I have seen how both the interviews and the research helped me to reorient my professional life. I came to understand more completely that if I wished to accomplish things, my drive for "more and faster" had to be tempered by what a given situation would tolerate. I can now judge more accurately how to deal with authority figures, when to push those who are bright, when to move cautiously so as not to be a threat or a nuisance.

The same is true of social relations. Those moments of "connection" described by Pearl are no longer so disconcerting. I have learned to accept and enjoy them, fleeting though they may be. I have also come to admit that I may have a similar effect on others, and with that comes a serious responsibility.

The ability to spot gifted persons has become very helpful in judging people in public life. Watching and listening beyond the sound bites can allow one to sort out candidates for office based on how intelligent they seem to be. Can giftedness sometimes explain the conduct of national and international leaders? Think about how you might apply the information in this book to the president, the vice president, the first lady, your senator or congressional representative, your mayor, or the president of your school board.

Before I began the research for this book, I knew certain things were true about gifted people. What I didn't expect was that no matter where I looked—education, gifted studies, general psychology, industrial relations, business, social criticism—all the voices would say the same thing about the needs of the twenty-first century and the needs of highly intelligent people. A management consultant warns that a whole new civilization—superindustrialism—will implode in our midst in the next forty years, and that its chief characteristic will be its speed. At the same time, an educational researcher

tells us that gifted people are complex, systems thinkers who can move rapidly in the face of change. A variety of writers note that throughout history, successful civilizations are the ones which have known how to honor and use their gifted people, while humorist (and gifted advocate) Steve Allen criticizes us for the way we treat gifted people in our society. And industrial psychologist David Willings warns us that "the gifted are a significant factor, if not THE significant factor in the national economy of any country and . . . most of the countries with which I am acquainted are recklessly squandering this resource." No one was putting these voices together and allowing them to speak to a wider audience, and this has been one of the major reasons for writing this book.

Suggestions for the commitment of large resources for the gifted often provoke the question, "Isn't that elitist?" Does acknowledging that people are different cause them to conclude that they are better than other human beings? Not the people who were interviewed for this book. One of the most frequently mentioned answers to the question of what gifted grownups should remember about themselves was that they are not better than other people. It was Thomas Jefferson who reminded us that nothing is more unequal than the equal treatment of those with unequal capabilities.

Think about how much of our national energy is focused on the production of talented athletes. We make progress physically because of recognition of talent, careful coaching, training, and support for this effort by society with both money and fame. Where are we in relation to our intellectual resources: great cries and lamentations about the state of education in our nation. Can there be any connection between this state of affairs and the recognition, coaching, training, and respecting of the "brain team" in any given school or workplace?

In attempting to dramatize the value of our gifted citizens, other writers have described the works of art not created, the human problems not solved, the inventions never developed. Consider the following scenario: He or she is out there somewhere—the person who will put together all the pieces of the puzzle and give us, finally, the insight that will synthesize our knowledge into a definitive cure for AIDS. It would be comforting to think that he or she is moving

through one of the ideal school programs scattered around the country, or working happily for an open and innovative employer, with that lifesaving idea ticking away. But what if he is working in a stifling environment where odd suggestions are punished, possibly by dismissal? What if that key is kicking around loose in the racing brain of a restless tenth-grade girl who has just been told by her threatened biology teacher to stop asking such strange questions and stick to the lesson for the day?

By encouraging the gifted people in our world, we benefit the rest of society. Can't we free all women from the career-driven success model and honor their function as nurturing parents? Won't all students rise higher in educational systems which encourage and allow for movement at one's own intellectual pace? If all workers who want to can work in systems that let the brightest forge ahead, why not allow for the most creative and the most practical ones to find an audience for their solutions to problems in manufacturing and social service? And don't we enrich the lives all older citizens by recognizing that age is no barrier to creative intellectual production?

Psychologist Abraham Maslow put it bluntly: "We have come to the point in biological history where we are now responsible for our own evolution." If you believe, as many do, that humanity is continually evolving to greater levels of accomplishment and development, then at least one tentative conclusion is possible. Wherever the race is going, the gifted grownups are probably on the leading edge. Should we not do all that we can to free them to run on ahead?

Resources and Recommended Readings

You will quickly note that many of these books are directed toward gifted children—another indication that not enough attention is being paid to the problems of gifted adults. However, you can gain much insight into your life by acquiring a background on the early life of gifted grownups. Some of these selections are fun; some are technical, but all are worth the effort. New books are appearing all the time; these are a small sampling of what is available if you are willing to look.

Advanced Development: A Journal on Adult Giftedness. Published annually by the Institute for the Study of Advanced Development (see organizations).

An international forum for the exploration of new knowledge about gifted people.

Alvino, James, and the editors of *Gifted Children Monthly: A Parent's Guide to Raising a Gifted Child*. New York: Ballantine Books, Inc., 1996.

Comprehensive and practical, this book is notable for specifics: lists of organizations, publications, and an extensive bibliography of books for gifted kids to read.

Canfield, Jack, and Harold Wells. *100 Ways to Enhance Self-Concept in the Classroom: A Handbook for Teachers, Counselors and Group Leaders.* Boston: Allyn and Bacon, Inc., 1994.

Can be adapted for home or school; helpful for communication skills.

Clark, Barbara. *Growing Up Gifted: Developing the Potential of Children at Home and at School,* 5th edition. Englewood Cliffs, NJ: Prentice-Hall, Inc., 1997.

A comprehensive book on giftedness, written by a parent and educator; contains directory of tests and how they should be used.

Csikszentmihalyi, Mihalyi, Kevin Rathunde, and Samuel Whalen. *Talented Teenagers: The Roots of Success and Failure.* Cambridge: Cambridge University Press, 1983.

Directed by the author of *Flow*, this report charts the development of gifted adolescents through high school in an effort to understand how personality, habit, and motivation help to keep them involved in their area of talent. A provocative look back at your own adolescence, or forward with your children.

Delisle, James. *Gifted Children Speak Out: Hundreds of Kids 6–13, Talk About School, Friends, Their Families and the Future.* Minneapolis: Free Spirit Publishing Co., 1988.

If you are a parent or teacher, you may be uncomfortable with what you hear, but there is much wisdom in what these children say so honestly.

Delisle, James, and Judy Galbraith. *The Gifted Kid's Survival Guide, II.* Minneapolis: Free Spirit Publishing Co., 1988.

Designed for kids 11 to 18, this sequel to the original ego-boosting guide is very helpful for opening dialogue about problems.

Directory of Centers for Older Learners. American Association of Retired Persons: Stock No. d13973: Fulfillment 233, P.O. Box 2400, Long Beach, CA 90801.

There are many opportunities out there. Don't stay at home!

Eby, Judy, and John F. Smutny. *A Thoughtful Overview of Gifted Education.* New York: Longman Publishing Group, 1990.

If you are a confused as well as concerned parent, this will give you up-to-date information. Don't overlook the older books, however; they contain much in the way of consolation and common sense.

Engel, Joel. *It's OK to Be Gifted and Talented!* New York: Tom Doherty Associates, 1989.

This book explains, through brief stories that offer solutions, some of the problems faced by intellectually gifted or artistically talented children. It also offers advice to parents on how to use these stories to help their children.

Galbraith, Judy. *The Gifted Kid's Survival Guide*. Minneapolis: Free Spirit Publishing Co., 1987.

There are two versions of this ego-boosting guide. This one is for kids under 10. *Note:* Free Spirit's catalogue is an excellent source for parents and educators.

Gallagher, James, and Shelagh Gallagher. *Teaching the Gifted Child*, 4th edition. Boston: Allyn and Bacon, 1994.

The classic in the field, it helps to make school more understandable. This new edition by Gallagher and his daughter is useful for anyone who wants to understand and improve gifted education.

Gifted Child Quarterly, 1701 L Street, NW, Suite 550, Washington, DC 20036.

This research-based publication is published by the National Association for Gifted Children (see helpful organizations) and is a good source for keeping up with the latest developments in gifted education. It can be found in college libraries, and back issues from the last several years can be enlightening for a smart kid of any age.

Halstead, Judith Wynn. *Some of My Best Friends Are Books*. Scottsdale, AZ: Gifted Psychology Press, 1995.

A guide to over 300 appropriate titles for high-ability children, suiting age, ability, and experience level.

Heacox, D. *Up From Underachievement: How Teachers, Students and Parents Can Work Together to Promote Student Success*. Minneapolis: Free Spirit Publishing, 1991.

Common sense advice for dealing with one of the most agonizing problems the parent of a gifted child can face.

Kerr, Barbara. *Smart Girls: A New Psychology of Girls, Women and Giftedness*, 3rd edition. Scottsdale, AZ: Gifted Psychology Press, 1997.

Essential for parents and daughters. Provides new insights for adult women about themselves. Read it with another woman.

McLeod, John. *Fostering Academic Excellence*. Oxford: Pergamon Press, 1989.

A thoughtful discussion of a sometimes controversial idea.

Miller, Alice. *The Drama of the Gifted Child: The Search for the True Self*, 3rd edition. New York: Basic Books, 1996.

An important book for any adult to read. The author is a noted European psychologist.

Olenchak, Richard. *They Say My Kid's Gifted, Now What?* Washington, DC: National Association for Gifted Children, 1996.

An easy-to-use guide to dealing with educational bureaucracy.

Piirto, Jane. *Talented Children and Adults: Their Development and Education*, 2nd edition. Columbus, OH: Charles E. Merrill Publishing Co., 1998.

Although primarily designed as a text for teachers, this volume is a good source for information about research in cognition.

Reis, Sally. *Work Left Undone: Choices and Compromises of Gifted Females*. Mansfield Center, CT: Creative Learning Press, 1998.

The newest work by a principal researcher for the National Research Center for Gifted Education and Talent Development, and the president-elect of the National Association for Gifted Children. Her work on gifted females is outstanding.

Schwartz, Lita L. *Why Give Gifts to the Gifted?* New York: Corwin Press, 1994.

If you are arguing to change things, this will give you much ammunition.

Takacs, Carol Addison. *Enjoy Your Gifted Child*. Syracuse, NY: Syracuse University Press, 1986.

Written by a university professor who is also a mother and a grandmother, it offers much practical advice for carrying out the title.

Torrance, Paul E. *Education and the Creative Potential*. University of Minnesota Press (available through Georgia Studies in Creative Behavior, 183 Cherokee Ave., Athens, GA 30606).

—*Multicultural Mentoring of the Gifted and Talented*. Waco, TX: Prufrock Press.

—*Why Fly? A Philosophy of Creativity*. Greenwich, CT: Ablex Publishing Corporation.

This is a small sample of what "The Creativity Man" has contributed to our knowledge of human learning. (These are in print as of 1998.)

> Vail, Priscilla. *Smart Kids With School Problems: Things to Know and Ways to Help.* New York: E.P. Dutton, 1989.

The title says it all; a marvel of a book if you have a gifted child of any age who is struggling with school.

> Webb, James T., Elizabeth Meckstroth, and Stephanie Tolan. *Guiding the Gifted Child.* Columbus, OH: Ohio Psychology Publishing Co., 1982.

A down-to-earth guide; answers many commonly asked questions.

> Whitmore, Joanne Rand, and C. June Maker. *Intellectual Giftedness and Disabled Persons.* Rockville, MD: Aspen Publications, 1985.

Case histories and helpful advice from two outstanding advocates for the gifted. This book deals with *adults* as well as children.

> Winner, Ellen. *Gifted Children: Myths and Realities.* New York: Basic Books, 1996.

Especially helpful if you have a highly gifted child, or if you are such a person.

Important Sources out of Print

The following are classics in the field, and well worth a search through interlibrary loan:

> Feldman, Ruth Duskin. *What Ever Happened to the Quiz Kids? The Perils and Profits of Growing Up Gifted.* Chicago: Chicago Review Press, 1982.

A real quiz kid tracked down and interviewed 85 of her peers. Interesting case histories.

> Greenlaw, M. Jean. *Educating the Gifted: A Sourcebook.* Chicago: American Library Association, 1988.

Good information for organizing parent groups.

> Graue, Elizabeth Brownrigg. *Is Your Child Gifted?* San Diego, CA: Oak Tree Publications, Inc., 1982.

Filled with helpful advice and specific information; upbeat and very readable.

Grost, Audrey. *Genius in Residence.* New York: Prentice-Hall, Inc., 1970.
An inside look, honestly told, of how a family adjusted as their math prodigy son grew up.

Moore, Linda P. *Does This Mean My Kid's a Genius?* New York: McGraw-Hill Book Co., 1981.
A wise and wonderfully funny book about one parent's struggle to find the best for her son; good background material.

Vail, Priscilla. *The World of the Gifted Child.* New York: Walker and Co., 1979.
Focused on the child from the point of view of a parent.

Whitmore, Joanne Rand. *Conflict, Giftedness and Underachievement.* Boston: Allyn and Bacon, Inc., 1982.
A must if you have a child experiencing difficulty in the early grades, or if you were such a child yourself.

Organizations

Though these sources may be widely scattered geographically, contact with them can often lead to help closer to home. Currently, a large number of colleges and universities offer special programs for younger gifted students and for senior citizens who want to continue learning. Check with those institutions that are within reach.

American MENSA, Ltd.
2626 East 14th Street
Brooklyn, NY 11235

Center for the Gifted, Ltd.
3324 Midvale Ave.
Philadelphia, PA 19129

Council for Exceptional
   Children
1920 Association Drive
Reston, VA 22091

Council of State Directors of
   Programs for the Gifted
Suite 526, Hall of the States
444 N. Capitol St., NW
Washington, DC 20001

ELDERHOSTEL
75 Federal Street
3rd floor
Boston, MA 02112

Gifted Advocacy Information Network, Inc. (GAIN)
225 West Orchard Lane
Phoenix, AZ 85021

Institute for the Study of Advanced Development
1452 Marion St.
Denver, CO 80218

National Association for Creative Children and Adults
8080 Spring Valley Drive
Cincinnati, OH 45236

National Association for Gifted Children*
1707 L Street, NW
Suite 550
Washington, DC 20036

Supporting the Emotional Needs of the Gifted (SENG)
405 White Hall
Kent State University
Kent, OH 44242

And on the Internet:

GT World†
www.gtworld.org

*(A directory of graduate degree programs in gifted and talented education can be ordered from the association.)
†This is an online support community for gifted and talented individuals. It is intended for anyone interested in sharing the issues involved in being a gifted adult and who agrees to abide by rules for promoting a civilized environment.

Notes

Chapter One: What Makes You Gifted?

Page 5: Lewis M. Terman, "The Discovery and Encouragement of Individual Talent," *American Psychologist* (June 1954): 221–230.

Page 5: Leta Hollingworth, *Children above 180 IQ* (Chicago: World Book Co., 1942); Dean K. Simonton, *Genius, Creativity and Leadership* (Cambridge: Harvard University Press, 1984), 58.

Page 5: Lewis M. Terman, "The Discovery and Encouragement of Individual Talent,"*American Psychologist*(June 1954): 221–230.

Page 5: George T. Betts and Maureen Neihart, "Profiles of the Gifted and Talented," *Gifted Child Quarterly* 32, no. 2 (1988).

Page 6: Elizabeth Drews, "The Four Faces of Able Adolescents," *Saturday Review*, 46 (1963): 69.

Page 8: Ibid.

Page 10: Linda P. Moore, *Does This Mean My Kid's a Genius?* (New York: McGraw-Hill, 1981), xi.

Page 12: Dorothy Sisk, "What If Your Child Is Gifted?" in *Readings in Gifted and Talented Education* (Guilford, Conn.: Special Learning Corp., 1978), 52.

Page 13: Dean K. Simonton, *Genius, Creativity and Leadership* (Cambridge: Harvard University Press, 1984), 58.

Page 13: Michael Piechowski, "Developmental Potential," in *New Voices in Counseling the Gifted*, eds. Nicholas Colangelo and Ronald T. Zaffran (Dubuque: Kendall/Hunt Publishing Co., 1979), 29–31.

Page 14: Michael Piechowski, "Developmental Potential," in *New Voices in Counseling the Gifted*, eds. Nicholas Colangelo and Robert T. Zaffran (Dubuque: Kendall/Hunt Publishing Co., 1979), 29.

Page 14: M. Kay Ogburn and Nicholas Colangelo, "Giftedness as Multi-Level Potential: A Clinical Example," in *New Voices in Counseling the Gifted* (Dubuque: Kendall/Hunt Publishing Co., 1979), 165–186.

Page 14: James Gallagher, *Teaching Gifted Students* (Boston: Allyn & Bacon, 1965), 18.

Page 14: J. W. Getzels and P. W. Jackson, "The Meaning of Giftedness—An Examination of an Expanding Concept," in *Psychology and Education of the Gifted*, eds. Walter Barbe and Joseph Renzulli (New York: Irvington Publishers, Inc., 1975); Deanna H. Berg and William D. DiMartini, "Uses of Humor in Counseling the Gifted," in *New Voices in Counseling the Gifted* (Dubuque: Kendall/Hunt Publishing Co., 1979).

Page 15: Paul Torrance, "Creative Teaching Makes a Difference," in *Psychology and Education of the Gifted* (New York: Irvington Publishers, Inc., 1975), 48–49.

Page 16: Mary Racamora, "Counseling Issues with Recognized and Unrecognized Creatively Gifted Adults," *Advanced Development* 4 (1992): 147–161.

Page 16: Joseph Khatena, "The Gifted Child in the U.S. and Abroad," in *Readings in Gifted and Talented Education* (Guilford, Conn.: Special Learning Corp., 1978), 54.

Page 17: Raymond E. Francher, *The Intelligence Men: Makers of the IQ Controversy* (New York: W.W. Norton & Co., 1985), 104.

Page 18: Ibid., p. 77; Barbara Clark, *Growing Up Gifted* (Columbus: Charles E. Merrill Publishing Co., 1983), 8.

Page 19: Abraham Tannenbaum, "Pre-Sputnik and Post-Watergate Concern about the Gifted," in *Psychology and Education of the Gifted* (New York: Irvington Publishers, Inc., 1975), 9.

Page 19: Daniel Coleman, "1528 Geniuses and How They Grew," *Psychology Today* (February 1980): 54.

Page 20: John J. Phillips, *The Origins of Intellect: Piaget's Theory* (San Francisco: W.H. Freeman and Company, 1975).

Page 20: J. P. Guilford, *Way Beyond the IQ* (Buffalo: The Creative Education Foundation Inc., 1977), 23.

Page 20: J. W. Getzels and P. W. Jackson, "The Meaning of Giftedness—An Examination of an Expanding Concept," in *Psychology and Education of the Gifted* (New York: Irvington Publishers, Inc., 1975), 49.

Page 21: Paul Torrance, "Emerging Concepts of Giftedness," in *Psychology and Education of the Gifted* (New York: Irvington Publishers, Inc., 1975), 49.

Page 21: Barbara Clark, *Growing Up Gifted* (Columbus: Charles E. Merrill Publishing Co., 1983), 16.

Page 21: Howard Gardner, *Frames of Mind: The Theory of Multiple Intelligences* (New York: Basic Books, 1993).

Page 22: Barbara Clark, *Growing Up Gifted* (Columbus: Charles E. Merrill Publishing Co., 1983), 2.

Page 22: Paul Torrance, "Emerging Concepts of Giftedness," in *Psychology and Education of the Gifted* (New York: Irvington Publishers, Inc., 1975), 50.

Page 23: Donald Sellin and Jack W. Birch, *Psychoeducational Development of Gifted and Talented Learners* (Rockville, Md.: Aspen Systems Corporation, 1981), 37.

Page 23: Richard Bach, *Illusions* (New York: Delacorte Press, 1982), 51.

Page 23: Ernest T. Newland, *The Gifted in a Socioeducational Perspective* (Englewood Cliffs, N.J.: Prentice-Hall, 1976), 71.

Page 24: Judy W. Eby and Joan F. Smutny, *A Thoughtful Overview of Gifted Education* (New York: Longman, 1990), 119.

Page 24: Joanne Rand Whitmore and C. June Maker, *Intellectual Giftedness in Disabled Persons* (Rockville, Md.: Aspen Publications, 1985).

Chapter Two: Inside the Gifted Brain/Mind

Page 25: Barbara Clark, *Growing Up Gifted* (Columbus: Charles E. Merrill Publishing Co., 1983), 21.

Page 26: David Bohm, "Physics and Perception," in *The Special Theory of Relativity* (New York: W.A. Benjamin, Inc., 1965); Richard Restak, *The Brain: The Last Frontier* (Garden City, N.Y.: Doubleday, 1979).

Page 26: David Bohm, "Physics and Perception," in *The Special Theory of Relativity* (New York: W.A. Benjamin, Inc., 1965), 198.

Page 27: Barbara Clark, *Growing Up Gifted* (Columbus: Charles E. Merrill Publishing Co., 1983), 30.

Page 27: Lynn Waterhouse, "Speculation on the Neuroanatomical Substrate of Special Talents," in *The Exceptional Brain: Neuropsychology of*

Talent and Special Abilities (New York: Guilford Press, 1988), 509; Michael Hutchinson, *Megabrain* (New York: Beech Tree Books, 1986), 39; Barbara Clark, *Growing Up Gifted* (Columbus: Charles E. Merrill Publishing Co., 1983), 30.

Page 29: Hutchinson, 177.

Page 29: Richard Restak, *The Brain: The Last Frontier* (Garden City, N.Y.: Doubleday, 1979), 23.

Page 29: Timothy Teylor, *A Primer of Psychobiology: Brain and Behavior* (New York: W.H. Freeman and Co., 1984), 55.

Page 29: Donald Lindsley, "Common Factors in Sensory Deprivation, Sensory Distortion and Sensory Overload," in *Sensory Deprivation* (Cambridge: Harvard University Press, 1961), 176.

Page 30: Barbara Clark, *Optimizing Learning* (Columbus: Charles E. Merrill Publishing Co., 1986), 112.

Page 30: Michael Hunt, *The Universe Within* (New York: Simon & Schuster, 1982), 89.

Page 30: Deane McGuiness and Karl H. Pribram, in *The Brain and Psychology*, ed. M. C. Whittrock (New York: Academic Press, 1980), 122.

Page 31: David Bohm, "Physics and Perception," in *The Special Theory of Relativity* (New York: W.A. Benjamin, Inc., 1965), 212.

Page 31: Ibid., 46

Page 31: Philip Solomon et al., eds., *Sensory Deprivation* (Cambridge: Harvard University Press, 1961), 235.

Page 31: Ibid., 237.

Page 31: Ibid., 229.

Page 32: Ibid., 199.

Page 33: Barbara Clark, *Growing Up Gifted* (Columbus: Charles E. Merrill Publishing Co., 1983); Richard Restak, *The Brain: The Last Frontier* (Garden City, N.Y.: Doubleday, 1979).

Page 33: Carolyn Trevarthan, "Functional Organization of the Human Brain," in *The Brain and Psychology* (New York: Academic Press, 1980), 69; Richard Thompson et al., "An Introduction to the Anatomy, Physiology and Chemistry of the Brain," in *The Brain and Psychology* (New York: Academic Press, 1980), 26.

Page 33: Barbara Clark, speech to the annual conference of the Pennsylvania Association for Gifted Education, Philadelphia, April 1987.

Page 34: Michael Hutchinson, *Megabrain* (New York: Beech Tree Press, 1986).

Page 34: Barbara Clark, speech to the annual conference of the Pennsylvania Association for Gifted Education, Philadelphia, April 1987.

Page 34: Timothy Teylor, in *Growing Up Gifted* (Columbus: Charles E. Merrill Publishing Co., 1983), 31.

Chapter Three: In Hiding

Page 36: Gail Sheehy, *Passages* (New York: E.P. Dutton and Co., 1974), 35.

Page 37: Abraham Maslow, *Toward a Psychology of Being* (New York: VanNostrand Rheinhold Co., 1968), 51.

Page 37: Barbara Clark, *Growing Up Gifted* (Columbus: Charles E. Merrill Publishing Co., 1984), 3.

Page 45: Walter Shiras, "In Hiding." in *Great Science Fiction Stories* (New York: Dell Publishing Company, Inc., 1964).

Chapter Four: The Gifted Family

Page 52: James Webb, personal communication, 1984.

Page 56: Marshall P. Sanborn, "Working with Parents," in *New Voices in Counseling the Gifted* (Dubuque: Kendall/Hunt Publishing, 1979), 396.

Page 56: Dewey G. Cornell and Ingrid W. Grossberg, "Family Environment and Personality Adjustment in Gifted Program Children," *Gifted Child Quarterly* 31, no. 2 (1987), 59.

Page 62: Alice Miller, *The Drama of the Gifted Child* (New York: Basic Books, 1981), 97.

Chapter Five: School: Hard Times, Easy As

Page 74: William Saroyan, *Places Where I've Done Time* (New York: Praeger Publishers, 1972), 33.

Page 74: Joanne Rand Whitmore, *Conflict, Giftedness and Underachievement* (Boston: Allyn & Bacon, 1980), 3.

Page 74: Victor Goertzel and Mildred Goertzel, *Cradles of Eminence* (Boston: Little, Brown and Co., 1962).

Page 74: George T. Betts, "Development of the Emotional and Social Needs of Gifted Individuals," *Journal of Counseling and Development*, 64 (1986), 587.

Page 74: Paul Witty, "The Education of the Gifted and Creative in the USA," in *Psychology and Education of the Gifted* (New York: Irvington Publishers, Inc., 1975), 40.

Page 74: June Cox, Neil Daniel, and Bruce Boston, "A Study of MacArthur Fellows," for *Sid W. Richardson Foundation of Texas* (Austin: University of Texas Press, 1985).

Page 81: Nicholas Colangelo and Ronald T. Zaffran, *New Voices in Counseling the Gifted* (Dubuque: Kendall/Hunt Publishing Co., 1979), 90.

Page 82: Ernest T. Newland, *The Gifted in a Socioeducational Perspective* (Englewood Cliffs, N.J.: Prentice-Hall, 1976), 88.

Page 92: Robert J. Havighurst, "Conditions Productive of Superior Children" in *The Intellectually Gifted* (New York: Grune and Stratton, 1976), 261.

Page 92: A Nation at Risk: National Commission on Excellence in Education (Washington, D.C.: U.S. Government Printing Office, 1983), np; *National Excellence: A Case for Developing America's Talents* (Washington, D.C.: U.S. Government Printing Office, 1993).

Page 93: np.

Page 93: "Carnegie Report Describes Teachers for Twenty-First Century," *The New York Times* (May 16, 1986), 17.

Page 93: Lynn Fox and Jerilene Washington, "Programs for the Gifted and Talented: Past, Present and Future," in *The Gifted and Talented: Developmental Perspectives* (Washington, D.C.: American Psychological Association, 1985), 214.

Page 95: M. Jean Greenlaw, *Educating the Gifted: A Sourcebook* (Chicago: American Library Association, 1988), 421.

Page 97: John Feldhusen and Sidney M. Moon, "Grouping Gifted Students: Issues and Concerns," *Gifted Child Quarterly* 36, no. 2 (1992).

Page 98: John Feldhusen, ed., *Toward Excellence in Gifted Education* (Denver: Love Publishing Co., 1985), 119.

Page 100: Julian Stanley and Ann M. McGill, "More about Young Entrants to College: How Did They Fare?" *Gifted Child Quarterly* 30, no. 2 (1986), np.

Page 100: Linda Brady and Camilla Benbow, "Acceleration Strategies: How Effective Are They for the Gifted?" *Gifted Child Quarterly* 31, no. 3 (1987), 105; Paul M. Jonas, "A Fifty-Year Follow-up of Terman's Youngest College Students and IQ-Matched Age Mates," *Gifted Child Quarterly* 31, no. 2 (1987), 55.

Page 100: Dewey Cornell, Carolyn Callahan, and Brenda Loyd, "Personality Growth of Female Early College Entrants," *Gifted Child Quarterly* 37, no. 1 (1993).

Page 101: David Irvine, "Gifted Education without a State Mandate: The Importance of Vigorous Advocacy," *Gifted Child Quarterly* 35, no. 4 (1991).

Page 104: By permission of Herbert Perkins-Frederick.

Chapter Six: Young Adults: The Extra Mile

Page 105: John Gowan and Catherine Bruch, *The Academically Talented Student and Guidance* (New York: Houghton Mifflin, 1971), 33.

Page 106: Gail Sheehy, *Passages* (New York: E.P. Dutton and Co., Inc., 1974).

Page 107: Alan Levitt, telephone interview, 1984.

Page 111: David Willings, "The Gifted at University," proceedings of the Conference on the Gifted at University. New Brunswick, Canada, 1982, np.

Page 113: Wayne Dennis and Margaret Dennis, eds., *The Intellectually Gifted* (New York: Grune and Stratton, 1972), 248.

Page 113: J. M. Tolliver, "The Gifted at University," mimeograph of proceedings of the Conference on the Gifted at University. New Brunswick, Canada, 1982, np.

Page 113: Ziolkowski, Theodore, "The Ph.D. Squid" in *American Scholar*, Spring, 1990, p. 195.

Page 113: David Willings, "The Gifted at University," mimeograph of proceedings of the Conference on the Gifted at University. New Brunswick, Canada, 1982, np.

Page 113: Ibid.

Page 129: Eve Curie and Vincent Sheehan, trans., *Madame Curie* (New York: Doubleday, Doran & Co., 1937), 166.

Chapter Seven: Bored, Bored, Bored: The Quest for
Challenging Work

Page 132: David Willings, "The Gifted at Work," paper presented at the Fourth World Conference on Gifted and Talented Children, 1981, np.

Page 133: Dean C. Dauw and Alan C. Fredian, eds., *Creativity and Innovation in Organizations* (Dubuque: Kendall/Hunt Publishing Co., 1971), 111.

Page 133: Ibid., 79.

Page 133: George S. Swope, *Dissent—The Dynamic of Democracy* (New York: Amacom, 1972), 141.

Page 134: Robert Waterman, *The Renewal Factor: How the Best Get and Keep the Competitive Edge* (New York: Bantam Books, 1987), 13.

Page 139: Felice Kauffman, "The 1964–68 Presidential Scholars: A Follow-up Study," *Exceptional Children* 48, no. 2 (1981), np.

Page 141: David Willings, "The Gifted at Work," paper presented at the Fourth World Conference on Gifted and Talented Children. Montreal, Canada, 1981, np.

Page 143: Ibid.

Page 144: Dean C. Dauw and Alan C. Fredian, eds., *Creativity and Innovation in Organizations* (Dubuque: Kendall/Hunt Publishing Co., 1971), 15.

Page 153: By permission of Herbert Perkins-Frederick.

Page 154: Dennis Kinlaw, *Developing Superior Work Teams* (Lexington, Mass.: Lexington Books, 1991), xiii.

Page 154: Thomas Peters and Robert Waterman, *In Search of Excellence* (New York: Warner Books, 1982), 24–26.

Page 155: Dean C. Dauw and Alan Fredian, eds., *Creativity and Innovation in Organizations* (Dubuque: Kendall/Hunt Publishing Co., 1971), 134.

Page 155: Alan Kantrow, *Survival Strategies for American Business* (New York: John Wiley & Sons, Inc., 1983), 433.

Page 156: Richard Walton, "How to Counter Alienation in the Plant," in *Survival Strategies for American Business* (New York: John Wiley & Sons, Inc., 1983), 501.

Page 157: David Willings, "The Gifted at Work," paper presented at the Fourth World Conference on Gifted and Talented Children, 1981, np.

Page 159: Tom Peters, *Liberation Management: Necessary Disorganization for the Nanosecond Nineties* (New York: Alfred Knopf, 1992), 761.

Page 159: Ibid., 762.

Page 159: Ibid.

Chapter Eight: The Dark Side

Page 164: J. Kent Hollingsworth, telephone interview, May 1993.

Page 165: Donald Dowd, telephone interview, December 1984.

Page 165: Carl Frankenstein, *Varieties of Juvenile Delinquency* (New York: Gordon and Breach Science Publishers, 1970), 95.

Page 166: Alan Levitt, telephone interview, December 1984.

Page 166: Ibid.

Page 166: Don Crouthamel, personal interview, July 1984.

Page 166: Hervey Cleckley, *The Mask of Sanity* (New York: New American Library reprint, 1982), 152.

Page 167: Ibid., 148.

Page 167: Ibid., 166.

Page 167: Ibid., 182.

Page 167: Sean Ryan, personal interview, July 1984.

Page 168: Travis Hirschi, *Causes of Delinquency* (Berkeley: University of California Press, 1969), 177.

Page 168: Don Crouthamel, personal interview, July 1984.

Page 169: Alan Levitt, telephone interview, December 1984.

Page 169: Don Crouthamel, personal interview, July 1984.

Page 169: Sean Ryan, personal interview, July 1984.

Page 173: Alan Levitt, telephone interview, December 1984.

Page 173: Ibid.

Page 174: Don Crouthamel, personal interview, July 1984.

Page 176: Ibid.

Page 176: Sean Ryan, personal interview, July 1984.

Page 176: Ibid.

Page 183: Ibid.

Chapter Nine: Finding the Others: Friends and Lovers

Page 194: Dierdre Lovecky,"Can You Hear the Flowers Singing? Issues for Gifted Adults," *Journal of Counseling and Development* (May 1986), 574.

Page 195: Harriet O'Shea, "Friendship and the Intellectually Gifted Child," in *Psychoeducational Development of Gifted and Talented Learners* (Rockville, Md.: Aspen Systems Corp., 1981), 228.

Page 198: Frederick Franck, *The Supreme Koan* (New York: Crossroads Publishing Co., 1982), 178.

Page 199: Richard Bach, *Illusions* (New York: Delacorte Press, 1977), 51.

Page 200: Barbara Clark, *Growing Up Gifted* (Columbus: Charles E. Merrill Publishing Co., 1981), 393–410.

Page 201: John C. Gowan and George Demos, *The Education and Guidance of the Ablest* (Springfield: Charles C. Thomas, Publisher, 1964); John C. Gowan, *Development of the Creative Individual* (San Diego: Robert R. Knopp, 1972); John C. Gowan, *The Guidance and Measurement of Intelligence, Development and Creativity* (Northridge, Calif.: Gowan, 1972); John C. Gowan, *Development of the Psychedelic Individual* (Northridge, Calif.: Gowan, 1974); John C. Gowan et al., eds., *Educating the Ablest* (New York: F.E. Peacock Publishers, Inc., 1979).

Page 201: Dierdre Lovecky, "Can You Hear the Flowers Singing? Issues for Gifted Adults," *Journal of Counseling and Development* (May 1986), 572–575.

Page 201: William James, *Varieties of Religious Experience* (New York: Penguin Books, 1961), 304.

Page 204: David Willings, "Helping the Gifted at University," lecture reprint. University of New Brunswick, Canada, 1981, np.

Page 211: Gail Sheehy, Passages (New York: E.P. Dutton and Co., Inc., 1974), 19.

Chapter Ten: Gifted Women

Page 213: Linda Kreger Silverman, "Giftedness and the Development of the Feminine," *Advanced Development*, 5 (January 1993), 42.

Page 214: Barbara Kerr, *Smart Girls, Gifted Women* (Columbus: Ohio Psychology Publishing Co., 1985), 155.

Page 214: Ibid., 73.

Page 214: Patricia Casserly, "Helping Young Women to Take Math and Science Seriously in School," in *New Voices in Counseling the Gifted* (Dubuque: Kendall/Hunt Publishing Co., 1979); Sally M. Reis, "We Can't Change What We Don't Recognize: Understanding the Special Needs of Gifted Females," *Gifted Child Quarterly* 31, no. 2 (1987), 83; Susan Chira, "Bias against Girls Found Rife in Schools, with Lasting Damage," *The New York Times* (February 12, 1992), 1.

Page 214: Judith Rodenstein and Carol Glickhauf-Hughes, "Career and Lifestyle Determinants of Gifted Women," in *New Voices in Counseling the Gifted* (Dubuque: Kendall/Hunt Publishing Co., 1979), 370–380.

Page 215: Trudi Ferguson and Joan Dunphy, *Answers to the Mommy Track* (Far Hills, N.J.: New Horizon Press, 1993). The term "mommy track" comes from a 1989 article in the *Harvard Business Review* by Felice Schwartz, president of Catalyst, titled "Management Women and the New Facts of Life," in which she suggested that anyone with children be relegated to a separate career tracks and fewer opportunities.

Page 215: Carol Gilligan, *In a Different Voice* (Cambridge: Harvard University Press, 1982), 15.

Page 215: Ibid., 9–11.

Page 215: Ibid., 7.

Page 215: Ibid., 8.

Page 216: Ibid., 9–11.

Page 216: Ibid., 172.

Page 216: Ibid, 18.

Page 216: Ibid.

Page 216: Elizabeth Drews, "The Gifted Student—A Researcher's View," in *Readings in Foundations of Gifted Education* (Guilford, Conn.: Special Learning Corp., 1980), 35.

Page 217: Betty Friedan, "The Second Stage," *Redbook Magazine* (May 1980).

Page 217: Linda Schierse Leonard, *Meeting the Madwoman* (New York: Bantam Books, 1993).

Page 217: Lynn Gilbert and Gaylen Moore, *Particular Passions* (New York: Clarkson N. Potter, Inc., 1981), 333.

Page 217: Trudi Ferguson and Joan Dunphy, *Answers to the Mommy Track* (Far Hills, N.J.: New Horizon Press, 1993), 23.

Page 218: Judith Rodenstein and Carol Glickhauf-Hughes, "Career and Lifestyle Determinants of Gifted Women," in *New Voices in Counseling the Gifted* (Dubuque: Kendall/Hunt Publishing Co., 1979), 370–380.

Page 218: Sally Reis, "We Can't Change What We Don't Recognize: Understanding the Special Needs of Gifted Females," *Gifted Child Quarterly* 31, no. 2 (1987), 88.

Page 218: Jacquelynne Eccles, "Why Doesn't Jane Run? Sex Differences in Educational and Occupational Patterns," in *The Gifted and Talented: Developmental Perspectives* (Washington, D.C.: American Psychological Association, 1985), 290.

Page 218: Trudi Ferguson and Joan Dunphy, *Answers to the Mommy Track* (Far Hills, N.J.: New Horizon Press, 1993), 26.

Page 220: Patricia Wolleat, "Guiding the Career Development of Gifted Females," in *New Voices in Counseling the Gifted* (Dubuque: Kendall/Hunt Publishing Co., 1979), 331–342.

Page 220: Judith D. Schwartz, *The Mother Puzzle* (New York: Simon & Schuster, 1993), 123.

Page 229: Jacquelynne Eccles, "Why Doesn't Jane Run? Sex Differences in Educational and Occupational Patterns," in *The Gifted and Talented: Developmental Perspectives* (Washington, D.C.: American Psychological Association, 1985), 240.

Page 229: Barbara Kerr, *Smart Girls, Gifted Women* (Columbus: Ohio Psychology Publishing Company, 1985), 121.

Page 230: Trudi Ferguson and Joan Dunphy, *Answers to the Mommy Track* (Far Hills, N.J.: New Horizon Press, 1993), 128.

Page 230: Sally Reis, "We Can't Change What We Don't Recognize: Understanding the Special Needs of Gifted Females," in *Gifted Child Quarterly* 31, no. 2 (Spring 1987), 84.

Page 230: Steven Carter and Julia Sokol, *What Smart Women Know* (New York: M. Evans and Co., Inc., 1990), 195.

Page 232: J. T. Spence and R. Helmreich, "Achievement-Related Motives and Behaviors," in *Achievement and Achievement Motives: Psychological and Sociological Approaches* (San Francisco, Calif.: Freeman, 1983); Sally Reis and C. M. Callahan, "Gifted Females, They've Come a Long Way—Or Have They?" *Journal for the Education of the Gifted* 12, no. 2 (1989); Constance Hollinger and Elyse Fleming, "The Longitudinal Examination of the Life Choices of Gifted and Talented Women," *Gifted Child Quarterly* 36, no. 4 (Fall 1992).

Page 232: Barbara Ehrenreich, "Strategies of Corporate Women," *New Republic* (January 1986), 28.

Page 233: Carol Tavris, *The Mismeasure of Woman* (New York: Simon & Schuster, 1992), 38.

Page 233: Lawrence M. Miller, *American Spirit: Visions of a New Corporate Culture* (New York: William Morrow & Co., Inc., 1984) 120–121.

Page 233: Ibid., 121.

Page 233: Betty Walker, Sally Reis, and Janet Leonard, "A Developmental Investigation of the Lives of Gifted Women," *Gifted Child Quarterly* 36, no. 4 (Fall 1992).

Page 234: Trudi Ferguson and Joan Dunphy, *Answers to the Mommy Track* (Far Hills, N.J.: New Horizon Press, 1993), 60.

Page 234: Kevin Kelly, "The Relation of Gender and Academic Achievement to Career Self-Efficacy and Interests," *Gifted Child Quarterly* 37, no. 2 (1993), 63.

Page 235: Trudi Ferguson and Joan Dunphy, *Answers to the Mommy Track* (Far Hills, N.J.: New Horizon Press, 1993), 270.

Chapter Eleven: Young in Mind: The Later Years

Page 250: Susan L. Crowley, "Aging Brain's Staying Power," *AARP Bulletin* 37, no. 4 (Washington, D.C., April 1996), 1.

Page 252: By permission of Pamela Perkins-Frederick.

Chapter Twelve: The Value of the Gift

Page 254: Dean C. Dauw, "Bridging the Creativity Gap," in *Creativity and Innovation in Organizations* (Dubuque: Kendall/Hunt Publishing Co., 1971), 236.

Page 255: Dorothy Sisk, "What If Your Child Is Gifted?" in *Readings in Gifted and Talented Education* (Guilford, Conn.: Special Learning Corp., 1978).

Page 255: Steve Allen, "A Speech on Creativity," in *Readings in Gifted and Talented Education* (Guilford, Conn.: Special Learning Corp., 1978).

Page 255: David Willings, "The Gifted at Work," paper presented at the Fourth World Conference on Gifted and Talented Children. Montreal, Canada, 1981, np.

Page 256: Abraham Maslow, *The Farther Reaches of Human Nature* (New York: Penguin Books, 1976), 10.

References

Albrecht, K. 1979. *Stress and the manager.* Englewood Cliffs, N.J.: Prentice-Hall.

Allen, Steve. 1978. From a Speech on Creativity. In *Readings in gifted and talented education.* Guilford, Conn.: Special Learning Corporation.

Alvino, James, and *The Gifted Children Newsletter* staff. 1985. *Parents guide to raising a gifted child.* Boston: Little, Brown and Co.

Anastasi, A. 1958. *Differential psychology—individual and group behavior.* 3d ed. New York: Macmillan.

A nation at risk: National commission on excellence in education. Washington, D.C.: U.S. Government Printing Office, 1983.

Bach, Richard. 1977. *Illusions.* New York: Delacorte Press.

Barbe, Walter, and Joseph Renzulli, eds. 1975. *Psychology and education of the gifted.* New York: Irvington Publishers, Inc.

Bell, Lee Anne. January 1990. The gifted woman as imposter. *Advanced Development,* 4.

Berg, Deanna H., and William D. DeMartini. 1979. Uses of humor in counseling the gifted. In *New voices in counseling the gifted,* edited by Nicholas Colangelo and Ronald T. Zaffran. Dubuque: Kendall/Hunt Publishing Co.

Betts, George T. May 1986. Development of the emotional and social needs of gifted individuals. *Journal of Counseling and Development,* 64.

Betts, George T., and Maureen Neihart. Spring 1988. Profiles of the gifted and talented. *Gifted Child Quarterly,* 32(2).

Binet, Alfred, and Theophile Simon. 1976. The development of intelligence in the child. In *The intellectually gifted, an overview,* edited by Wayne and Margaret Dennis. New York: Grune and Stratton.

Bohm, David. 1965. Physics and perception. In *The special theory of relativity*. New York: W. A. Benjamin, Inc.

Brady, Linda E., Susan G. Assouline, and Julian Stanley. Fall 1990. Five years of early entrants: Predicting successful achievement in college. *Gifted Child Quarterly*, 34(4).

Brady, Linda E., and Camilla Benbow. Summer 1987. Acceleration strategies: How effective are they for the gifted? *Gifted Child Quarterly*, 31(3).

Brown, Scott W., and Mary E. Yakimowski. Summer 1987. Intelligence scores of gifted students on the WISC-R. *Gifted Child Quarterly*, 31(3).

Bruch, Catherine. 1979. Counseling girls for the development of creativity. In *New voices in counseling the gifted*, edited by Nicholas Colangelo and Ronald T. Zaffran. Dubuque: Kendall/Hunt Publishing Co.

Bruner, Jerome S. 1961. The cognitive consequences of early sensory deprivation. In *Sensory deprivation*, edited by Philip Solomon. Cambridge: Harvard University Press.

———. 1984. *In search of mind: Essays in autobiography*. New York: Harper-Collins.

Burt, Cyril. 1975. *The gifted child*. London: Holder and Stoughton.

Campbell, Frank, and George Singer. 1983. *Stress, drugs and health: Recent brain behavior research*. Sidney: Pergamon Press.

Capra, Fritjof. 1982. *The turning point*. New York: Simon & Schuster.

Carter, Steven, and Julia Sokol. 1990. *What smart women know*. New York: M. Evans & Co., Inc.

Casserly, Patricia Lund. 1979. Helping able young women to take math and science seriously in school. In *New voices in counseling the gifted*, edited by Nicholas Colangelo and Ronald T. Zaffran. Dubuque: Kendall/Hunt Publishing Co.

Chira, Susan. 1992. Bias against girls found rife in schools, with lasting damage. *The New York Times*, 12 February, p. 1.

Clark, Barbara. 1983. *Growing up gifted*. 2d ed. Columbus: Charles E. Merrill Publishing Co.

———. 1986. *Optimizing learning*. Columbus: Charles E. Merrill Publishing Co.

———. April 1987. Speech to the annual conference of the Pennsylvania Association for Gifted Education. Philadelphia, Pa.

Cleckley, Hervey. 1982. *The mask of sanity*. New York: New American Library.

Cohen, Joseph, ed. 1966. *The superior student in American higher education*. New York: McGraw-Hill.

Colangelo, Nicholas, and Ronald T. Zaffran, eds. 1979. *New voices in counseling the gifted.* Dubuque: Kendall/Hunt Publishing Co.

Coleman, Daniel. February 1980. 1528 geniuses and how they grew. *Psychology Today.*

Cornell, Dewey G., Carolyn M. Callahan, and Brenda H. Loyd. Winter 1993. Personality growth of female early college entrants. In *Gifted Child Quarterly,* 37(1).

Cornell, Dewey G., and Ingrid W. Grossberg. Spring 1987. Family environment and personality adjustment in gifted program children. *Gifted Child Quarterly,* 31(2).

Cox, Catherine. 1976. Early mental traits of geniuses. In *The intellectually gifted,* edited by Wayne and Margaret Dennis. New York: Grune and Stratton.

Cox, Catherine, and Lewis M. Terman. 1976. Excerpts from the early writings of geniuses, selected and arranged by Lewis M. Terman. *The intellectually gifted,* edited by Wayne and Margaret Dennis. New York: Grune and Stratton.

Cox, June, Neil Daniel, and Bruce Boston. 1985. A Study of MacArthur fellows for Sid W. Richardson Foundation of Texas. Austin: University of Texas Press.

Crowley, Susan L. 1996. Aging brain's staying power. *AARP Bulletin,* 4(4).

Curie, Eve. 1937. *Madame Curie,* translated by Vincent Sheen. New York: Doubleday, Doran & Co.

Dauw, Dean C., and Alan C. Fredian, eds. 1971. *Creativity and innovation in organizations.* Dubuque: Kendall/Hunt Publishing Co.

Deakin, Michael. 1972. *The children on the hill.* New York: Bobbs/Merrill Co., Inc.

Delp, J., and R. Martinson. 1977. *A handbook for parents of the gifted and talented.* Ventura, Calif.: Superintendent of Schools.

Dennis, Wayne, and Margaret W. Dennis, eds. 1976. *The intellectually gifted.* New York: Grune and Stratton.

Dettmer, Peggy. Spring 1993. Gifted education: Window of opportunity. *Gifted Child Quarterly,* 37(2).

Dewar, Donald L. 1979. *Quality circles.* Red Bluff, Calif.: Quality Circle Institute.

Diamond, M. C., and A. B. Scheibel. July 1985. Research on the structure of Einstein's brain in W. Reich's, *The stuff of genius. New York Times Magazine.*

Dixon, John. 1982. *The spatial child.* Springfield: Charles C. Thomas, Publisher.

Dowd, Donald. December 1984. Telephone interview.

Drews, Elizabeth. 1963. The four faces of able adolescents. *Saturday Review of Literature*, 46:68–71.

———. 1980. The gifted student—a researcher's view. In *Readings in Foundations of Gifted Education*, edited by David M. Jackson. Guilford, Conn.: Special Learning Corporation.

Eby, Judy W., and Joan F. Smutny. 1990. *A thoughtful overview of gifted education*. New York: Longman.

Eccles, Jacquelynne. 1985. Why doesn't Jane run? Sex differences in educational and occupational patterns. In *The gifted and talented: Developmental perspectives*, edited by Frances D. Horowitz and Marion O'Brien. Washington, D.C.: American Psychological Association.

Ehrenberg, Miriam, and Otto Ehrenberg. 1985. *Optimum brain power*. New York: Dodd, Mead and Co.

Ehrenreich, Barbara. January 1986. Strategies of corporate women. *New Republic*.

Feldhusen, John, ed. 1985. *Toward excellence in gifted education*. Denver: Love Publishing Co.

Feldhusen, John, and Sidney M. Moon. Spring 1992. Grouping gifted students: Issues and concerns. In *Gifted Child Quarterly*, 36(2).

Ferguson, Marilyn. 1980. *The Aquarian Conspiracy*. Los Angeles: J. P. Tarcher, Inc.

Ferguson, Trudi, and Joan S. Dunphy. 1993. *Answers to the mommy track*. Far Hills, N.J.: New Horizon Press.

Fox, Lynn H., and Jerilene Washington. 1985. Programs for the gifted and talented: Past, present and future. In *The gifted and talented: Developmental perspectives*, edited by Frances D. Horowitz and Marion O'Brien. Washington, D.C.: American Psychological Association.

Francher, Raymond E. 1985. *The intelligence men: Makers of the IQ controversy*. New York: W. W. Norton and Co.

Franck, Frederick. 1982. *The supreme koan*. New York: Crossroads Publishing Co.

Frankenstein, Carl. 1970. *Varieties of juvenile delinquency*. New York: Gordon and Breach Science Publishers.

French, Joseph L. 1975. The highly intelligent dropout. In *Psychology and education of the gifted*, edited by Walter Barbe and Joseph Renzulli. New York: Irvington Publishers, Inc.

Friedan, Betty. January 1980. The second stage. *Redbook Magazine*.

Friedman, Sonya. 1985. *Smart cookies don't crumble*. New York: G. P. Putnam's Sons.

Gallagher, James. 1964. *Teaching the gifted child*. Boston: Allyn & Bacon.

———. Winter 1986. A proposed federal role: Education of gifted children. *Gifted Child Quarterly*, 30(1).

———. Fall 1991. Programs for gifted students: Enlightened self-interest. *Gifted Child Quarterly*, 35(4).

Gallagher, James, ed. 1965. *Teaching gifted students*. Boston: Allyn & Bacon.

Galton, Francis, 1976. The classification of men according to their natural gifts. In *The intellectually gifted: An overview*, edited by Wayne and Margaret Dennis. New York: Grune and Stratton.

Gardner, Howard. 1983. *Frames of mind: The theory of multiple intelligences*. New York: Basic Books.

Gardner, John W. 1976. Excellence: Can we be equal and excellent too? In *The intellectually gifted*, edited by Wayne and Margaret Dennis. New York: Grune and Stratton.

Getzels, J. W., and P. W. Jackson. 1975. The meaning of giftedness—an examination of an expanding concept. In *Psychology and education of the gifted*, edited by Walter Barbe and Joseph Renzulli. New York: Irvington Publishers, Inc.

———. 1975. A study in giftedness: A multidimensional approach. In *Psychology and education of the gifted*, edited by Walter Barbe and Joseph Renzulli. New York: Irvington Publishers, Inc.

Gilbert, Lynn, and Gaylen Moore. 1981. *Particular passions*. New York: Clarkson N. Potter, Inc.

Gilligan, Carol. 1982. *In a different voice*. Cambridge: Harvard University Press.

Goertzel, Victor, and Mildred Goertzel. 1962. *Cradles of eminence*. Boston: Little, Brown and Co.

Gowan, John C. 1972. *Development of the creative individual*. San Diego: Robert R. Knopp.

———. 1972. *The guidance and measurement of intelligence, development and creativity*. Northridge, Calif.: Gowan.

———. 1974. *Development of the psychedelic individual*. Northridge, Calif.: Gowan.

———. 1975. Identification—responsibility of both principal and teacher. In *Psychology and Education of the Gifted*, edited by Walter Barbe and Joseph Renzulli. New York: Irvington Publishers, Inc.

Gowan, John C., and Catherine Bruch. 1971. *The academically talented student and guidance*. New York: Houghton Mifflin Co.

Gowan, John C., and George D. Demos. 1964. *The education and guidance of the ablest.* Springfield: Charles C. Thomas, Publisher.

Gowan, John C., Joe Khatena, and E. Paul Torrance, eds. 1979. *Educating the ablest.* New York: F. E. Peacock.

Greenlaw, M. Jean. 1988. *Educating the gifted: A sourcebook.* Chicago: American Library Association.

Gruber, Howard E. 1985. Giftedness and moral responsibility. In *The gifted and talented: Developmental perspectives,* edited by Frances D. Horowitz and Marion O'Brien. Washington, D.C.: American Psychological Association.

Gryna, Frank M., Jr. 1981. *Quality circles: A team approach to problem solving.* New York: Amacom.

Guest, Robert H. 1983. Quality of work life: Learning from Tarrytown. In *Survival strategies for American business,* edited by Alan M. Kantrow. New York: John Wiley & Sons, Inc.

Guilford, J. P. 1979. Intellect and the gifted. In *Educating the ablest,* edited by Gowan et al. New York: F. E. Peacock.

———, 1975. Three facets of intellect. In *Psychology and education of the gifted,* edited by Walter Barbe and Joseph Renzulli. New York: Irvington Publishers, Inc.

———. 1977. *Way beyond the IQ.* Buffalo: The Creative Education Foundation, Inc.

Havighurst, Robert J. 1976. Conditions productive of superior children. In *The intellectually gifted,* edited by Wayne and Margaret W. Dennis. New York: Grune and Stratton.

Hirschi, Travis. 1969. *Causes of delinquency.* Berkeley: University of California Press.

Hollinger, Constance L., and Elyse S. Fleming. Fall 1992. A longitudinal examination of life choices of gifted and talented young women. *Gifted Child Quarterly,* 36(4).

Hollingworth, Leta S. 1942. *Children above 180 IQ.* Chicago: World Book Co.

Hollingsworth, J. Kent. May 1993. Telephone interview.

Horowitz, Frances D., and Marion O'Brien, eds. 1985. *The gifted and talented: Developmental perspectives.* Washington, D.C.: American Psychological Association.

Hunt, M. 1982. *The universe within.* New York: Simon & Schuster.

Hutchins, David. 1985. *Quality circles handbook.* New York: Nichols Publishing Co.

Hutchinson, Michael. 1986. *Megabrain.* New York: Beech Tree Books.

Irvine, David J. Fall 1991. Gifted education without a state mandate: The importance of vigorous advocacy. *Gifted Child Quarterly*, 35(4).

Jackson, David M. 1980. *Readings in foundations of gifted education.* Guilford, Conn.: Special Learning Corporation.

James, William. 1982. *Varieties of religious experience.* New York: Penguin Books.

Janos, Paul M. Spring 1987. A fifty-year follow-up of Terman's youngest college students and IQ-matched age mates. *Gifted Child Quarterly*, 31(2).

Jarecky, Roy K. 1975. Identification of the socially gifted. In *Psychology and education of the gifted*, edited by Walter Barbe and Joseph Renzulli. New York: Irvington Publishers, Inc.

Kantrow, Alan M., ed. 1983. *Survival strategies for American business.* New York: John Wiley & Sons, Inc.

Karczmar, A. G., and J. C. Eccles, ed. 1972. *Brain and human behavior.* New York: Springer-Verlag.

Karnes, Frances, and Herschel Q. Peddicord. 1980. *Programs, leaders, consultants and other resources in gifted and talented education.* Springfield: Charles C. Thomas, Publisher.

Kaufmann, Felice. 1981. The 1964–1968 presidential scholars: A follow-up study. *Exceptional Children*, 48(2).

Keirauz, Kathryn S. Spring 1990. Concerns of parents of gifted children. *Gifted Child Quarterly*, 34(2).

Kelly, Kevin R. 1993. The relation of gender and academic achievement to career self-efficacy and interests. *Gifted Child Quarterly*, 37(2).

Kerr, Barbara. 1985. *Smart girls, gifted women.* Columbus: Ohio Psychology Publishing Co.

Khatena, Joseph. 1978. The gifted child in the U.S. and abroad. In *Readings in gifted and talented education.* Guilford, Conn.: Special Learning Corporation.

Kinlaw, Dennis C. 1991. *Developing superior work teams.* Lexington, Mass.: Lexington Books.

Krippner, Stanley, and Gardner Murphy. 1976. Extrasensory perception and creativity. In *The creativity question*, edited by Rothenberg and Hausman. Durham: Duke University Press.

Larson, Carl E., and Frank M. J. LaFasto. 1989. *Teamwork: What must go right/what can go wrong.* London: Sage Publications.

Lawrence, Paul R., and Davis Dyer. 1983. *Renewing American industry.* New York: The Free Press.

Laycock, Frank. 1979. *Gifted children.* Glenview, Ill.: Scott, Foresman and Co.

Leonard, Linda Schierse. 1993. *Meeting the madwoman.* New York: Bantam Books.

Levitt, Al. December 1984. Telephone interview.

Lincoln, James R., and Arne L. Kalleberg. 1990. *Culture, control and commitment.* Cambridge, England: Cambridge University Press.

Lindsley, Donald. 1961. Common factors in sensory deprivation, sensory distortion, sensory overload. In *Sensory deprivation,* edited by Philip Solomon et al. Cambridge: Harvard University Press.

Lovecky, Deirdre. May 1986. Can you hear the flowers singing? Issues for gifted adults. *Journal of Counseling and Development.*

———. January 1993. Creative connections: Perspectives on female giftedness. *Advanced Development,* 5.

Lyon, Harold C., Jr. 1971. *Learning to feel—feeling to learn.* Columbus: Charles E. Merrill Publishing Co.

Maker, C. June, ed. 1986. *Critical issues in gifted education.* Rockville, Md.: Aspen Publications.

Martinson, Ruth A., and Leon M. Lessinger. 1975. Problems in the identification of intellectually gifted pupils. In *Psychology and education of the gifted,* edited by Walter Barbe and Joseph Renzulli. New York: Irvington Publishers, Inc.

Maslow, Abraham H. 1971. *The farther reaches of human nature.* New York: Penguin Books.

———. 1968. *Toward a psychology of being,* 2d ed. New York: VanNostrand Reinhold Co.

McGuiness, Deane, and Karl H. Pribram. 1980. In *The brain and psychology,* edited by M. C. Wittrock. New York: Academic Press.

McLeod, John. 1989. *Fostering academic excellence.* New York: Pergamon Press.

Miller, Alice. 1981. *The drama of the gifted child.* New York: Basic Books.

Miller, Lawrence M. 1984. *American spirit: Visions of a new corporate culture.* New York: William Morrow and Co., Inc.

Moore, Linda P. 1981. *Does this mean my kid's a genius?* New York: McGraw-Hill.

Newland, Ernest T. 1976. *The gifted in a socioeducational perspective.* Englewood Cliffs, N.J.: Prentice-Hall.

Noble, Kathleen D., and Julie E. Drummond. Spring 1992. But what about the prom? Students' perceptions of early college entrance. *Gifted Child Quarterly,* 36(2).

————. January 1989. Living out the promise of high potential. *Advanced Development*, 1.

Obler, Loraine K., and Deborah Fein. 1988. *The exceptional brain: Neuropsychology of talent and special abilities*. New York: Guilford Press.

Ogburn, M. Kay, and Nicholas Colangelo. 1979. Giftedness as multilevel potential: A clinical example. In *New voices in counseling the gifted*, edited by Nicholas Colangelo and Ronald T. Zaffran. Dubuque: Kendall/Hunt Publishing Co.

O'Shea, Harriet. 1981. Friendship and the intellectually gifted child. In *Psychoeducational development of gifted and talented learners*, edited by Donald Sellin and Jack W. Birch. Rockville, Md.: Aspen Publications.

Parnes, Sidney J. 1967. *Creative behavior workbook*. New York: Charles Scribner's Sons.

Perrone, Philip A., and Robert A. Male. 1981. *The developmental education and guidance of gifted learners*. Rockville, Md.: Aspen Publications.

Peters, Tom. 1987. *Thriving on chaos: A handbook for a management revolution*. New York: Alfred A. Knopf.

————. 1992. *Liberation management: Necessary disorganization for the nanosecond nineties*. New York: Alfred A. Knopf.

Peters, Thomas J., and Robert H. Waterman. 1982. *In search of excellence*. New York: Warner Books.

Phillips, John L. 1975. *The origins of intellect: Piaget's theory*. San Francisco: W.H. Freeman & Co.

Piechowski, Michael. 1979. Developmental potential. In *New voices in counseling the gifted*, edited by Nicholas Colangelo and Robert T. Zaffran. Dubuque: Kendall/Hunt Publishing Co.

Pressy, Sidney L. 1976. Skipping grades vs. acceleration. In *The intellectually gifted*, edited by Wayne and Margaret W. Dennis. New York: Grune and Stratton.

Prigogene, Ilya. 1984. *Order out of chaos: Man's new dialogue with nature*. New York: Bantam Books.

Progress in neuroscience—Readings from Scientific American. 1986. New York: W.H. Freeman & Co.

Racamora, Mary. January 1992. Counseling issues with recognized and unrecognized creatively gifted students. *Advanced Development*, 4.

Readings in gifted and talented education. 1978. Guilford, Conn.: Special Learning Corporation.

Reich, Walter. July 1985. The stuff of genius. *New York Times Magazine*.

Reis, Sally M. Spring 1987. We can't change what we don't recognize: Understanding the special needs of gifted females. *Gifted Child Quarterly*, 31(2).

Reis, S. M., and C. M. Callahan. 1989. Gifted females: They've come a long way—or have they? *Journal for the Education of the Gifted*, 12(2).

Renzulli, Joseph. 1979. *What makes giftedness? A reexamination of the definition of the gifted and talented*. Ventura, Calif.: Ventura County Superintendent of Schools.

———. Spring 1991. The national research center on the gifted and talented: The dream, the design and the destination. *Gifted Child Quarterly*, 35(2).

Restak, Richard. 1979. *The brain: The last frontier*. Garden City, N.Y.: Doubleday.

Rice, Joseph P. 1985. *The gifted—developing total talent*. Springfield: Charles C. Thomas, Publisher.

Rodenstein, Judith, and Cheryl Glickhauf-Hughes. 1979. Career and lifestyle determinants of gifted women. In *New voices in counseling the gifted*, edited by Nicholas Colangelo and Robert T. Zaffran. Dubuque: Kendall/Hunt Publishing Co.

Roe, Anne. 1975. A psychologist examines sixty-four eminent scientists. In *Psychology and education of the gifted*, edited by Walter Barbe and Joseph Renzulli. New York: Irvington Publishers, Inc.

Ross, Alan O. 1979. The gifted child in the family. In *New voices in counseling the gifted*, edited by Nicholas Colangelo and Robert T. Zaffran. Dubuque: Kendall/Hunt Publishing Co.

Rostow, Jerome, ed. 1985. *Views from the top*. New York: Facts on File Publications.

Rothenberg, Albert, and Carl L. Hausman, eds. 1976. *The creativity question*. Durham: Duke University Press.

Runcie, John R. 1983. By day I make the cars. In *Survival strategies for American business*, edited by Alan M. Kantrow. New York: John Wiley & Sons, Inc.

Sanborn, Marshall P. 1979. Career development: Problems of gifted and talented students. In *New voices in counseling the gifted*, edited by Nicholas Colangelo and Robert T. Zaffran. Dubuque: Kendall/Hunt Publishing Co.

———. 1979. Working with parents. In *New voices in counseling the gifted*, edited by Nicholas Colangelo and Robert T. Zaffran. Dubuque: Kendall/Hunt Publishing Co.

Saroyan, William. 1972. *Places where I've done time*. New York: Praeger Publishers.

Schwartz, Judith D. 1993. *The mother puzzle*. New York: Simon & Schuster.

Scobel, Donald N. 1983. Doing away with the factory blues. In *Survival strategies for American business*, edited by Alan M. Kantrow. New York: John Wiley & Sons, Inc.

Sellin, Donald, and Jack W. Birch. 1981. *Psychoeducational development of gifted and talented learners*. Rockville, Md.: Aspen Publications.

Selye, Hans. 1956. *The stress of life*. New York: McGraw-Hill.

Shankland, Robert, ed. 1981. *The faces and forms of creativity*. Ventura, Calif.: Ventura County Superintendent of Schools.

Sheehy, Gail. 1974. *Passages*. New York: E. P. Dutton and Co., Inc.

Shiras, Wilmar. 1964. In hiding. In *Great science fiction stories*. New York: Dell Publishing Co., Inc.

Silverman, Linda Kreger. January 1993. Giftedness and the development of the feminine. *Advanced Development*, 5.

Simonton, Dean K. 1984. *Genius, creativity and leadership*. Cambridge: Harvard University Press.

Sisk, Dorothy. 1978. What if your child is gifted? In *Readings in gifted and talented education*. Guilford, Conn.: Special Learning Corporation.

Skinner, Wickham. 1983. The anachronistic factory. In *Survival strategies for American business*, edited by Alan M. Kantrow. New York: John Wiley & Sons, Inc.

Solomon, Philip, ed. 1961. *Sensory deprivation*. Cambridge: Harvard University Press.

Spence, J. T., and R. Helmreich. 1983. Achievement-related motives and behaviors. In *Achievement and achievement motives: Psychological and sociological approaches*, edited by J. T. Spence. San Francisco: Freeman.

Stanley, Julian C., and Ann M. McGill. Spring 1986. More about young entrants to college: How did they fare? *Gifted Child Quarterly*, 30(2).

Sternberg, Robert J., and Todd I. Lubart. Winter 1993. Creative giftedness: A multivariate investment approach. In *Gifted Child Quarterly*, 37(1).

Stevens, Charles F. 1986. The neuron. In *Progress in neuroscience*. New York: W. H. Freeman & Company.

Swope, George S. 1972. *Dissent—the dynamic of democracy*. New York: Amacom.

Tannenbaum, Abraham. 1983. *Gifted children: Psychological and educational perspectives*. New York: Macmillan.

———. 1975. Pre-Sputnik and post-Watergate concern about the gifted. In *Psychology and education of the gifted*, edited by Walter Barbe and Joseph Renzulli. New York: Irvington Publishers, Inc.

Targ, Russell, and Keith Harary. 1984. *The mind race: Understanding and using psi*. New York: Random House.

Tart, Charles T. August 1982. The meaning of life: Values in science and transpersonal psychology. Abstract of address at the American Psychological Association Conference.

Tavris, Carol. 1992. *The mismeasure of woman.* New York: Simon & Schuster.

Taylor, John. 1971. *The shape of minds to come.* New York: Weybright & Talley.

Terman, Lewis M. June 1954. The discovery and encouragement of individual talent. Reprint from *American Psychologist.*

———. 1975. A new approach to the study of genius. In *Psychology and education of the gifted,* edited by Walter Barbe and Joseph Renzulli. New York: Irvington Publishers, Inc.

Terman, Lewis M., and Melita H. Oden. 1976. The Terman study of intellectually gifted children. In *The intellectually gifted,* edited by Wayne and Margaret W. Dennis. New York: Grune and Stratton.

———. 1947. *The gifted child grows up: Twenty-five year followup of a superior group.* Stanford: Stanford University Press.

———. 1959. *The gifted group at mid-life: Thirty-five year followup of the superior child.* Stanford: Stanford University Press.

Teylor, Timothy. 1984. *A primer of psychobiology: Brain and behavior,* 2d ed. New York: W.H. Freeman & Co.

Thompson, Richard, Theodore Berger, and Stephen D. Berry. 1980. An introduction to the anatomy, physiology and chemistry of the brain. In *The brain and psychology,* edited by M. C. Wittrock. New York: Academic Press.

Tiellhard de Chardin, Pierre. 1965. *Building the earth.* New York: Avon Books.

Todd, Sally M., and Ann Larson. Summer 1992. In what ways might statewide advocates for gifted and talented education coordinate and focus their efforts? *Gifted Child Quarterly,* 36(3).

Tolliver, J. M. 1982. The gifted at university. Mimeograph. University of New Brunswick, Canada.

Torrance, Paul. 1975. Creative teaching makes a difference. In *Psychology and education of the gifted,* edited by Walter Barbe and Joseph Renzulli. New York: Irvington Publishers, Inc.

———. 1961. Problems of highly creative children. *Gifted Child Quarterly.*

Treffinger, Donald J. Winter 1991. School reform and gifted education: Opportunities and issues. *Gifted Child Quarterly,* 35(1).

———. 1962. *Guiding creative talent.* Englewood Cliffs, N.J.: Prentice-Hall.

————. 1975. Emerging concepts of giftedness. In *Psychology and education of the gifted*, edited by Walter Barbe and Joseph Renzulli. New York: Irvington Publishers, Inc.

Trevarthen, Carolyn. 1980. Functional organization of the human brain. In *The brain and psychology*, edited by M. C. Wittrock. New York: Academic Press.

Tuttle, Frederick, and Laurence A. Becker. 1983. *Program design and development for gifted and talented students*. Washington, D.C.: National Education Association.

Vail, Persila. 1979. *The world of the gifted child*. New York: Walker and Co.

————. 1987. *Smart kids with school problems*. New York: E.P. Dutton.

VanTassel-Baska, Joyce, ed. 1983. *A practical guide to counseling in a school setting*. Reston, Va.: The Council for Exceptional Children.

Walker, Betty A., Sally M. Reis, and Janet S. Leonard. Fall 1992. A developmental investigation of the lives of gifted women. *Gifted Child Quarterly*, 36(4).

Walker, Charles R., and Robert H. Guest. 1983. The man on the assembly line. In *Survival strategies for American business*, edited by Alan M. Kantrow. New York: John Wiley & Sons, Inc.

Walton, Richard E. 1983. How to counter alienation in the plant. In *Survival strategies for American business*, edited by Alan M. Kantrow. New York: John Wiley & Sons, Inc.

————. 1983. Work innovations in the United States. In *Survival strategies for American business*, edited by Alan M. Kantrow. New York: John Wiley & Sons, Inc.

Ward, Virgil S. 1980. *Differential education for the gifted*. Ventura, Calif.: Ventura County Superintendent of Schools.

Waterhouse, Lynn. 1988. Speculations on the neuroanatomical substrate of special talents. In *The exceptional brain: Neuro-psychology of talent and special abilities*, edited by Loraine K. Obler and Deborah Fein. New York: Guilford Press.

Waterman, Robert H. 1987. *The renewal factor: How the best get and keep the competitive edge*. New York: Bantam Books.

Webb, James. April 1986. Personal communication.

Webb, James, Elizabeth Meckstroth, and Stephanie Tolan. 1982. *Guiding the gifted child*. Columbus: Ohio Psychology Publishing Co.

Whitmore, Joanne Rand. 1980. *Giftedness, conflict and underachievement*. Boston: Allyn & Bacon.

Whitmore, Joanne Rand, and C. June Maker. 1985. *Intellectual giftedness in disabled persons*. Rockville, Md.: Aspen Publications.

Wiener, Norbert. 1953. *The autobiography of an ex-prodigy.* Cambridge: MIT Press.

Willings, David. 1982. The gifted at university. Proceedings of the Conference on the Gifted at University. University of New Brunswick, Canada.

————. The gifted child grows up. Lecture reprint. University of New Brunswick, Canada.

————. 1981. The gifted at work. Paper presented to the Fourth World Conference on Gifted and Talented Children. Montreal, Canada.

————. 1981. Helping the gifted at university. Lecture reprint. University of New Brunswick, Canada.

Wittrock, M. C., ed. 1980. *The brain and psychology.* New York: Academic Press.

Witty, Paul, ed. 1972. *The gifted child.* Westport, Conn.: Greenwood Press.

Wolleat, Patricia L. 1979. Guiding the career development of gifted females. In *New voices in counseling the gifted,* edited by Nicholas Colangelo and Robert T. Zaffran. Dubuque: Kendall/Hunt Publishing Co.

Ziolkowski, Theodore. Spring 1990. "The Ph.D. Squid" in *American Scholar.*

Acknowledgments

The largest measure of my thanks must go to the one hundred men and women who gave me their time and shared their lives with me in the writing of this book. For help in obtaining some of the most fascinating of the interviews, I am especially grateful to Pamela Wallenstein, "Gus" Linton, Sean Ryan, Marina Streznewski, and Dr. Earl McWilliams. Dr. Corinne Cody, James LoGuidice, and Kathleen Kelly Mazza provided valuable insights and supportive criticism of the manuscript. My research assistant, Andrea Schraffron, lent her skills and her smile to speed the project along. I am grateful also to the Central Bucks School District for granting me sabbatical time to work on this project. Special thanks are due to my mother, for her unfailing encouragement; to my husband Tom, for serving as my technical guide through the mysterious world of word-processing; and to my children, Marina, Tom, Andrew, and Alex. Without the support and encouragement of my own family of gifted grownups, this book would never have been written. Without the encouragement of Liz Aleshire and the members of the International Women's Writing Guild, I would have given up on the struggle to find a publisher. Finally, without the help of Dr. Joan Barth, Dr. Florence Kaslow, my editor Kelly Franklin, and assistant editor Dorothy Lin, this book would never have become a reality.

M.K.S.

About the Author

Marylou Kelly Streznewski received her M.Ed. from the College of New Jersey in Trenton. Certified as a program specialist in gifted education, she has taught gifted teenagers for twenty years at Central Bucks East High School in Bucks County, Pennsylvania.

The author's perspective on gifted adults has been informed by a lifetime as a member of a three-generation extended family of smart kids and gifted grownups. A long-standing marriage to a gifted gentleman and the raising of her own four gifted children has provided experience in the realities of the life of a gifted family. As an educator, she has counseled gifted students and their families in a variety of settings.

In addition to her work as an educator, Ms. Streznewski's career in communications has included theater, journalism, fiction, and poetry. She has taught writing at the high school and college levels. Her fiction and poetry have appeared nationally, and she has won awards in a number of competitions. Currently, she gives poetry readings and is at work on her second novel. She and her husband Tom reside in Bucks County, Pennsylvania.